APR 2 8 2003

Women at Work
The Transformation of Work and Community in
Lowell, Massachusetts, 1826–1860

WOMEN

View of Lowell, c. 1850. From a lithograph on a cloth sampler of the
Merrimack Manufacturing Company in Lowell.
COURTESY OF THE MERRIMACK VALLEY TEXTILE MUSEUM.

AT
WORK

The Transformation of Work and Community
in Lowell, Massachusetts, 1826-1860

Thomas Dublin

New York   Columbia University Press   1979

As a dissertation this book was awarded the Bancroft Dissertation Award by a committee of the faculty of the Graduate School of Arts and Sciences of Columbia University.

Library of Congress Cataloging in Publication Data
Dublin, Thomas, 1946–
Women at work.

Bibliography: p.
Includes index.
1. Women—Employment—Massachusetts—Lowell—History.
2. Textile workers—Massachusetts—Lowell—History.
3. Cotton manufacture—Massachusetts—Lowell—History.
4. Labor and laboring classes—Massachusetts—Lowell—
History. 5. Lowell, Mass.—Social conditions. I. Title.
HD6073.T42U52   331.4'87'70097444   79-10701
ISBN 0-231-04166-7

Columbia University Press
New York   Guildford, Surrey

Copyright © 1979 Columbia University Press
All rights reserved
Printed in the United States of America

Acknowledgments

OVER THE YEARS that I have been exploring the lives of working women in early Lowell, I have benefited from the support, advice, and criticism of what seem by now almost countless individuals. Among archivists and curators, William Copeley, Robert Lovett, and Helena Wright went out of their way numerous times to assist me in getting and using primary sources. Robert Bristol, David Plourde, and Dorothy Sanborn made available rare local records that proved invaluable in the social origins study. Steven Dubnoff, Bryn Evans, Marc Harris, Gary Kulik, Harold Luft, Jonathan Prude, Mildred Tunis, and Lise Vogel shared unpublished papers that broadened my vision. Harry and Mary Dinmore, Aileen Eurich, Joanne Preston, and Mildred Tunis shared precious family letters and kindly permitted me to quote from these sources. Kathie Galotti and Margaret Moran shared research skills that sped up record linkage for the social origins study immeasurably. The entire staff of the Computer Center at the University of California, San Diego, have been helpful in initiating me into the mysteries of their craft.

For permission to reproduce maps, photographs, and paintings used in the illustrations of this book, I would like to acknowledge the Lowell Historical Society and the Merrimack Valley Textile Museum. The following libraries and archives have kindly permitted me to quote from manuscripts in their collections: Baker Library, Harvard Graduate School of Business Administration, Brown University Library, Haverhill (Mass.) Public Library, the Lowell Historical Society, Massachusetts Historical Society, Merrimack Valley Textile Museum, New Hampshire Historical Society, Old Sturbridge Village, Schlesinger Library, Radcliffe College, University of Lowell, and the Vermont Historical Society.

Sections of this book draw upon earlier published articles and permission to reprint portions is gratefully acknowledged. Ideas elaborated in chapters 4-7 first appeared in "Women, Work, and Protest in the Early

Lowell Mills," *Labor History*, XVI (1975), 99-116. Chapter 10 is based in part on material first appearing in "Women, Work, and the Family," *Feminist Studies*, 3, nos. 1/2 (Fall 1975), 30-39, and appears by permission of the publisher, Feminist Studies Inc., c/o Women's Studies Program, University of Maryland, College Park, MD 20742. Finally portions of chapter 11 draw upon "Women Workers and the Study of Social Mobility," *The Journal of Interdisciplinary History*, IX (1979), 647-665, and appear by permission of *The Journal of Interdisciplinary History* and The M.I.T. Press, Cambridge, Massachusetts.

In addition, I have benefited from the comments, suggestions, and criticisms of friends and colleagues who have read earlier drafts of the book. Susan Benson, Steven Dubnoff, Bryn Evans, Paul Faler, Eric Foner, Michael Katz, Alice Kessler-Harris, Mary Lou Locke, Arthur McEvoy, Michael Merrill, David Montgomery, Mary Beth Norton, Robert Ritchie, Mary Ryan, and Carole Srole all read and shared thoughts on this study as it evolved from an earlier dissertation into the present book. Their support has meant a lot to me as a historian and as a person.

In the final process of writing and rewriting, a number of individuals have read, and sometimes reread, the entire manuscript and made particularly important contributions to the final product. I would especially like to thank Victoria Brown, Stuart Bruchey, Earl Pomeroy, and Harry Scheiber for their helpful suggestions and criticism on the final manuscript. Stuart Bruchey, in particular, has provided valuable guidance and support. He has given me a rare blend of criticism and distance that have helped me grow as a historian.

A historian does not live entirely in the past, and in the course of this work a Danforth Fellowship and an NEH Summer Fellowship freed me to devote full time to study. Grants-in-aid from the Center for Research on Women in Higher Education and the Professions, at Wellesley College, and the American Council of Learned Societies provided helpful funds. In addition, the Research Committee of the Academic Senate, University of California, San Diego, provided crucial support.

And finally, since I began on this project, almost eight years ago, Penny Dublin has shared its tortuous ways, its numerous ups and downs, every detail from computer cards to commas. Our shared life has made this a better book and me a richer person, for both of which I am very grateful.

Contents

Tables

Illustrations

Women at Work

The Transformation of Work and Community in
Lowell, Massachusetts, 1826–1860

A Note on Quotations

TO CONVEY a sense of what early women workers were like, I have avoided modernizing or correcting their spelling or grammar in quotations. The only changes I have made are ending sentences with a period and beginning them with capitals. Otherwise, any additions are noted within brackets. I have avoided use of the admonitory [sic] except in quoting published sources or in cases of particularly literate writers where errors stand out.

CHAPTER ONE

Women Workers and Early Industrialization

WOMEN have always worked, but until the past century their work has been confined almost entirely to the domestic setting, and it has been for the most part unpaid labor. Women's work was an element in the larger family economy that predominated in preindustrial society. Although this work proved crucial to family subsistence, it also constituted the basis for women's subordinate position in patriarchal society. In the American colonies, for instance, women made substantial contributions to both agricultural production and domestic manufacture; still, married women could not own property, nor could they make contracts on their own.[1] This legal framework reinforced the economic subordination of colonial women; without means for self-support, women's place was clearly in the home.

The nineteenth century saw crucial changes in this dominant pattern. With the rise of the cotton textile industry in New England in the years between 1820 and 1860, large numbers of young, single women left their parental homes to work in the expanding mill towns. Employment in the mills enabled women to enjoy social and economic independence unknown to their mothers' generation. At the same time it created new pressures—in both the economic and cultural spheres—to which Yankee women had to respond. In responding to the novel demands of industrial capitalism, women workers relied upon familiar cultural traditions and yet moved beyond the culture in which they were raised. In this book I focus on the experiences of the first generation of American women to work outside of the home setting, examining, in turn, their newfound independence, the unprecedented demands industrial capitalism placed on them, and women's responses to the changing order in which they lived and worked.

At the outset let me state the basic conceptual framework within which this study has evolved. An understanding of historical change requires, it seems to me, an appreciation of human beings as both objects and subjects. Marx expressed the first element of this dialectic in his preface to *A Contribution to the Critique of Political Economy*: "In the social production which men carry on they enter into definite relations that are indispensable and independent of their will. . . . "[2] Intrinsic to the view expressed here is the belief that broad social and economic relations shape our beliefs and actions. We are born into a world not of our own making or choice, and society provides the raw materials that shape all our efforts to recast it. But just as men and women are acted upon by a world they have inherited from the past, they act in turn upon that world. As it makes them, they also make themselves and transform their world.[3] Human agency is as important in this framework as the larger forces that appear to be independent of individual human will.

This perspective proves useful in examining the lives of women workers in the early cotton textile industry in the United States. Much of the world these women experienced in New England's mill towns had to be taken as given; the level of technology, the organization of production, and management paternalism were facts of life to which women had to accommodate as they left their homes and entered mill employment. But, although millowners and managers may have viewed workers simply as a factor or cost of production, the women were never an inert mass. They both accommodated to the demands of industrial capitalism and rebelled against those demands. Generally they accepted the new discipline required in factory employment, but on occasion they rejected the authority of their employers and challenged their power head-on. In a number of early strikes and in the growth of a movement to reduce the hours of labor in the mills, women workers organized collectively to contest the power of the textile corporations. While the protests were largely unsuccessful, they reveal alternative values and beliefs that helped shape women's responses during a period of transition.

Thus this study will examine both the broad economic and social changes that led to a transformation of women's work in the first half of the nineteenth century and the attitudes and responses of women workers themselves that shaped and modified the larger processes. As both objects and subjects in the historical process, working women merit our attention.

The economy of the United States underwent profound transformation in the years from 1820 to 1860. At the start of the period the economy was based mainly on two sectors—agriculture and foreign trade. In 1820 almost three fourths of the labor force worked in agriculture.[4] In the Northeast and the West family farming predominated. While a market orientation is clearly evident, the lack of substantial urban markets and the inadequacies of overland transportation limited long-distance trade. On New England's hill-country farms, in particular, much of the family's work went into producing goods for home consumption that later generations would buy in the marketplace.[5]

Only 7 percent of Americans resided in cities with 2,500 or more residents in 1820. With urban centers concentrated on the eastern seaboard, economic activity was closely tied to foreign commerce; shipyards, ropeworks, shops, and taverns, for instance, all depended on the success of foreign trade for their prosperity.[6] While each city developed trade with its immediate hinterland, such trade was limited by the difficulties of land and river transport in the first decades of the nineteenth century.

The growth of manufacturing was stunted under these circumstances. The extent of the domestic market was effectively limited by the high cost of transport. Further, the availability of undeveloped land and the small size of the urban population limited the growth of an industrial work force and meant that unskilled labor was relatively expensive. Prospects for industrialization under these circumstances were not bright.

Given these hindrances, manufacturing before 1820 was concentrated in homes and in small establishments serving the immediate, local market. As late as 1820 women working in their own homes made two thirds of all clothing produced in this country.[7] Only in those processes that called for waterpower and extensive machinery did production outside of the household predominate. In rural communities, typically small mills dotted flowing streams—sawing wood, grinding flour, carding flax and wool, or fulling cloth for local customers. These early factories, however, did not so much replace household manufacture as complement it. By mechanizing the slowest, most laborious steps in the production process, the carding and fulling mills actually contributed to increasing production of cloth in the home. Early factory-based industry was well integrated into the larger preindustrial economy.

Women had an assured and important place in the preindustrial household economy of the agricultural North in this period. Farm wives and daughters carried out much of the domestic manufacturing conducted in the home. They produced a variety of goods consumed at home, traded with neighbors, or sold at nearby country stores. Milk, eggs, butter and cheese, garden produce, soap, candles, yarn, and cloth constituted the chief products of women's domestic labor. Women's diaries and letters reveal the quantity and variety of their home manufactures and the importance of this work to the family farm economy at the beginning of the nineteenth century.[8]

These activities gave women a respected place in the family economy but placed severe limits on their independence. Women's work was almost entirely confined within the home, and they rarely earned a cash wage for their labors. Women undoubtedly kept some of the income from the sale of products they had made, but the largest share probably went to the family as a whole and more particularly to the husband and father as household head. More importantly, opportunities outside of the family setting were so limited that few women could conceive of living beyond its bounds. Women were largely confined within a patriarchal framework, first as daughters in their fathers' households and later as wives in their husbands'. Those who did not marry remained in their parents' households or lived with married siblings. For a woman in a subsistence farming economy, the option of living alone was hardly a viable one.

Such was the place of women on the family farm in the first years of the nineteenth century, but the American economy was by no means static. The period from 1820 to 1860 saw the first decisive steps from the preindustrial to the industrial economy. The proportion of the work force employed outside of agriculture increased from 28 to 41 percent over these years. Reflecting both this increase and the numerous improvements in industrial technology, the value of manufactured goods increased at a rate more than twice that of population growth.[9] New factory industries concentrated on the production of standardized consumer goods for a wide market. By 1860 the cotton textile and boot and shoe industries were well developed and dominated the domestic market for coarse grades of finished goods.

In no area of the nation were these changes more strongly felt than in New England. The agri-mercantile economy that predominated at the outset of the century soon felt the inroads of industrial growth. At first the establishment of small spinning mills in southern New England did not threaten traditional economic activities. Relying in part on a domestic putting-out system, the early mills offered considerable household employment to women and children. But after 1813, with the founding of the first fully integrated textile factory in Waltham, Massachusetts, factory textile production began to compete with, and displace, household manufactures.[10]

By undermining the bases of economic stability in the rural countryside and by creating a new demand for labor in the growing factories, textile manufacturing contributed to a dramatic demographic shift in New England in these years. The movement of the young from hill-country farms into urban centers, the Yankee emigration to the West, and the Irish immigration all played a part in this shift of population within the region. Between 1810 and 1860 the proportion of New Englanders living in cities increased from 7 to 36 percent.[11] Textile manufacturing had ushered in both industrialization and urbanization.

No group felt the impact of early industrialization more than young women in the New England countryside. On the one hand, the new mills undermined the primary economic activities of farmers' daughters—the spinning of yarn and weaving of cloth. On the other hand, the mills offered employment to these young women and tempted them to leave their rural homes to work in the growing factory towns. This combination of factors led to a mass movement of women into the early mills, until by 1860 more than sixty thousand women were employed in the cotton textile industry in New England alone. [12]

Yet much of the historical literature on the Industrial Revolution in this country reads as if only workingmen experienced the wrenching changes of this transformation. Existing accounts stress the impact of the changing social relations and technology of production on skilled, male artisans. [13] We know relatively less about their sisters in the textile factories of the period. This study seeks to redress the present imbalance and examine the experience of women workers.

Such a study can make an important contribution to our understanding of American labor history in a number of respects. Much of the recent literature in this field has drawn on the pathbreaking work of E. P. Thompson, *The Making of the English Working Class*, with its emphasis on working-class culture in a period of transition. Faler, Dawley, Laurie, and others have sought to examine within the American setting the survival of preindustrial traditions and values that informed workers' reactions to the novel economic and cultural demands of industrial capitalism. [14] While the new work represents a major advance over the earlier studies of John R. Commons and others of the "Wisconsin School" of labor historians, women still occupy only a minor role in these analyses. In this context the study of women textile workers affords the opportunity of looking at the process from another angle. Women's preindustrial social and economic roles differed from those of men, and industrialization posed somewhat different challenges and opportunities for them. Finally, women brought different values, attitudes, and expectations into the industrial setting. By examining the experience of women workers in the early mills and by tracing their responses to the novel demands they encountered, we may gain a broader view of the impact of industrial capitalism in this period.

Consideration of the experience of workingwomen also contributes to an understanding of factors influencing labor protest. The years between 1820 and 1860 are particularly interesting ones in this respect because they offer important examples of both protest and acquiescence among workers. In the 1830s and 1840s women textile workers took part in a number of major strikes and contributed to the growth of an organized labor movement in New England. The 1850s, in contrast, stand out as a period of industrial peace in which mill management was able to transform the labor process with little or no opposition from workers. This study will explore the reasons why under certain conditions women workers struck or protested while under others they acquiesced in changes that degraded working conditions and undermined their standard of living.

Just as this study draws on the work of labor historians, it also relates to the growing number of studies of women's history in the antebellum period. A lively debate has developed in the past five years over the impact of industrial capitalism on women. Edward Shorter set off the first sparks when he argued that industrialization provided women with a new economic independence and encouraged a new individualism. According to this view, the new individualism led to a greater sexual freedom reflected in the rising rates of illegitimacy in European countries in the eighteenth and nineteenth centuries. [15] Shorter's argument has generated considerable opposition, and Louise Tilly, Joan Scott, and others have taken up his challenge. Tilly and Scott have offered a very different interpretation of the impact of industrial capitalism on women, arguing that the new work opportunities for women were largely confined within the traditional household family economy and that even when women moved outside the home to find employment, they usually did so for traditional familial reasons. [16]

Given the debate among European historians, it makes sense to examine the American context with these questions in mind. To this date few studies have examined specific work situations in the United States to consider the extent to which women's wage labor outside of the home served traditional or nontraditional purposes. [17] Since the cotton textile industry in New England offered one of the first opportunities for large numbers of American women to work outside of the domestic context, this study should shed light on these concerns as well.

While some of the questions I raise are rather new, motivated as they are by the recent work of Thompson, Tilly, Scott, and others, there is fortunately a rich secondary literature concerning the early New England textile mills. Economic historians have studied the business organization and administration of the industry and have traced its growth in the antebellum period. They have analyzed the wages, earnings, and productivity of textile workers, the profits and investment policies of management, and the broader contributions of the textile industry to economic growth in the period. Although much of this work has little explicit concern with the social history of women workers in the early mills, it provides an important context for such a study. [18]

Social historians have shown more interest than economists in the texture of women's experiences in the early mills. Caroline Ware, in *The Early New England Cotton Manufacture*, and Hannah Josephson, in *The Golden Threads*, stand out for their treatment of women operatives. Although Ware covers somewhat more ground that Josephson, examining developments in northern and southern New England between 1790 and 1850, they both focus on the same principal issues: the founding of the mills, work and housing of operatives, changing conditions of work, labor unrest in the 1830s and 1840s, and the coming of the Irish at the end of the period. Furthermore, both authors rely on the same principal sources: contemporary newspaper reports, observers' accounts, and a scattering of corporation records. [19]

These studies have two major shortcomings, however. The authors' reliance on contemporary literary evidence limits their analysis of the transformation of women's work in the mills. They touch on the primary discontents expressed by women in their protests, but they fail to place the protests within the changing structure and composition of the mill work force. Furthermore, by halting their studies just as the Irish began to displace native-born workers in the mills, Ware and Josephson fail to explore the relationship between native- and foreign-born during the period of transition. Their limited time-frame means that the studies focus exclusively on a period of labor militancy and fail to consider the forces that led to a decline in visible labor unrest in the 1850s.

We may be better able to understand the early protests by simultaneously broadening and narrowing the scope of the inquiry. By extending the time-frame to 1860, it becomes possible to contrast the experience of native-born women workers in the 1830s and 1840s with that of their counterparts—Yankee and immigrant—in the 1850s. We can gain insights into the roots of labor activity among Yankee women by analyzing the factors that undermined it in the 1850s. To focus the study more narrowly, I will concentrate on the experience of women workers in a single community, the mill town of Lowell, Massachusetts.

This work is unashamedly a case study. It is an attempt to examine the lives and experiences of women workers in the early New England textile mills by close analysis of Lowell, the largest of the mill towns in the antebellum years. I have chosen to focus on a single community in order to gain access to those human experiences that tend to disappear among the larger generalizations and aggregates of economic history. Particularly in the study of labor struggles and the growth of labor organizations among women, it is helpful to narrow the focus and examine the process in some detail. But the purpose of the inquiry on such an intensive basis is to enable one to draw broader conclusions and generalizations relevant beyond the confines of Lowell.

Of all the New England mill towns in this period, Lowell is the most appropriate choice for these purposes. Before the Civil War Lowell was, in two senses of the term, the leading center of textile production in the nation. In the first place it was the largest center, in terms of capital invested, workers employed, and cloth produced. In the second, it was the center of innovation: the basic technology, organization of production, and systems of housing, wage payment, and work discipline adopted by the Lowell firms became the standards for much of New England. Lowell set the pace for, and was representative of, the most rapidly growing and innovative sector of the industry. [20]

In addition to focusing on Lowell, I shall at times draw considerable quantitative evidence from the records of a single major firm in Lowell, the Hamilton Manufacturing Company. I have chosen the Hamilton Company for more detailed analysis principally because it has a uniquely rich surviving collection of labor-related records. Virtually complete payroll records, register books, and rental volumes, and substantial company correspondence permit one to examine the changing makeup and residence of the work force and the changing structure and wages of mill occupations over the antebellum period. [21] This detailed analysis of the transformation of the work force and employment at a single company provides evidence that is crucial in understanding the broader patterns of labor protest that emerged throughout New England in this period.

Given the focus on the experience of women workers in Lowell, and on the Hamilton Company in particular, it is important to demonstrate that the picture which emerges is indicative of patterns throughout the New England textile industry. There is considerable evidence that the Hamilton Company was representative of the other Lowell mills and that these firms, in turn, were representative of the broader industry in the region.

The textile corporations in Lowell, including the Hamilton Company, adopted a unified set of policies from the outset. They shared waterpower rights, technological developments, labor policies, and marketing strategies. Mill architecture, the organization and technology of production, and the regulations adopted for workers were virtually identical. They made repeated efforts to ensure that the various establishments did not compete with one another in wages or working conditions. Periodically, in times of crisis, mill managers met together to formulate and implement joint policies. In February 1834, for instance, all the Lowell firms reduced wages at the same time, a procedure they followed on numerous occasions thereafter. In 1847 and 1853 they jointly reduced the hours of labor in the mills. It is clear that management acted so as to promote the interests of all the Lowell firms. [22]

The willingness of millowners and managers to cooperate so fully with one another undoubtedly stemmed from the fact that the textile firms in this period were owned and directed by a narrow circle of capitalists, known collectively as the Boston Associates. Stocks in the early companies were narrowly held, concentrating enormous economic power in a limited number of hands. Stock ownership patterns, though, actually understate the concentration of power, for among stockholders power fell to those who owned the largest blocks of stock and who were involved in the initial organization of the firms. A few men appear time and again among the directors of these companies. Nathan Appleton served on the boards of directors of a dozen firms; William Appleton and George Lyman served on eleven; Patrick T. Jackson on ten. Further, leading stockholders often served as treasurer, the chief executive officer, of several firms at the same time. Henry Hall acted as treasurer of three Lowell firms—the Tremont, Suffolk, and Lawrence companies—in the 1830s and 1840s, while Henry Ward occupied the same posts in the 1850s. Similarly, Thomas G. Cary held the top positions at the Hamilton and Appleton companies in the 1840s. These interlocking directorates assured that no single firm would place its own interests above those of the larger group of firms. The common policies adopted by the New England mills reflected the common interests of the stockholders and officers of the firms. [23]

The bonds of common interest among stockholders and directors led to a sharing of technology, resources, and information that was remarkable. Companies routinely shared architectural drawings, wage lists, figures on costs of production, even pieces of equipment and extra cotton stock. Each company kept track of developments elsewhere, and none tried to hide secrets from the others. Each firm clearly sought to maximize its profits, but cutthroat competition was forbidden by the gentlemanly rules of the game. [24]

While every firm tried to keep abreast of developments elsewhere, companies looked particularly to Lowell for leadership. One Nashua, New Hampshire, agent cautioned against a proposed wage cut by noting: "for us to think of reducing wages before they do at Lowell would in my opinion be bad policy." Another agent, this time in Lancaster, Massachusetts, similarly referred to a Lowell wage reduction when he wrote: "I wish our girls and others in the factory to understand that whatever reduction we may make shall be done at least as well." When Lowell firms cut wages in 1834 and raised the price of room and board in company boardinghouses two years later, other companies throughout New England followed suit. Similarly, when they reduced the hours of labor in 1847 and 1853, operatives throughout the region soon benefited as other firms followed the Lowell example. [25]

One might argue that the evidence presented so far has shown only that mill managers sought to impose uniform standards. Perhaps they were unsuccessful because of factors beyond their control. Robert Layer, an economic historian, studied surviving payrolls of four major northern New England firms—including two in Lowell—and demonstrated that patterns of wages and earnings were remarkably similar. The daily earnings of workers in each firm showed similar short- and long-run trends between 1825 and 1914, and the indices of average daily earnings and total days worked for individual companies moved in parallel fashion. Correspondence reveals that the firms attempted to standardize wages and working conditions; Layer indicates that they were successful. [26]

Taken together, the evidence provides assurance that in examining the experience of women workers in the Lowell mills we are also addressing broader trends and issues relevant to workingwomen in other factory towns of New England in this period. When, in subsequent chapters, the focus shifts even more narrowly to women's wages, the ethnic makeup of the mill work force, and careers of workers at the Hamilton Company in Lowell, we can have confidence that the patterns revealed for that firm reflect what was going on throughout much of New England—not that the patterns at Hamilton are repeated identically, and at exactly the same dates, in all other firms but that they correspond to general trends within the broader industry in the antebellum years.

The study which follows examines the experience of women workers in the early Lowell mills, with a view toward understanding the human impact of early industrial capitalism in the United States, particularly as it was felt by women. Chapters 2 and 3 situate the Lowell mills and their women workers within the broader New England context of the period. The first chapter traces the events that led to the founding of the Lowell mills in the early 1820s, while the next examines the social origins of women workers in the early mills and considers the reasons they left their rural homes and the place of the mill experience in their larger lives. With the foundation laid the scene shifts more directly to Lowell, and chapters 4 and 5 examine the bases of what I call a close-knit community among women workers. I argue there that bonds among women that developed at the workplace and in the boardinghouses provided women with a solidarity that later played a major part in the growth of collective protest. Chapters 6 and 7 trace the evolution of that protest and examine the changing consciousness of Yankee women evident in their labor struggles.

The final chapters of the study, beginning with chapter 8, concern the transformation of work and the work force in the Lowell mills in the 1840s and 1850s and the consequent decline in labor protest in the decade before the Civil War. Here the focus shifts to the Hamilton Company in Lowell, and I explore, in turn, the integration of the Irish into the the mill work force, the emergence of a family labor system, the transformation of the wage and occupational structure of the female work force, and the changing nature of women's careers in these years. The final chapter then examines how these broader changes led to a decline in the level of protest among women workers.

While I am convinced that the experience of women workers in the Lowell mills is representative of that of women throughout the northern New England textile industry in this period, it is also important to acknowledge that this experience was not shared by all working women in the period. Until almost the turn of the twentieth century, domestic service remained the largest occupation of female labor. In the antebellum period teaching and sewing employed almost as many women as did textiles. [27] In none of these other occupations was work nearly as social an experience as work in the mills, nor did women live in a female peer group as they did in the early mill towns. In these respects, women workers in the early mills were socialized in a way that not all other women shared. Until there are additional studies focusing on women workers in these other occupational groups, we can have only a limited sense of how the experience of women textile workers fits into the larger whole. This book is offered as an initial contribution to what must eventually become a much broader history of working women in this country.

CHAPTER TWO

The Early Textile Industry and
the Rise of Lowell

IN THE LATE eighteenth century and for several decades into the nineteenth, the spinning of yarn and the weaving of cloth remained primarily domestic industries performed by women within the home. As late as
1820 two thirds of all the clothing produced in the United States was of
home manufacture.[1] Not only was the work done in the home, but it
was carried out with a view toward home consumption for the most part.
Such work was tedious but necessary. It constituted a major element of
women's contribution to the family economy in this period and filled a
good portion of women's domestic activity.

Diaries give an indication of the way in which textile manufacture
could dominate women's work at home. Fifteen-year-old Elizabeth Fuller was evidently skilled in all the operations necessary to convert raw
wool into finished cloth, as her diary, kept between October 1790 and
December 1792, reveals. She began by picking and breaking the wool to
remove impurities and separate the individual fibers. Judging from her
diary entries, these steps took little time in comparison to spinning and
weaving. Beginning April 27, 1791, Elizabeth Fuller spun yarn steadily
for three straight weeks. Her diary records no other work in that time,
and she seems to have spun every day except on the Sabbath. In that
time she spun 74 skeins of yarn, according to her own count, for a total
of more than 40,000 yards. For three months in the spring of 1792,

weaving dominated her life, though not so totally as the earlier spinning had done. She kept track of her production and recorded weaving 176 yards of cloth. As she completed her weaving she sighed, "Welcome Sweet Liberty, once more to me. How I have longed to meet again with thee." [2]

At the same time that Elizabeth Fuller was busily engaged in hand spinning and weaving in her own household in Princeton, Massachusetts, the first steps were being taken that would eventually lead to the removal of these activities from the domestic sphere. In January 1790 Samuel Slater, an emigrant who had completed an apprenticeship in the English cotton textile firm of Arkwright and Strutt, arrived in Pawtucket, Rhode Island. There he agreed to work for William Almy and Moses Brown, proprietors of the mercantile firm of Almy and Brown. The merchants set up Slater in a small workshop, provided him with materials, an assistant, and a dollar a day in wages; in return Slater agreed to construct a machine to spin yarn by waterpower. Using imperfect models purchased earlier by Almy and Brown, Slater fashioned a functioning Arkwright water frame, similar to the ones he had worked with in Derbyshire. With the completion of a carding machine as well, Slater was ready to begin operations. [3]

In December 1790, eleven months after arriving in Pawtucket, Slater set up the first permanent spinning mill in the United States. Nine children, seven boys and two girls, all between the ages of 7 and 12 years old, constituted the first work force of this mill. It was a small beginning in rented quarters along the Blackstone River, but the firm of Almy, Brown, and Slater soon made enough profit to justify expansion. In 1793 operations moved into a new two-and-a-half story mill and an enlarged dam provided additional waterpower. Still, in July 1793 the machinery was most modest, three carding machines and two spinning frames with a total of seventy-two spindles in all. [4]

As the first American firm marketing yarns produced by waterpower and utilizing the Arkwright machinery, Almy, Brown, and Slater enjoyed considerable success. With Slater concentrating his efforts on supervising daily operations and improving the machinery, Almy and Brown exploited their mercantile contacts to expand the market for their yarns. At first they sold yarns on a consignment basis to retailers and weavers in the Providence area, but soon the market spread out along the eastern seaboard from Maine to Maryland. By 1800 the labor force in the mill had expanded from the original nine to more than one hundred. [5]

This first venture prospered and soon gave rise to numerous other spinning mills in the Providence area. In 1799 Slater built his own mill, though he continued to supervise operations at both sites. By 1805 three more mills had been established in Pawtucket, and here too Slater's influence played its part. According to one contemporary: "[N]early all the cotton factories in this country from 1791 to 1805, were built under the direction of men who learned the art or skill of building machinery, in Mr. Slater's employ." [6]

The early spinning mills in Rhode Island expanded rapidly in the years before 1815, their business aided greatly by the cessation in English imports that came with the Embargo and Non-Intercourse Acts and the war with England. [7] Still, these mills did not drive textile production entirely out of the household; in fact they created a considerable demand for household labor. For only the carding and spinning steps were fully mechanized, and mills continued to be dependent on children and adults, working in their own homes, to clean the raw cotton and weave the finished cloth. Women who had previously produced cloth for their own family needs now began weaving on consignment for the local spinning mills. One traveler in eastern Connecticut wrote that he encountered "every few miles a factory from which yarn is furnished to every female able to weave in the vicinity." [8] Companies that started relatively late often had to search at a distance for weavers to take their yarns. A Fall River firm apparently found "the neighboring farmers' wives so fully employed by Providence spinners that it opened a store in Hallowell, Maine, as a weaving center and outlet for goods." [9] In this way the early spinning mill was well integrated within the rural economy.

Practices in the spinning mills of southern New England were enough alike to be described by contemporaries as the Rhode Island system. The labor force consisted of whole families, with manufacturers giving preference to those with large numbers of children. [10] As late as 1820, for instance, children comprised more than two thirds of the Pawtucket textile work force. [11] The mills remained relatively small affairs, with limited capital, and were generally owned by local merchants and mechanics. They relied exclusively on waterpower and utilized machinery patterned after that developed by Arkwright and copied by Slater. They concentrated almost entirely on the carding and spinning steps, and even as late as 1826 only about a third of the Rhode Island mills had adopted power looms. [12]

While the Rhode Island firms, sheltered from the competition of English imports, enjoyed boom times, events in northern New England pointed toward even more dramatic changes in the future. In an attic room in Boston in 1813, a merchant, Francis Cabot Lowell, and a mechanic, Paul Moody, were at work constructing a power loom. Recently returned from a trip to England and Scotland, Lowell attempted to reconstruct the loom from memory, much as Slater had reproduced an Arkwright frame some twenty years earlier. [13] With the help of Moody he succeeded, and Lowell and a number of other Boston merchants obtained a charter from the state legislature to establish a cotton manufactory in Waltham, Massachusetts. The Boston Manufacturing Company presented a radical departure from prevailing practice in the industry. First, it operated on a scale far beyond that of competing firms. Capitalized initially at $400,000, it was more than ten times larger than the typical Rhode Island mill. [14] Moreover, by utilizing the power loom, it integrated all the steps in the manufacturing process at a single location, thus eliminating the loss of time, labor, and materials associated with the putting-out system. Whereas the Rhode Island firms marketed yarns and handwoven cloth, the Waltham company commanded the American market in cheap, coarse goods for the mass market.

Additional differences distinguished the Waltham and the Rhode Island systems of cotton manufacture. The owners of the Waltham company resided in Boston and delegated responsibility at the plant to a resident agent. Furthermore, few children were hired by the new corporation. This practice may have resulted from technical problems encountered in operating the new machinery, or it may have been due to the swifter pace of production that would have overtaxed the strength of children. [15] In any case, the firm turned to adult labor, particularly to single, young women recruited from the surrounding countryside. When it did so, however, it found that its relatively remote location on the Charles River made it impossible to secure a labor force from adjoining towns. The firm, therefore, sought to recruit labor within a wider radius and erected company boardinghouses where the women resided while working in the mills. [16]

The high level of capitalization gave the Waltham firm a number of advantages over its smaller southern New England competitors. It was able to purchase and stock large amounts of raw cotton at favorable prices and extend credit to purchasers of the finished cloth. The large scale of operations and the integrated nature of production led to additional economies of scale. Finally, the Waltham mill proved particularly attractive to potential workers as it paid cash wages monthly, rather than offering credit at a company store, a practice common in the Rhode Island mills. Although the smaller spinning mills advertised repeatedly to attract sufficient workers, there is no evidence that management at Waltham had to do so. [17]

From the outset the Boston Manufacturing Company prospered. Production began in a limited way in 1814, but within three years the firm had paid its first dividend of 20 percent. Annually, until 1825, dividends maintained this average. Sales skyrocketed from $3,000 annually in 1814 to more than 100 times this figure eight years later. Between 1814 and 1823 assets grew almost twentyfold, increasing from $39,000 to $771,000. The Boston merchants, turned manufacturers, had hit upon an enormously profitable investment. [18]

The Boston Manfacturing Company achieved this success in the face of difficult times. With the return of peace in 1815, English manufacturers dumped cloth exports on the American market in an effort to recapture the markets they had lost during the war. Many mills ceased operations, and, as Slater noted in a letter to a Philadelphia merchant, prospects were "very gloomy." [19] But because the Waltham firm utilized power looms, it produced a coarse, cheap cloth that could compete with English imports, and sales increased briskly. By 1821 the Boston Manufacturing Company had added another mill and had expanded operations until it utilized all available waterpower at its Charles River site. Further growth was clearly in the offing; only the location and the timing remained unsettled.

In the fall of 1821 the directors of the Waltham Company, after several unsuccessful scouting trips into northern New England, learned of the little-used Pawtucket Canal and the adjoining falls of the Merrimack River, where, within the space of a mile, the river fell 32 feet. Working through an agent, they quietly purchased a majority of the shares in the canal and most of the land between the canal and the river (see figure 1). In November the leading figures in the venture made their first trip to the East Chelmsford site. Thinking on a grand scale, as they always did, one of them remarked that they might "live to see the place contain twenty thousand inhabitants."[20]

At that date, however, only a dozen family farms lined the banks of the Merrimack and Concord rivers at their junction just below the Pawtucket Falls. A small woolen mill and a powder mill provided work for those not primarily engaged in farming. The Pawtucket Canal skirted the falls in a wide loop and linked the upper Merrimack River Valley to Newburyport at the river's mouth. Completed in the last decade of the eighteenth century, the canal had fallen rapidly into disuse after 1804 with the completion of the Middlesex Canal, which originated just a few miles upstream and provided easy transportation to the much larger Boston market twenty-seven miles away. The site was ideal for the Boston capitalists. It offered a large waterpower site, the Pawtucket Canal, that could easily be enlarged for waterpower purposes, and the Middlesex Canal, with daily freight and passenger service to Boston.[21]

Following the purchase of land and waterpower rights and their initial visit to East Chelmsford, the new directors set to work realizing their vision. They drew up articles of incorporation and petitioned the state legislature for a charter. Capitalized at $600,000 initially, the Merrimack Manufacturing Company was destined to dwarf its Waltham predecessor. In 1822 work began at the site under the direction of the Merrimack's first agent, Kirk Boott, who brought more than five hundred Irish common laborers to the site and housed them in tent camps, while they worked at widening and deepening the canal and building the first mills and boardinghouses. By the fall of 1823, the mills had turned out their first finished cloth.[22]

The Merrimack Manufacturing Company was essentially a branch plant of the Waltham firm. Merrimack directors paid $75,000 in cash and $150,000 in stock to the Boston Manufacturing Company (and indirectly to themselves as stockholders in that firm) for patent rights, initial machinery, and the services of Paul Moody, the parent company's chief mechanic. They moved the Waltham machine shop, including its skilled machinists, up to East Chelmsford in 1824 to service the new company.

Even the first operatives were recruited from Waltham. The extent of cooperation was reflected in a vote of the boards of directors of the two firms in 1823 to equalize dividends paid to their respective stockholders. The two companies were one in all but name. [23]

Planning to advance the mutual interests of the two companies went beyond these efforts. The Merrimack directors decided at the outset to manufacture printed cloth goods and thus not offer direct competition with the plain shirtings produced in Waltham. [24] The new company pioneered in the manufacture of printed calicoes and enjoyed preeminence in this high-priced market, while the Boston Manufacturing Company maintained its dominant position in cheaper goods.

The Boston Associates, as the owners of the Merrimack and Boston Manufacturing companies came to be called, had much more than a second profitable textile mill in their East Chelmsford plant; they had a valuable real estate investment as well. Immediately after production began, the directors transferred title to land and waterpower rights to the Proprietors of the Locks and Canals on the Merrimack River, the body that had been established originally to operate the Pawtucket Canal. This corporation—owned by the same group of investors—became the major developer of the growing mill town. The Locks and Canals company sold land, leased waterpower rights, and built mills, boarding-houses, and textile machinery for the new firms established in Lowell. The profits of this development company dwarfed those of the mills themselves, averaging fully 24 percent annually between 1825 and 1845. [25]

The immediate success of the Merrimack Company and the expansionist vision of the Boston Associates led to the founding of new firms in rapid succession. The Hamilton Corporation (1825), the Appleton and Lowell corporations (1828), and the Suffolk, Tremont, and Lawrence corporations (1831) followed one right after the other. All were owned by this slowly expanding circle of Boston capitalists. By 1836 investment totaled more than $6.2 million in eight major firms employing more than 6,000 workers. [26] By 1839 the last remaining waterpower sites had been occupied. Thereafter expansion depended on additions to existing mills, improvements in machinery, and more efficient use of waterpower (see figure 2).

With the expansion of the mills, the community surrounding the factories grew as well. In 1820 the population of East Chelmsford had been about 200. By 1826, when the community was incorporated as the town of Lowell, the population had reached 2,500. With the continued growth of the mills, the population spiraled, reaching 6,000 in 1830, 18,000 in 1836, and 33,000 in 1850. At that date Lowell was the leading textile center in the nation and the second largest city in Massachusetts. [27]

The active agents in the expansion of Lowell were the textile corporations. They controlled development by the ownership of almost three fourths of the land in the city. As principal taxpayers in the community, the corporations kept a watchful eye on the activities of local government. [28] As described earlier, numerous ties joined the Lowell firms into a unified group. Narrow concentration of stock ownership and interlocking directorates concentrated power in the hands of a relatively small number of stockholders. In addition, the corporations shared patent and water rights, and all had access to the Locks and Canals machine shop. They marketed their cloth through the same few Boston commission houses. They paid identical wages, set the same hours of work, established the same regulations for their operatives, and housed their workers in company houses and tenements. [29]

The corporations also shared the same basic organization of management. The chief executive officer of each company was invariably the treasurer. The company president presided over the annual meetings of stockholders but otherwise had little responsibility. The treasurer, on the other hand, received a substantial salary and, from his office in Boston, was responsible for the overall operations of the firm. He ordered cotton from the South, supplied the Lowell mill with cash for monthly payrolls and miscellaneous expenses, and received payment from commission houses upon the sale of the company's cotton goods. He prepared semiannual financial statements and advised the board of directors on the state of company affairs. [30]

The board of directors appointed an agent who directed the day-to-day operations of the company in Lowell. The agent resided in Lowell in a substantial house near the mills provided by the firm. He supervised all aspects of the company's operations: construction of new mills, replacement of worn machinery, inventories of raw cotton and finished goods, as well as production. He was in daily mail contact with the treasurer, informing him about operations and making requests for the purchase of additional cotton or other supplies. Through weekly reports he advised the treasurer of the level of production. The agent communicated his needs to the board of directors through the treasurer, who, in turn, transmitted decisions of the board to the agent. The agent was generally afforded a good deal of latitude in implementing company policy. When the directors instructed him to reduce costs or to expand production, they usually left the specific means to his own judgment.

A number of salaried officials assisted the agent in the daily management of company affairs. A superintendent oversaw production in the numerous departments in the mills. A clerk kept accounts of production, recorded the entries and departures of operatives, and prepared the payroll volumes for the paymaster who disbursed the monthly wages.

In each room of the mills an overseer, assisted by a "second hand," supervised production. The overseer had responsibility for the conduct and productivity of workers under his charge. Weekly he reported the output produced in his room. Monthly he reported the number of days worked and the output of each operative to the paymaster who made up the payroll. With the assistance of the second hand, he saw that machinery was maintained and adjusted and that operatives were supplied with materials. Although formal hiring was done by the clerk in the counting room, operatives generally spoke to overseers first when they were looking for work. Furthermore, overseers had authority to dismiss operatives under their charge for poor work, frequent absence from the mill, insubordination, or other cause. [31]

The final link in the chain of command in the mill was the operative. The operative came to Lowell and had to work within a fixed corporate structure. The vast majority of operatives in the early mills were women. Before examining the nature of their experience in early Lowell, however, we need to determine who these workers were and the backgrounds they came from. Only when we have a better sense of the identity of women workers and of the traditions they brought into the mills, can we fully understand their responses to the novel demands and opportunities posed by the mill experience.

CHAPTER THREE

The Lowell Work Force, 1836, and the Social Origins of Women Workers

ACCORDING to the conventional view, women in the early Lowell mills were young, single women attracted from the surrounding New England countryside. They entered and left the mills frequently, working for repeated short stretches in the years before marriage. While in Lowell they resided in company boardinghouses, erected by the textile corporations and managed by boardinghouse keepers. These are time-honored generalizations, enunciated initially by contemporary observers and corroborated by the research of subsequent historians.[1]

This description is basically correct and uncontroversial, but it does not take the analysis of the early work force in the Lowell mills far enough. In the first place, it is possible to quantify these generalizations more carefully, determining the actual proportions of men and women, native-born and immigrant, children and adults, and boardinghouse residents and family members in the overall work force. Determination of these proportions for the mid-1830s provides a base line for later discussion of the transformation of the Lowell labor system in succeeding decades.

In the second place, it is possible to extend this framework beyond the confines of Lowell by tracing workers back to the rural families and communities from which they came. Such tracing illuminates the social origins, and also the motivations, of women workers in the early mills, besides placing the mill experience within the broader life cycle of rural women. Taken together, these approaches establish the human context of life and work in early Lowell and point to the broader significance of the experience in the lives of women workers.

The lives of two women show in microscopic detail the interacting themes that the quantitative evidence demonstrates for Lowell women as a whole. The diary of Mary Hall and the autobiography of Harriet Hanson Robinson offer rare glimpses into the personal lives and attitudes of women in the early mills. Let us begin the analysis, then, with brief sketches of these two women.

Mary Hall first came to Lowell in September 1831 at the age of 23. The diary she kept during this period reveals an unsettledness common among mill operatives at this time. Over the next six years, Mary Hall worked short stretches in the mills, ranging from four to eleven months at a time, for three different firms in Lowell. Interspersed with her work were numerous visits back home to Concord, New Hampshire, including one stay at home that lasted a year and a half. During the Lowell years, she remained in close touch with her family. Frequent letters helped sustain the bond; her father and brothers visited repeatedly; a sister and two cousins also worked in the mills, and another sister and an uncle lived in Lowell. Finally, Mary Hall's residence in Lowell extended well beyond her six years in the mills. In 1838 she married Albert Capen, a railroad worker, and the couple continued to reside in Lowell at least until 1855. In all, she lived in Lowell for more than two decades.[2]

Why did Mary Hall go to Lowell in the first place? Though her diary reveals little in the way of personal feelings, company payrolls may provide part of the answer. Mary Hall made good wages in the mills. As a weaver at the Lawrence Company, she earned $115 during an eight-month period in 1834, and in 11 months in 1836 and 1837 her wages totaled more than $150.[3] Over the course of her mill career, Hall averaged about $3.25 per week. Given a weekly charge of $1.25 for room and board in company boardinghouses over most of this period, these earnings must have enabled Hall to support herself quite well. The economic and social independence which her wages provided must have been important to Mary Hall, a 29-year-old, single woman in her final year of employment in the mills.

Harriet Hanson Robinson did not keep a diary during her years in the mills, but her autobiography, *Loom and Spindle*, published in 1898 when she was 73 years old, provides a rich source for the social historian. Harriet came to Lowell as a child when her widowed mother took a boardinghouse at the Lawrence Corporation. At first she attended school and helped her mother with household chores, but in 1834, at the age of 10, she began work as a doffer, or bobbin girl, in a spinning room in the Lawrence mills. Though a child she took an active part in a strike in 1836, and her reminiscences provide a vivid, firsthand account of the affair. Her career also affords evidence of the occupational mobility common for women in the early mills. After working several years she moved up to tend a spinning frame, where she earned regular adult wages. Still later, she learned drawing in, one of the more skilled and better-paid occupations open to women. Her mill career came to an end in 1848, when at the age of 24 she married a young newspaper editor, William Robinson. [4]

These sketches of the lives of Mary Hall Capen and Harriet Hanson Robinson are much more complete than those that can be reconstructed for most mill operatives. But even if other surviving accounts were equally full, it would be risky to generalize about the makeup of the early mill work force or the social origins of women workers solely on the basis of letters, diaries, and reminiscences. The two dozen literary accounts that are available to us are indeed valuable, but they remain simply the stories of twenty or so women out of the tens of thousands who worked in the Lowell mills in these years. Luckily for the historian, however, other sources are available. The Lowell textile firms were pioneers in the development of business accounting procedures in the decades before the Civil War, and they kept remarkably complete payroll records. These sources enable the historian to reconstruct the mill work force in the mid-1830s and to trace a sample of workers back to their native homes in rural New England. Analysis of these systematic business records provides a strong foundation for generalizations about the makeup of the early mill work force and the social origins of operatives. When supplemented by a consideration of the beliefs and attitudes of women as expressed in surviving literary accounts, they illuminate the place and significance of the mill experience in the lives of women workers.

The richest available evidence on the composition of the mill work force in the mid-1830s is contained in the labor records of the Hamilton Manufacturing Company of Lowell.[5] Hamilton records enable one to determine the sex, nativity, place of residence, literacy, occupation, wage rates, and overall earnings of mill employees. The records must be sampled, however, as the survival of almost complete payroll records over the period 1830-1860 means that there are on the order of 400,000 individual monthly payroll entries. Thus the single payroll months of July 1836, August 1850, and June 1860 were chosen for detailed study. A full discussion of the reasoning behind these choices, the methods utilized in preparing the data for analysis, and the representativeness of these sources can be found in appendix 1. For the present the discussion will focus on the basic findings themselves.

The work force of the Hamilton Company in July 1836 was overwhelmingly female.[6] More than 85 percent—881 of 1030—of those employed in the company's three mills were women. Less than 4 percent of the work force were foreign-born.[7] As table 3.1 indicates, the proportion of immigrants among men, 6.1 percent, was considerably greater than the corresponding figure among women. The overall total of immigrants was very small; the Irish, numbering 20 in all, comprised the largest single group.[8]

Another factor unifying the female work force was its homogeneity in terms of age. Of females 10 years of age or older who were resident in Hamilton Company boardinghouses in 1830 and 1840, more than 80

TABLE 3.1. ETHNIC MAKEUP OF THE HAMILTON COMPANY
WORK FORCE, JULY 1836

Nativity	Males	Females	Overall
United States	93.9%	96.6%	96.3%
Ireland	2.0	2.4	2.3
England	2.0	0.3	0.5
Canada	2.0	0.8	0.9
Total cases	98	765	863
Missing cases[a]	51	116	167

NOTE: Columns may not add up to 100.0% due to rounding.
[a]Missing cases include individuals unlinked in company register books, and individuals successfully linked but for whom the clerk failed to record nativity. For further discussion see appendix 1.

percent were between 15 and 30 years of age.[9] Company records suggest
that only about 3 percent of Hamilton workers were children under 15
years old. Thus children were a small and not very significant part of the
work force of the early Lowell mills. Women in their teens and twenties
dominated the work force of the Hamilton Company in these years.[10]

Most workers at Hamilton resided in company-owned housing. Almost three fourths, 73.7 percent, lived in housing provided by the Hamilton or the adjacent Appleton Company. Males and females resided in
company housing in similar proportions, 70 and 74 percent respectively,
but there remained important differences in housing patterns for the two
groups. Male workers living in company housing were divided almost
evenly between single, adult men in boardinghouses and married men
with families in company tenements. In contrast, about 95 percent of
women workers in Hamilton Company housing were single residents of
female boardinghouses.[11]

More than a fourth of the women employed at Hamilton resided in
private housing, but considerably fewer lived with their own families.
Only 11.5 percent—about one in nine—of the females at Hamilton lived
at home with their families; the remainder, 88.5 percent, resided in either company-owned or private boardinghouses.[12] This separation of
women workers from their immediate families heightened the importance of the peer group among Lowell operatives, a phenomenon that
will be examined further in succeeding chapters.

These data on the composition of the mill work force at the Hamilton
Company in the mid-1830s are crucial to an understanding of the nature
of community and the growth of labor protest in Lowell in this period.
To limit the analysis to Lowell, however, is to gloss over the fact that the
work force was the product of a rural-urban migration that linked the
factory town to numerous villages in the surrounding countryside. Tracing women workers back to the families and communities from which
they came will more clearly place the Lowell work force in a broader
context and contribute to a fuller understanding of the meaning of the
mill experience in the lives of women workers.[13]

Here again the register volumes of the Hamilton Company provide a
starting point for the analysis. These volumes recorded the entrances
and departures of operatives, noting their nativity as well. Seven hundred workers entered the Hamilton mills in the first six months of 1836,

and New Hampshire towns predominated among those sending large numbers into the company's employ. Excluding Lowell itself, twelve of the fourteen towns that sent the largest numbers of workers to Hamilton were found in New Hampshire, five of these in central Merrimack County. From the communities in Merrimack County that supplied so many workers to Hamilton, I selected three towns with particularly complete published vital records—Boscawen, Canterbury, and Sutton—for detailed examination. [14]

These towns were long-settled agricultural communities by the second third of the nineteenth century. The initial land grants for all three towns had been made by 1750; first settlement and incorporation of the towns were complete by 1784. They moved rapidly beyond the frontier stage and reached relative population peaks before 1830. Their populations held steady between 1830 and 1850, ranging from about 1,400 for Sutton to a bit more than 2,000 for Boscawen. The steady growth of previous decades halted as the good lands were absorbed and the local economies stagnated. [15] Unable to fulfull their ambitions at home, the young people departed to more fertile western lands or to the growing cities of New England. In this respect the three sample communities shared an experience common to a majority of the hill-country towns of central Vermont and New Hampshire in the period: rapid growth followed by decline and outmigration. [16]

In economic as in demographic terms, Boscawen, Canterbury, and Sutton had much in common. All three were overwhelmingly agricultural communities. The vast majority of adult men worked in farm occupations, the proportions in 1840 varying from 82 percent for Boscawen to 87 percent for Canterbury. All three had, however, a small number of artisans—blacksmiths, shoemakers, carpenters, and furniture makers were most numerous—providing needed services for the local community. A number of grist and saw mills, carding and fulling mills, and tanneries dotted the banks of local streams, but they were invariably small affairs and generated few jobs. In fact the most significant "industry" reported in an 1833 census of manufactures was sheepraising. Boscawen counted some 5,000 sheep, Sutton another 4,000, and both communities derived considerable cash income from the sale of wool in Lowell and Boston. The 1830s saw a rapid growth in the size of herds in central New Hampshire as the price of wool rose substantially. By 1836 the number of sheep in Boscawen, Canterbury, and Sutton was reliably reported to be greater than 18,000. Increasingly, the communities looked toward urban markets for their wool. Treading the same paths were the many young women who sought employment in the Lowell mills. [17]

While all three towns were primarily farming communities, there were differences among them. Boscawen and Canterbury were river valley settlements, located just across the Merrimack River from one another. They had lush, flat farm land periodically enriched by deposits from spring flooding, while in sharp contrast, Sutton was a hill town, marred by steep hills that minimized the prime farmlands. As a result sheep and dairy farming were more important in the Sutton economy than in the other two towns. [18] Sutton was also a far poorer community, as evidenced in the low property valuations of taxpayers in 1830. The mean valuation of individual taxed property in that year for Sutton was $362, well below the comparable figures of $518 and $685 for Boscawen and Canterbury respectively. [19]

Despite these differences among the towns, large numbers of young women from all three set out for Lowell and found employment in the Hamilton Company. Between 1830 and 1850 at least 75 women left Boscawen to work in the mills of the Hamilton Company, while 55 and 45 came from Canterbury and Sutton respectively. In contrast to the total of 175 women recorded in company register volumes, only 9 men from these communities came to work at Hamilton, although larger numbers

TABLE 3.2. FIRST ENTRANCES OF NEW HAMPSHIRE WOMEN
AT HAMILTON, 1827–1850

Entrance Date	Proportion (%)
1827–1834	47.7
1835–1839	30.8
1840–1844	12.8
1845–1850	8.7
Total cases	172
Missing cases	3

NOTE: Although the sample consisted of women recorded in register volumes between 1830 and 1850, a few actually entered earlier, necessitating the 1827 beginning date for the table.

worked elsewhere in Lowell as city directory and marriage records make clear.[20]

The women began employment at the Hamilton Company primarily in the 1830s, particularly in the first half of that decade. Table 3.2 indicates the distribution of their first entrances into the mill work force at Hamilton.

Women from these three New Hampshire towns were a representative cross section of the female work force at Hamilton. Since almost 80 percent of the women entered employment before 1840, it is reasonable to compare the group with women employed at Hamilton in July 1836. In terms of the rooms they worked in, their age and marital status, and the length of their careers, they did not deviate significantly from the work force as a whole.

The New Hampshire women were distributed throughout the major rooms of the Hamilton Company in proportions quite similar to those for the overall female work force. Table 3.3 makes this point clear.

There were slightly more weavers and proportionately fewer carders and spinners among the New Hampshire sample members than in the female work force as a whole. This occupational distribution suggests that sample members were probably earning wages somewhat higher than those of the female work force as a whole. These differences were not great enough, however, to indicate that they were a privileged stratum within the mills.

The ages of the New Hampshire operatives are consistent with the findings presented earlier for residents of Hamilton Company boarding-

TABLE 3.3. ROOM DISTRIBUTION OF NEW HAMPSHIRE WOMEN AT
FIRST ENTRANCE AT HAMILTON, COMPARED TO
OVERALL FEMALE WORK FORCE, JULY 1836

	Proportion	
Room	NH women	Female work force
Carding	10.9%	14.3%
Spinning	20.0	26.1
Weaving	51.4	43.0
Dressing and others	17.7	16.5
Total cases	175	880

TABLE 3.4. AGE DISTRIBUTION OF NEW HAMPSHIRE WOMEN
AT FIRST ENTRANCE AT HAMILTON

Age Group	Proportion[a] (%)
Under 15	14.3
15.0–19.9	46.2
20.0–24.9	25.2
25.0–29.9	9.2
30.0 and over	5.0
Total cases	119
Missing cases	56

[a] Column may not add up to 100.0% due to rounding.

houses. Few children or older women came to the mills from these three rural communities. The mean age for beginning work at the company was 19.8, and women on the average completed their careers at Hamilton when they were 22.4 years old. Table 3.4 provides data on the age distribution of New Hampshire women at the beginning of their employment at Hamilton.

As with the boardinghouse residents enumerated in the 1830 and 1840 censuses of Lowell, about 80 percent of the women were between the ages of 15 and 29 when they began work at Hamilton. The proportion under 15, 14.3 percent, seems on the high side, but this age distribution catches the group at first entrance into the mills. By the time of their departures, only 4.5 percent of the women were under 15 years of age.

The data on age suggest that mill work attracted young women seeking employment for a brief period before marriage, and the evidence on marital status confirms this supposition. Almost 97 percent—124 of the 128 with usable marriage linkage—were single, never married at the beginning of their careers at Hamilton. At the end of their employment, fully 93 percent remained single. In terms of actual numbers, only 5 married women and 3 widows were included in this group of mill workers.

The married women in the sample group present a special and interesting case, and although their absolute numbers are small, they deserve some additional consideration. Their careers reveal a number of striking elements. As a group they tended to have very brief stays in the mills.

Mary Morrill worked for three months at Hamilton in 1835. Later she married George Chase, a housewright in Lowell, and returned to Hamilton for four months during the depression months of the winter of 1839-40. Similarly, Naomi Herriman, wife of an overseer at the carpet factory in Lowell, worked two months in 1831-32. Other evidence makes it clear that these married women worked before the birth of children. The living situations of the married working women were also unusual. Two of the women, Mary Morrill Chase and Lydia Currier Bickford, lived with sisters in Lowell during their stints in the mill. Perhaps their husbands' work, or the search for work, had taken them out of the city for a period. Also, the married couples may have been separated, as in the case of Mary Morrill Chase whose earnings were "trusteed"—that is, garnished—by a grocery firm. This practice was common in dealing with men who absconded leaving bad debts behind. All in all, the little that is known about married women workers at Hamilton suggests that such employment was infrequent, that the work periods were brief, that women with children did not work, and that unusual family circumstances were often associated with employment.

Mill employment represented a stage in a woman's life cycle before marriage; this was demonstrated by the fact that the vast majority of operatives did marry after their sojourn in Lowell. Of the 115 women for whom adequate data survive, 98 married. About 15 percent—17 of 115—definitely did not marry, either because they died at a relatively young age—one while working at Hamilton, for instance—or because they chose to remain single. Despite the claims of some contemporary critics of the mills, it is clear that mill employment did not disqualify young women for marriage.[21]

These women came to the mills, of course, as individuals, but they also brought along with them a social position and cultural outlook from their home towns. Nominal record linkage, which provides evidence on the age and marital status of women workers, also enables the historian to place them and their families within the economic and social structure of their home towns. What kinds of generalizations may be made about the families of women operatives? What sort of place did they occupy in their rural communities? And how did millhand daughters fit within their families? It is possible to move beyond the solely individual focus and examine the women and their families within a broader context.

The vast majority of women came from farming families. Almost two thirds of their fathers traced in the 1850 manuscript censuses of these three towns—21 of 32—were listed as farmers by census enumerators. This proportion was slightly higher than that for all male household heads in the three communities. The remainder of the fathers of mill-hands filled a variety of skilled occupations—blacksmith, stonemason, and wheelwright among others. The occupations of the fathers suggest that the women came from rather typical rural families. [22]

Tax inventories reinforce this conclusion. In all, the parents of 62 women workers were successfully linked to tax inventories for Boscawen, Canterbury, or Sutton for 1830. The composition of this group of linked parents and their property holdings indicate that the women were drawn from almost the entire range of families in these towns. Five of the 62 linked parents were widows, 8 percent of the group as a whole. Looking at the data in another way permits a somewhat different perspective. For the three towns taken together, 11 percent of tax-paying female heads of households had a daughter working at Hamilton; among males the comparable figure was 7.7 percent. Even though female-headed families were somewhat more likely to have a daughter working in the mills, more than 90 percent of linked operatives came from typical male-headed households. The female millhand supporting her widowed mother is hardly as common in actuality as contemporary sources suggest.

Property valuations of the fathers of operatives place them in the broad middle ranges of wealth in their home towns. None of the linked fathers was propertyless in 1830 or among the very richest in their communities. Table 3.5 compares the distribution of taxable property among linked fathers with that of all male household heads. [23]

If those fathers linked in tax inventories are representative, then it is evident that women workers did not come from families near destitution. Fully 86 percent of linked fathers had property valued at $100 or more; for all male household heads in these towns the comparable proportion was less than 80 percent. On the whole, however, the typical millhand father was less wealthy than other taxpayers around him. The median property holding of millhand fathers in 1830 was only $338, compared to $459 for all male household heads taxed in the three towns. [24] Even if the typical sample father was somewhat below this

TABLE 3.5. ASSESSED PROPERTY VALUATIONS OF FATHERS OF HAMILTON
OPERATIVES, COMPARED TO MALE HOUSEHOLD HEADS,
BOSCAWEN, CANTERBURY, AND SUTTON, 1830

	Proportions[a]	
Assessed Value of Property	Millhand fathers	Male household heads
$0	0.0%	5.1%
1–99	14.0	15.3
100–499	43.9	32.8
500–999	26.3	27.8
1000–1999	15.8	13.7
2000+	0.0	5.1
Total cases	57	746

[a] Columns may not add up to 100.0% due to rounding.

town median, he remained a propertied member of the community.
That only three parents were ever traced to Lowell is indicative of the
fact that absolute poverty did not drive these families into the factory
town.

Tax inventories list not only the total amount of property owned by
families sending daughters into the mills but also reveal what kind of
property it was. Benjamin Kendrick of Sutton, a rather typical father as
far as his 1830 tax assessment was concerned, had three daughters,
Mary, Judith, and Sarah, who worked at Hamilton between 1835 and
1840. The family also had four sons who undoubtedly helped their father with the work of the farm. Included in the Kendrick property assessed in 1830 were two horses, two oxen, four cows and three "stock,"
undifferentiated. In all, 15.5 acres were under cultivation, while another
50 unimproved acres rounded out the farm. The Kendrick family, like so
many others with daughters employed at Hamilton, was thus tied to a
system of mixed agriculture common in New Hampshire.

The fathers of millhands in 1830 did not comprise a depressed group
within the towns; nor is there any evidence that over time their economic conditions were worsening. For those who could be traced after
1830, property holdings increased steadily. The median value of their
property increased more rapidly than did that of other male household
heads in these three towns.[25] As table 3.6 shows, in 1830 their median
property holdings were $120 less than those of all male household heads;

TABLE 3.6. MEDIAN PROPERTY HOLDINGS OF LINKED MILLHAND FATHERS,
1830–1860, COMPARED TO MALE
HOUSEHOLD HEADS OF SIMILAR AGES

	Median Property Holdings	
	Millhand fathers	Male household heads of similar ages[a]
1830	$338 (57)	$459 (746)
1850	960 (33)	998 (386)
1860	1600 (14)	1203 (236)

SOURCES: 1830 tax inventories and 1850, 1860 Manuscript Censuses. Data for 1830 refer to all taxed property and for 1850 and 1860 to real property only.
[a] For 1830 all male household heads listed in tax inventories have been included; for 1850 and 1860 only those in the same age group as millhand fathers, those over 50 and 60 years of age respectively.

by 1860 they were almost $400 above those of other male household heads of similar ages.

There is some possibility that the findings here are an artifact of the linkage process, and I would not want to make too much of the apparent improvement of millhand fathers relative to other male household heads. Those fathers successfully linked in the 1850 and 1860 censuses had persisted in their home towns for two and three decades respectively, a fact that immediately sets them apart from all household heads of the same ages. If possible one would want to compare millhand fathers only to other persistent household heads within this age group, but this comparison would require extensive nominal record linkage of the manuscript censuses between 1830 and 1860, a task beyond the scope of this study.

Still the evidence undermines any argument that sheer economic need drove large numbers of women into the Lowell mills in the period 1830-1850. At least the economic needs of the families of operatives could not have been a compelling force. Some women, perhaps the 8 percent whose fathers had died, may well have worked in the mills in order to contribute to the support of their families. The evidence strongly suggests that most young women themselves decided to work in the mills. They were generally not *sent* to the mills by their parents to supplement low family incomes but went of their own accord for other reasons. When we also consider the distance separating mill operatives from their families, the probability is strong that it was the women themselves who decided how to spend their earnings. [26]

The correspondence of a number of operatives supports this view. Mary Paul, of Barnard, Vermont, began work in the Lowell mills at 15 or 16, in November 1845. Before going to the mills she had worked briefly as a domestic servant and then lived with relatives a short distance from her home; at that time she wrote seeking her father's permission to go to Lowell. In this letter she revealed the basic motivation that prompted her request: "I think it would be much better for me [in Lowell] than to stay about here. . . . I am in need of clothes which I cannot get about here and for that reason I want to go to Lowell or some other place." After getting permission, Mary Paul worked in Lowell off and on for at least four years. In 1850 she lived briefly with her father, but then went on her own again, this time working as a seamstress in Brattleboro, Vermont. She evidently felt some guilt at not contributing to her father's support. In an 1853 letter she wrote "I hope sometime to be able to do something for you and sometimes feel ashamed that I have not before this." But there were obstacles which she noted:

> I am not one of the *smart* kind, and never had a passion for laying up money, probably never shall have, can find enough ways to spend it though (but I do not wish to be extravagant). Putting all these things together I think explains the reason that I do not 'lay up' anything.

She expressed the wish that sometime she could live with her father and provide for him but always fell back on the argument that sent her to Lowell in the first place: "I . . . must work where I can get more pay." [27]

Sally Rice of Somerset, Vermont, left her home in 1838 at the age of 17 to take her first job "working out." Her work and her travels took her to Union Village, New York, where she supported herself on farm work, and led eventually to Thompson, Connecticut, where she found employment in a textile factory. That she was working for her own personal support and not to assist her family is evident in a poignant letter she wrote to her parents from Union Village in 1839 rejecting her familial home:

> I can never be happy there in among so many mountains. . . . I feel as though I have worn out shoes and strength enough riding and

walking over the mountains. I think it would be more consistent to save my strength to raise my boys. I shall need all I have got and as for marrying and settling in that wilderness, I wont. If a person ever expects to take comfort it is while they are young. I feel so. . . . I have got so that by next summer if I could stay I could begin to lay up something. . . . I am most 19 years old. I must of course have something of my own before many more years have passed over my head. And where is that something coming from if I go home and earn nothing. . . . You may think me unkind but how can you blame me for wanting to stay here. I have but one life to live and I want to enjoy myself as well as I can while I live. [28]

Sally Rice left home to earn "something of my own," which was obviously not possible in the family economy of her father's farm. The more fertile farm lands of neighboring New York created a demand for agricultural labor and offered wages high enough to attract Sally Rice away from the "wilderness" about Somerset. The wages in the textile mills of central and southern New England soon proved an even greater lure for this farmer's daughter eager to earn her own money.

Earning wages to provide for a dowry seems to have been Sally Rice's primary motivation for leaving home in 1838. Mill employment appealed to her principally because its wages were higher than those for farm laborers or domestic servants. She did not consider mill work a long-term prospect but intended to remain there only briefly: "I should not want to spend my days in a mill unless they are short because I like a farm too well for that." Finally, in 1847, probably with a sufficient dowry laid up, Sally Rice married the brother of a fellow operative and settled in Worcester, Massachusetts. [29]

If clothes and a dowry provided the motivation for Mary Paul and Sally Rice to leave home and work in textile factories, a desire for education stimulated the efforts of one mill worker in Clinton, Massachusetts, in 1851. One Lucy Ann had her sights set on using her wages to attend Oberlin College. In a letter to a cousin she wrote: "I have earned enough to school me awhile, & have not I a right to do so, or must I go home, like a dutiful girl, place the money in father's hands, & then there goes all my hard earnings." If she had to turn her wages over to her family she would consider them a "dead loss" and all her efforts would have been "spent in vain." Clearly mill employment could be turned to individualistic purposes. As Lucy Ann summed up her thinking: "I merely

wish to go [to Oberlin] because I think it the best way of spending the
money I have worked so hard to earn." [30]

Lucy Ann wrote in a belligerent, but defensive, tone which seemed to
say, "Others may find fault with me, and call me selfish, but I think I
should spend my earnings as I please." Her need to justify her conduct
suggests that others had not risen in her defense. One senses, however,
that she would spend her money as she chose, regardless of what others
had to say. Other letters reveal that it was often taken for granted, by
operatives and their parents alike, that women's earnings were their own
to spend as they pleased. Consider an 1840 letter from Elizabeth Hodgdon, of Rochester, New Hampshire, to her sister, Sarah, working in the
mills in nearby Great Falls:

> You say you want to come home when we all think you have staid
> long enough, but we do not know better than you or so well either
> when you have earned as much as you will want to spend. Yet it is
> Mothers opinion & mine that you have already as much as you will
> probably want to spend if you lay it out to good advantage which
> we doubt not but you will. [31]

Elizabeth suggests, and her mother evidently concurs, that Sarah should
work as long as necessary to earn as much as she felt she needed. When
Sarah returned to Rochester it is likely that she would not turn her
savings over to her parents, but would spend them as she chose. The
earnings would undoubtedly relieve her parents of certain expenses they
might have incurred had she simply lived at home, and in this way her
income was a help to them. The letter reinforces the distinct impression
that emerges from the correspondence as a whole that when daughters
left home and entered the mills they ceased to be "dependents" in the
traditional sense. They supported themselves while at work and used
their savings to maintain a certain independence even during the periods
they lived at home.

The Hodgdon correspondence is important because it suggests that
there was no great conflict between familial and individual interests for
most women workers. Parents gave their approval to daughters' plans to
work in the mills and were glad to see them earning money for themselves. Times were often hard in rural northern New England after 1830,
and even in prosperous years there were few opportunities for women to

earn anything while living at home. Whether or not working women actually contributed to support their families back home, each departure did mean one less mouth to feed. And with the growth of factory textile production, the contributions of farmers' daughters to the family economy declined significantly. Eben Jennison of Charleston, Maine, may have reflected the changing calculus of the family economy when, in 1849, he wrote to his daughter Elizabeth who was employed at the Merrimack Company in Lowell: "The season with us has been verry Dry and the Drough[t] verry severe. The crops are very light indeed and business verry Dull. If you should be blessed with your health and are contented I think you will do better where you are than you could do here." For Jennison, the decade of the 1850s appears to have been a difficult one, and by 1858 he had two daughters, Elizabeth and Amelia, working in the mills. In one of his letters to them he acknowledged the receipt of five dollars and expressed his hope that "some day or other" he would be able to repay them *with interest*. He needed the money but felt shame accepting it. Throughout his correspondence to his daughters, it is clear that he felt they should be in Lowell, but not because he expected them to contribute to his support as a matter of course. In fact his pride and sense of self-respect made it difficult for him to accept their apparently unsolicited aid, although need won out in the end. Still, even as he accepted their money, he viewed it as a loan to be repaid when his economic fortunes had improved.[32]

The view of women's motivations that emerges from analysis of their social origins and correspondence with their families stands in sharp contrast to contemporary writings, especially to the *Lowell Offering*, an operatives' literary magazine of the period.[33] In the repeated "factory tales" published in the *Offering*, writers stressed the selfless motivations that sent women into the mills. Characters in the stories were invariably orphans supporting themselves and younger brothers and sisters, or young women helping to pay off the mortgage on a family homestead or to send a brother to college, or widows raising and supporting families. Never, in the fiction at least, did an operative work in the mills in order to buy "new clothes" or to get away from a domineering father, though in real life these motivations must have been common enough. The more idealistic themes of the *Offering* presented the best possible case against those who argued that women should not work in the mills at all.

The data on the social origins of workers, together with their letters, tell a rather different story.

Mill work should not be viewed as simply an extension of the traditional family economy as work for women moved outside the home. Work in the mills functioned for women rather like migration did for young men who could see that their chances of setting up on a farm in an established rural community were rather slim. The mills offered individual self-support, enabled women to enjoy urban amenities not available in their rural communities, and gave them a measure of economic and social independence from their families. These factors made Lowell attractive to rural women and led them to choose to work in the mills. The steady movement of the family farm from a subsistence to a commercial basis made daughters relatively "expendable" and gave fathers who otherwise might have guarded the family labor supply reason to allow them a chance on their own.

The work patterns in Lowell are strikingly different from those evident for young, single European women in this period. Joan Scott and Louise Tilly have argued convincingly that women's work outside the home in nineteenth-century Europe should be viewed primarily as an extension of the traditional family economy within a changed economic setting. They argue that parents *sent* their daughters out to work and that daughters routinely turned over all or large portions of their earnings directly to their parents. [34] Such practices may have prevailed earlier in those spinning mills of southern New England that hired entire families, but there is little evidence of this sort of pattern in mill towns of the Waltham-Lowell variety. For the New Hampshire women traced here, only 3 of 175 parents were linked to Lowell. Furthermore, operatives' correspondence suggests that most women spent and saved their earnings as they chose with little pressure to contribute to their family's support.

Several factors are relevant in explaining the differences in the American setting. First, the nature of the traditional family economy in rural New England differed from its counterpart among European peasants. Diaries of American women suggest that daughters living at home often kept a portion of their earnings, indicating that they were not totally subordinated within the family economy even when living at home. [35] Secondly, as New England daughters sought mill employment they generally left home and accepted a considerable separation from their families, in terms of both distance and time. The physical separation of women and their residence in a peer-group community of other young, single women further encouraged their economic and social independence. Finally, their correspondence suggests they did not have to buck very strong parental counterpressures in this regard. Parents encouraged their daughters, or at least appear to have given their approval, and do not seem to have demanded that they place their earnings in the family till. Scott and Tilly point out that over time "more individualistic and instrumental" attitudes did develop among European working women, but these attitudes appear to have developed more rapidly and with less resistance in northern New England than in the European context. [36]

While Lowell women do not appear to have been working to support their families, analysis of family patterns among operatives reveals that family factors did influence entry into the mills. The families of women workers at Hamilton were large ones, but daughters did not enter the mills at random. On the average there were 7.2 children in completed families, 3.7 of whom were daughters. Employed daughters tended to be first or second daughters rather than younger ones. Among the families of millhands, 63 had two or more daughters who can be placed in their proper birth order. [37] In all, these 63 families had 244 daughters. From among these daughters, 90, or 36.9 percent, worked for the Hamilton Company at some point between 1830 and 1850, but as table 3.7 shows very clearly, firstborn daughters were much more likely to be employed at Hamilton than were their younger sisters.

TABLE 3.7. RANK BIRTH ORDER OF NEW HAMPSHIRE WOMEN
EMPLOYED AT THE HAMILTON COMPANY, 1830–1850

Rank Order among Daughters	Number of Daughters in Rank	Number of Daughters at Hamilton	Proportion (%)
1st	63	29	46.0
2d	63	27	42.9
3d	51	18	35.3
4th	35	11	31.4
5th or higher	32	5	15.6
Overall	244	90	36.9

NOTE: Includes only women drawn from families with two or more daughters for whom rank birth order is known.

Almost half of firstborn daughters, 46 percent, worked at the Hamilton Company in this period. The proportion declined steadily, though, for younger siblings, until fifth or later-born daughters, of whom only 15.6 percent went to Hamilton. Among these families oldest daughters were about three times as likely as the youngest to work away from home. This pattern may reflect a greater adventuresomeness among older girls in the family or a somewhat more protective attitude on the part of parents toward their younger daughters. Or perhaps a daughter's departure for the mills may have been tied in with the family cycle. Oldest daughters may have responded to a kind of population pressure within the family. The families may have been particularly crowded in small farmhouses, or the farm simply may have been unable to produce enough for such a large family. Their departures to the mills, and their subsequent marriages, would have relieved this pressure, thus enabling younger daughters to remain in the household. Since the millhands tended to come of age in the 1830s and younger sisters a decade later, the figures may reflect the declining attraction of the Lowell mills for Yankee women. While the explanations offered here must remain conjectures, the pattern of recruitment into the mills is clear.

An additional finding that emerges from the study of the families of operatives is evidence that women came to Lowell not as isolated individuals but as members of broader kin networks. [38] Almost two thirds— 71 of 111 for whom family reconstitution is possible—had other relatives employed at Hamilton at some time or other in the period 1830-1850. Sister pairs predominated among operatives, as is evident from the figures in table 3.7 that indicate that 90 daughters from 63 families worked in the Hamilton mills. But at least 13 operatives had cousins employed at Hamilton as well. Even these figures must be seen as minimum estimates, since vital records and genealogies shed little light on broader kin relations. For the most part it is only possible to trace networks on the father's side of the families.

Illustrations drawn from a number of individual cases illuminate the importance of kin networks for women workers. Lucinda and Abigail White of Sutton came to Lowell in June 1835 and worked together in Carding Room A at Hamilton. Abigail remained only 6 months, but her sister worked on and off until at least March 1840. Her entire family may have moved to Lowell, for her father died there in May 1841. Both sisters married Lowell men and continued to reside there after marriage. Thus the Whites as a family made the move from the countryside to the city, and for at least several family members the move proved to be a permanent one. [39]

Two other families came to Lowell from their rural homes; in each case the father's death appears to have been the precipitating event. Mary Woodward came from one of the poorer Sutton families. Her father, David Woodward, was assessed in 1830 for two cows, eight acres of "wild" lands, and one building worth $25. He had no other livestock and no cultivated land whatsoever. The exact date of his death is uncertain, but in June 1845, Mary Woodward began work at the Hamilton Company and lived with her mother, Ruth, on Cady Street in Lowell. Two brothers, Dana and David, married and died in Lowell. Mary herself died in Lowell in the cholera epidemic of 1849.

The Sawyer family, of Canterbury, also moved to Lowell. Apphia Sawyer, almost certainly a widow, kept a boardinghouse at the Appleton Company in 1830 and at the adjacent Hamilton Company between 1832 and 1836. Two daughters, Nancy and Mary, worked briefly at the Hamilton Company, living at their "Mom's" according to company registers. [40]

Apphia Sawyer, Ruth Woodward, and Henry White were the only parents of women operatives from Boscawen, Canterbury, and Sutton known to have lived in Lowell. They were unusual, as intergenerational kinship ties among workers in Lowell were rare. More frequently, sisters worked together in the mills. Eunice and Mary Austin, of Boscawen, for instance, worked in Upper Weaving Room C at Hamilton in 1830. They lived together in a company boardinghouse, and both left in July of that year. Two Canterbury sisters, Lucy Jane and Caroline Ames, began work together in April 1835 and resided in the same boardinghouse. They did not, however, work in the same room in the mills. Fourteen-year-old Caroline worked as a weaver, while her 18-year-old sister was employed in the dressing room. Usually dressing room hands were experienced operatives, suggesting that Lucy Jane Ames may have worked elsewhere before coming to Hamilton. In any event, Lucy remained at the company only a year, while Caroline worked off and on over the course of the next five years.

Kinship ties among mill operatives played a number of important roles for women workers in early Lowell. The existence of these bonds must have eased the shock of adjustment both to work in the factories and to the novel urban setting. The fact that so many pairs of sisters at Hamilton resided together in company boardinghouses and often worked in the same rooms at the mill strongly suggests the importance of a familial support network for newcomers. Experienced operatives probably arranged for housing accommodations ahead of time and may have been able to speak to the overseer on their sisters' behalf. Julia A. Dutton, of Clintonville, Massachusetts, described such arrangements in an 1847 letter to her mother in Vermont:

> I have engaged a place for Martha Coffren the first of Nov[ember]. The overseer sayed she might come at that [date] and if she is large enough for a weaver he will take her if not she can go into some other room. There is no doubt but she will work a plenty. She will have [$]1.25 [a week above board] while she is learning to weave.[41]

The presence of an older, more knowledgeable family member in Lowell must have comforted parents thinking about allowing a second child to make the journey. An 1849 letter from Eben Jennison of Charleston, Maine, to his daughter, Elizabeth, in Lowell, makes this point explicitly. Referring to a younger daughter, Emily, then sixteen, he noted:

> A few words in relation to Emily. She has got about ready to come to Lowel. Martha A. Marshall expects to return to Lowel in the course of some two or three weeks and if Emily comes she will come with hir. I should not consent to hir coming at any rate if you was not there. She is young and needs a mothers care and a mothers advise. You must se to hir and give hir such council as you thinks she needs. She may be Homesick for a spell but if you comfort hir up she will soon get the better of it.[42]

Since most of the women were in their teens when they first set off for the mills, family ties must have been a comfort for both the operatives and their parents.

Sisters or cousins working together constituted only the simplest of kin networks at the Hamilton Company. Groupings of this sort could in fact become quite intricate. The Danforth family of Boscawen was at the heart of one such network. Jedidiah and Rachel Danforth had eight children between 1803 and 1827, four boys and four girls. Twin oldest daughters, Rachel and Sarah, worked together in Weaving Room A at Hamilton between March 1830 and July 1832. Both resided at Number 6, Hamilton Company. A brother, Nathan, worked in Lowell as a stonemason and boarded at the Lawrence Corporation in 1834. The next year found him employed by the Tremont Company in Lowell.

Although Sophia Brown of Boscawen had no immediate kin at the Hamilton Company, she was not alone there. She worked in Weaving Room A alongside Rachel Danforth and lived in the same boardinghouse. In July 1833 she married Nathan Danforth, and thus the Brown and Danforth families of Boscawen were linked in Lowell. The young couple resided in Lowell for two years and then returned to Boscawen, where they raised five children.

Marriage also linked the Danforth and Fowler families of Boscawen and Lowell. Four Fowler sisters worked at Hamilton, sometimes together and sometimes sequentially between 1831 and 1842. Harriet and Sarah Fowler both worked in Weaving Room A in 1831, overlapping for a period with Sarah and Rachel Danforth. The eldest sister, Mary, came to Lowell in March 1836 and worked with her sister Harriet. Finally, a fourth sister, Elizabeth, came to Lowell in 1842, and after a stretch at the Lawrence Company, she too worked in Weaving Room A at Hamilton. Mary Fowler united the two mill families when she married Jedidiah Danforth, another brother of Rachel and Sarah, in Lowell in 1838.

The kin networks described here and traced through Hamilton Company records reveal only part of a dense thicket of relationships. First, they trace only blood relatives for the most part. Rachel and Sarah Danforth, for instance, had two future sisters-in-law working beside them at Hamilton, as did Mary Fowler and Sophia Brown. Furthermore, these operatives had additional relatives in Lowell, though they may never have worked at Hamilton. Only the marriages of Mary Fowler and Sophia Brown revealed that two Danforth brothers resided in Lowell.

Moreover, similar kin networks extending beyond the bounds of the Hamilton Company can be traced. Martha, Mary, and Nancy Emery of Canterbury all worked at Hamilton; one even lived in Mrs. Sawyer's boardinghouse for a time. In addition, four Emery brothers worked and married in Lowell, though none seems to have found his way to the Hamilton Company. Mary Morrill Chase had no relatives employed with her in the mills, but a sister, Sarah Morrill, married in Lowell and raised three children there between 1840 and 1849. Mary Woodward of Sutton had two cousins in Lowell, one a carpenter for many years, the other a "popular" teacher in Lowell, or at least so the compiler of Sutton's genealogies thought. Many more examples might be cited, but the point is clear. Rich kinship networks—along blood and marriage lines—joined women workers to one another while living and working in Lowell. They came to Lowell not as isolated individuals but as members of larger supportive groups. Those who did not come as part of a group seem to have been able to recreate such a network once arrived in Lowell.

From the vital records and local genealogies one can reconstruct the dimensions of the kinship network among women workers in early Lowell. But the support system extended beyond blood ties and included unrelated friends from the home towns as well. These sorts of bonds are not so easily traced through the kinds of records cited thus far, but literary sources can be particularly useful in this regard. Although none of the women in this sample left letters, diaries, or reminiscences describing their lives in Lowell, other New England women did. These sources confirm the importance of a support system based on kinship and friendship among rural women in urban, industrial Lowell.

Two sisters, Sarah and Elizabeth Hodgdon, worked in the textile mills of Lowell and Great Falls, New Hampshire, between 1830 and 1840. They came to Lowell together, and a family friend, Wealthy Page, took them in hand and aided them in the difficulties of their first months. The sisters lived together and worked in the same weaving room. They felt ill-treated by members of the Freewill Baptist Church, apparently because they could not afford to rent a pew. Wealthy Page stood by them during this crisis and assured mutual Rochester friends: "I am just the same friend to Sarah that I was when I promised to befriend her." [43]

Similarly, Mary Paul of Barnard, Vermont, went to Lowell in November 1845 and worked there periodically until at least July 1849. She went by stage to Lowell, the first time accompanied by a friend, Mercy Griffith. When in Lowell, Luthera Griffith took her to the mills and helped her find her first job. Here again, in the absence of kin in Lowell, friends from the rural home town played a supportive role for a newcomer. [44]

Surviving letters reveal the importance of continuing family ties for women in the mills. Family members often visited Lowell even when they did not reside there. Louisa Sawyer wrote a cousin that her brother had come to Lowell with her from her home in East Andover, New Hampshire, and that she expected he would come again soon. Her brother later lived in Lowell, himself, for she noted in a subsequent letter written from her rural home: "Brother Daniel came Home yesto-day and is well and left the Lowell friends all well." While Louisa and Daniel were home in New Hampshire one winter, their sister, Emeline, went to work in Lowell. [45]

Obviously, visits of relatives reinforced links between kin networks in Lowell and those back in the countryside. Mary Hall's diary, cited earlier, is remarkable for the repeated accounts it contains of visiting relatives. Two weeks after Mary began work, brother Learned visited briefly. Another brother, Robert, called at the countinghouse two weeks later and stayed for five weeks. Learned returned for a second visit while his brother was still there. Mary left the mills after seven months, and when she returned to Lowell, a year and a half later, two cousins accompanied her. An aunt resided in Lowell at this time, but Mary continued to board in company housing. Family visits quickly resumed. Mary's father and brother Robert appeared just two days after she started work, with her brother staying for two months. A third brother, Isaac, stopped in Lowell en route to Boston shortly thereafter. Learned visited one more time before Mary left Lowell, accompanied appropriately enough by brother Isaac. The visits came so often that one almost wonders whether the Hall family felt a need to keep a watch on Mary. [46]

Frequent visits kept Mary Hall in close touch with her family. Others, however, had to bridge the gap that separated them from their families with correspondence. The letters they wrote indicate that even when work in the mills took women away from family and friends, they continued to feel strong affection and concern for those at home. They felt distant but by no means estranged from loved ones.

Sarah Hodgdon's first letter home poignantly expresses the continuing bond that tied women to their families. It closed: "Give my love to farther. Tell him not to forget me and to my dear sister and to my brothers and to my grammother. Tell her I do not forget her. And to my Aunts and to all my enquiring friends." Her feelings welled into home-sickness in a poem she quoted in closing a subsequent letter:

I want to se you more I think
Than I can write with pen and ink.
But when I shall I cannot tell
But from my heart I wish you well.
I wish you well from all my heart
Although we are so far apart.
If you die there and I die here,
Before one God we shall apeare. [47]

Taken together, the family reconstitution data, the reconstruction of individual women's careers in Lowell, and the operatives' correspondence all indicate that women workers in the early mills were part of a social network of family and friends which had its roots in the countryside and which played an important role in their lives in Lowell. While women may not have been working expressly to contribute to their families back home, they were still operating within a familial context that is best viewed as a part of their traditional rural culture. Mill employment had not recast women within a completely individualistic mold. In Lowell women continued to provide crucial support to one another, as neighbors and family members had done for years in the countryside. They recruited one another into the mills, secured jobs for each other, and helped newcomers make the numerous adjustments called for in a very new and different setting. Here we see clear evidence of the maintenance of traditional kinds of social relationships in a new setting and serving new purposes. [48]

These kinship networks helped operatives adjust to urban life, but they also made a more direct contribution to women's success in the mills. Women operatives whose kin were also employed at Hamilton were able, on the whole, to secure better jobs in the mill. Table 3.8 contrasts the initial room assignment of those sample members who had relatives at Hamilton with the experience of those who did not.

More than 70 percent of women with relatives in the work force were hired initially to work in the high-paying weaving and dressing rooms, while only 52.5 percent of those without relatives began their mill careers there. These figures reinforce what Julia Dutton's letter quoted earlier pointed out: knowing someone already employed in the mills helped in securing one of the better-paying jobs. [49]

One of the consequences of better job placement of newcomers with

TABLE 3.8. INITIAL ROOM ASSIGNMENT OF NEW HAMPSHIRE WOMEN
AT THE HAMILTON COMPANY

Initial Room Assignment	Proportions[a]	
	With relatives	Without relatives
Carding	9.9%	17.5%
Spinning, winding	19.7	30.0
Weaving	54.9	42.5
Dressing	15.5	10.0
Total cases	71	40

[a] Columns may not add up to 100.0% due to rounding.

kin was that they remained longer at the company. Those with relatives worked at Hamilton an average of 3.66 years; those without kin remained only 2.21 years.[50] Having other members of the family at Hamilton clearly opened up opportunities for women and led them to stay longer in the mills. It also aided the companies. Because mill managers often complained that no sooner had they trained newcomers than they quit, encouraging family ties among workers made good business sense. Family networks reduced labor turnover and resulted in a more experienced and more productive labor force, which in turn contributed to greater profits. In the end, both workers and corporations benefited from the growth of kinship networks in the mill work force.

Clearly, then, the rural backgrounds as well as the kinship and friendship networks of these women were important factors in their entry into Lowell and their careers in the mills. It remains to examine the lives of these operatives after their years in the mills to ask how important the mill experience was to them. Did Lowell make any difference in their later lives, or was their experience there simply a brief and rather inconsequential episode? To answer this question it is necessary to look at the married lives of women in the sample group after they left the Hamilton Company.

Two contrasting illustrations may clarify the relevant issues. The marriages of Judith Kendrick and Abigail Hale provide the polar extremes for the marital experience of women workers in Lowell. Judith Kendrick of Sutton worked for two years at the Hamilton Company in the late

1830s. Two sisters worked at Hamilton as well. In April 1840 Judith Kendrick married James Peaslee of Sutton and the two settled in their home town. They followed a life much like that of their parents. By 1850 the census noted James's occupation as laborer and set the value of his real property at $600. Tax inventories for the same year agree with the census but indicate that he owned five cows and four sheep as well. He may in fact have inherited his father's farm, since his widowed mother resided with the family. The Peaslees prospered over the decade of the 1850s, and by 1860 James owned $2000 worth of real property and another $465 in personal property. His occupation, or rather his status, was that of yeoman farmer. Clearly, James and Judith Peaslee had a secure place in their rural community.

Abigail Hale of Boscawen took a somewhat different route after leaving the mills. She also worked two years at Hamilton in the early 1830s, but she evidently did not leave for good when she married Ebenezer Calef in Lowell in January 1837. Calef worked at the neighboring Appleton Company and boarded nearby. Upon marriage, the Calef family lived in a house on High Street. They continued to reside in Lowell at least until 1851, and Abigail Hale Calef gave birth to a son and a daughter during this period. Abigail had clearly forsaken her rural roots. It is unlikely that the Calefs, after fourteen years of married life in Lowell, returned to a rural home.

These two sketches raise an obvious question: which was more typical of the experience of women workers in early Lowell? Did most women return to their home towns, marry, and settle into the rural patterns of their childhood, or did they remain in Lowell or some similar urban setting? Clearly, their lives touched two worlds—that of the countryside and that of the city. Which one had the greater attraction?

The occupations of the husbands of millhands are instructive on this score. I have been able to determine the occupations of almost half of the known husbands—45 of 98—through linkage in the *Lowell Directory* or in the federal manuscript censuses of Boscawen, Canterbury, and Sutton. Whereas two thirds of the fathers of these operatives had held agricultural occupations, less than a third of their husbands did so, either at the time of marriage or at any time thereafter (see table 3.9). Skilled trades—carpenters, masons, and machinists among others—made up the largest single occupational group, accounting for fully a third of the jobs

TABLE 3.9. OCCUPATIONS OF HUSBANDS OF FORMER HAMILTON
OPERATIVES IN NEW HAMPSHIRE SAMPLE

Occupation	Proportion (%)
Skilled trades	33.3
Farmers, farm laborers	31.1
Textile mills	20.0
Others	15.6
Total cases	45

held by husbands of former millhands. Overall, more than two thirds of these men worked in nonagricultural occupations. [51]

Husbands' occupations reflect in part the simple fact that a large proportion of them resided in Lowell and that they could hardly have been farmers in that setting. However, a majority of even those husbands who lived in Boscawen, Canterbury, and Sutton after their marriages chose nonagricultural occupations. Of the 24 husbands living in these three towns in 1850, only 10—or 41.7 percent—were farmers. Nine were skilled artisans, and the remaining 5 were unskilled workers. Ten years later the proportion principally engaged in agriculture had increased, but still it reached only 50 percent—9 of 18.

One might argue that the difference between the fathers and the spouses of millhands was basically a generational one. Perhaps the occupational patterns of fathers and husbands simply reflected the fact that the fathers were 20 years older and more likely to have owned land upon which they could earn their living. However, if one compares husbands to male household heads of roughly the same age—between 30 and 50 years old in 1850—one finds that they were much less likely to be farmers than their peers. In 1850, for instance, 59.5 percent of male household heads in this age group were farmers, compared to only 41.7 percent of husbands of former millhands. Even controlling for age, these men were more likely to be working in artisan or unskilled manual occupations than were all males in their home towns. [52]

In yet another way the marriage patterns of women in the sample differed significantly from those of their parents—and of other rural women in their own generation. Former operatives tended to marry rather later than usual and to marry men who were on average the same

TABLE 3.10. AGE AT FIRST MARRIAGE OF MILLHANDS AND HUSBANDS

	Millhands (1)	Husbands (2)	Age Difference [a] (1) − (2)
Mean	26.3	25.3	+0.83
Median	25.2	24.5	+0.58
Total cases	80	36	35

NOTE: Table excludes ages at second marriages.
[a] Age differences calculated only for marriages for which ages of both mill-hand and husband are known.

age or slightly younger than themselves. Table 3.10 presents findings for the ages at first marriage for sample members and for their spouses. On average, these women workers married when they were 26 years old and tended to marry men who were ten months younger than themselves.

These figures stand in sharp contrast to data on age at first marriage for men and women throughout New England at this time. Vital registration data for Massachusetts between 1845 and 1860, for instance, indicate that on average men married 2.5 years later than did women. Vermont state figures for 1858 show men marrying at 24.6 years of age on average and women at 21.4, a difference of more than three years. Local community studies based on family reconstitution confirm these state-level findings. In Sturbridge, Massachusetts, between 1820 and 1849, women married for the first time at a mean age of 25.5; for men the comparable figure was 27.8. For Concord, Massachusetts, between 1831 and 1850 mean ages at first marriage for men and women were 26.5 and 23.4 respectively. Finally, for Hingham, Massachusetts, in a roughly comparable period, male and female figures came to 26.0 and 23.3 respectively. In every study *except* that of mill operatives in the Hamilton sample, the mean age at first marriage for men exceeded that for women by more than two years. [53]

The difference between the New Hampshire millhands and the other groups probably stems from the fact that in the years before marriage these women were separated from their families, living away from home and supporting themselves. It is likely that the economic and social independence that they achieved was reflected in their choice of spouse. Their parents probably had only a limited voice in the final selection, especially for those who met their husbands in Lowell. Furthermore, marrying a bit later than was typical for rural women in this period, the pool of men they chose from would have been younger (at least relative to themselves). The savings women brought with them and the similarity of ages of husband and wife in these couples may have placed the marriage partners on a more equal footing than would have been true in marriages for most rural women. In all, the data on marriage age of mill women suggest that the mill experience may have set them apart from others and prepared them for marriages that represented something of a departure from traditional patterns.

The evidence on the age of millhands at marriage suggests one important way in which early industrial capitalism changed the lives of women who worked in the early mills. It seems to have led women to marry considerably later than was general for rural women in this period. This pattern contradicts the conclusion that David Levine reached on examining similar data for the village of Shepshed, an industrial outwork community in Leicestershire, England. With increasing industrialization, Levine found a decline in the mean age at first marriage for both men and women. The growth of opportunities in framework knitting, according to Levine, led couples to marry earlier and begin having children immediately. Apparently children were viewed as an economic asset, and framework knitters sought to enjoy their contributions to the family economy as soon as possible. [54]

The New England social and economic setting varied on several counts from the English outwork environment, and these differences help explain the contrasting impact of industrial capitalism on marriage patterns. Industrial capitalism never seriously penetrated the local economies of Boscawen, Canterbury, and Sutton, which remained almost totally agricultural before 1850. Thus women had to migrate to find mill employment, in contrast to the scene at Shepshed, where framework knitters worked in their own homes. Because of its location, mill employment was never so totally integrated into the household economy of these New Hampshire towns as was framework knitting in Shepshed. With increasing economic opportunity, young men and women in Shepshed could marry and establish their own households much more easily than earlier. In Boscawen, Canterbury, and Sutton, in contrast, industrialization gave women a degree of economic and social independence that led them to postpone marriage. They put off marriage and by virtue of residence in Lowell and other mill towns had a wider range of men to choose among than women who remained at home. This greater choice is reflected in the varied occupations of the men they married. The different forms industrial capitalism took in New England and Leicestershire account for its contrasting impact on marriage patterns in the two regions.

As industrialization progressed, job opportunities within Shepshed increased, leading to a decline in outmigration and an increase in the proportion of young people marrying and settling in the village. In Boscawen, Canterbury, and Sutton, industrialization created job opportunities beyond the confines of the towns, luring increasing numbers of young people into the growing mill towns. With this migration we begin to see a widening gulf between the experiences of millhands and those of their parents. Residence patterns of women workers after marriage reflect their growing independence from parental dominance. They suggest that the Lowell experience was not just a passing moment, at least not in the lives of a fair proportion of the women. More than a third of the women married Lowell men and the same proportion continued to reside there after their marriages. For them life in Lowell was more than a brief sojourn in the years before marriage; work constituted an entry into the urban industrial world and signaled a permanent departure from the one in which they had grown up. [55]

For many of the women in the early mills, the world of their parents was not their world. The Lowell experience may have made them restless, made them unfit for the slower, more traditional life they had known. Or perhaps women who went to Lowell in the first place were particularly open and receptive to the urban, industrial world growing up nearby. In any event, the letters of women workers and the writings of New Englanders critical of the movement into the mills provide numerous indications that contemporaries were conscious of the tension between the two worlds and cultures—the urban world of Lowell and the rural world of the surrounding countryside.

One Sutton historian, herself the sister of two Lowell operatives, captured an element of this tension in a brief description of the experience of going to the mills for women of her town:

The girls began to go to work in the cotton factories of Nashua and Lowell. It was an all-day ride, but that was nothing to be dreaded. It gave them a chance to behold other towns and places, and see more of the world than most of the generation had ever been able to see. They went in their plain, country-made clothes, and after working several months, would come home for a visit, or perhaps to be married, in their tasteful city dresses, and with more money in their pockets than they had ever owned before. [56]

Augusta Worthen wrote these lines in 1890, looking back on the mill experience with an appropriate sense of distance. Other contemporaries, however, did not look so calmly upon their daughters returning with "tasteful city dresses, and more money . . . than they had ever owned before." Zadock Thompson, in his 1842 *History of Vermont*, described much the same phenomenon in a more judgmental tone: "It is too common for farmers' daughters to grow up young ladies, play the piano . . . and spend their father's surplus funds for fine clothing." [57] Perhaps the daughters Thompson decried had picked up their tastes in mill towns or from sisters who worked there. Whatever the causes, or whether such difficulties actually existed in fact is really beside the point; what is important is that contemporaries felt them to be matters of real concern.

The problem was not simply that some rural spokesmen observed their wayward daughters and found them wanting. Others felt that the judgment was mutual, that these young women rejected the values of their parents. An 1858 article, "Farming in New England," made just this point:

The most intelligent and enterprising of the farmer's daughters become school-teachers, or tenders of shops, or factory girls. They contemn the calling of their father, and will nine times out ten, marry a mechanic in preference to a farmer. They know that marrying a farmer is a serious business. They remember their worn-out mothers. [58]

The lines recall the marriage patterns of the women workers from the Hamilton Company. They were farmers' daughters, all right, but, seven times out of ten, they married a mechanic "in preference to a farmer." They chose not to follow in the footsteps of their "worn-out mothers."

The last example is particularly pointed because it shifts the emphasis away from the reaction of others and focuses on the attitudes of the women themselves. Passages in the letters of a number of mill women reveal that they did in fact make just these sorts of negative judgments about rural life. Maria and Lura Currier, two sisters from Wentworth, New Hampshire, worked in Lowell in the 1840s. In the winter of 1845-46 they wrote a number of letters to a friend and fellow operative in Lowell, Harriet Hanson. The sisters were most discontented. Their parents would not allow them to go to Lowell that winter and they felt penned up in the wilderness. As Lura wrote: "I cannot as you anticipated tell you of any pleasant sleigh rides . . . of the nice supper, and *turnovers* for they have no ambition for anything of that kind, up here in these *diggins*." Social life in Wentworth seemed barren indeed after all the excitement and bustle of city life: "It is extremely dull here now, there is nothing at all interesting going on here, save the orthodox have a singing school, but *that, we* do not attend." To the Currier sisters all the lively and interesting people in Wentworth seemed to be going to the mill towns. Wrote Maria: "A great many of our young people are leaving this Spring for Manchester and Lowell. Blaisdell will be about the only gentleman there will be left here and he is just about the same as a married man so we do not place any dependence upon him." It was indeed a long winter and spring for the two sisters who had their hearts set on returning to Lowell. [59]

Mary Paul, whose letters have been quoted earlier, also developed a degree of sophistication that led her to look down upon certain aspects of rural life and culture. Several years after she left Lowell, she moved to a utopian cooperative community in New Jersey. While working there she was surprised to meet a couple from her home town in Vermont, who were on something of a sightseeing tour that included this community. As Mary wrote to her father: "They are travelling for pleasure I expect and came here to *see* as people go to Niagara [Falls] to see." Mary expressed the distance between herself and her visitors when she noted: "They are real nice folks but seem rather countryfied in their ideas." [60]

The complaints of Zadock Thompson and the comments of the Currier sisters and Mary Paul provide contrasting views of the same basic dilemma. Women workers in the early mills were caught between two worlds. Born and raised in rural New England, they identified with the pride and independence of their yeoman farmer parents. At the same time, however, they experienced a new life in Lowell and enjoyed the social and economic independence it provided. They returned home with new clothes and with periodicals and more modern ideas picked up in the fluid urban setting. They also came back with money in their pockets and spending habits that surprised some of their rural neighbors. For many, work in Lowell proved to be a first, and an irreversible, step away from the rural, agricultural lives of their parents. Fully a third found the urban world and culture of Lowell and other cities too alluring to return to rural villages. And those who remained in their home towns tended to marry nonfarmers and thus did not follow in the footsteps of their mothers either. For both groups, for those who remained at home and those who settled in Lowell, the mill experience signaled the beginning of a new life. The world of their parents was the world of their past; they had moved beyond.

CHAPTER FOUR

The Social Relations of Production in the Early Mills

WHILE A vision of expanded economic and social opportunities motivated the young women who left their rural homes to work in Lowell in the 1820s and 1830s, a very different set of considerations was foremost in the minds of the millowners and managers who shaped the environment that these women entered. From the outset, managers of the Waltham-Lowell firms envisioned expansion and the creation of an industrial empire.[1] Toward this end management employed various strategies to increase the productivity of labor and generate the high rates of profit that would make expansion possible. Improvements in textile technology and tightening of labor discipline permitted the Waltham-Lowell firms to increase total output while reducing their unit costs of production. These developments assured the new companies steady, high levels of profit in comparison to the uneven returns of Rhode Island mills in this period.

While a strictly technological breakthrough—the reinvention of the power loom—provided the immediate stimulus to the founding of the Boston Manufacturing Company, innovations in the organization of production proved equally important for the early success of that firm. The existence of a working power loom enabled the Waltham company to adopt vertical integration—to centralize all of the steps in the production process from cleaning raw cotton to bleaching the finished cloth within a single mill. But vertical integation in turn necessitated further improvements in machine technology. By 1818 Paul Moody, chief mechanic of the Boston Manufacturing Company, had developed warping and dressing machines and had modified the spinning frame to enable it to spin filling yarn directly onto bobbins for use in the subsequent weaving step.[2] In the drive to increase productivity, technological and organizational innovations were closely interrelated and mutually reinforcing.

Through these developments the Waltham firm, and later its Lowell successors, sought to exercise greater control over the production process. Samuel Slater had been able to mechanize the early carding and spinning steps but remained dependent on skilled handloom weavers to transform his yarn into finished cloth. Since outworkers performed most of the weaving in their rural homes, Slater had little direct control over the quantity of work turned out. Piece rates gave outworkers some incentive to work steadily at their looms, but in years of plentiful harvests the motivation to take in weaving may well have been limited. The adoption of the power loom enabled the Boston Manufacturing Company to employ a full-time weaving work force under the company's supervision and discipline. This advantage probably contributed as much to the gains in productivity as mechanization itself.

Work took on a regularity lacking in the domestic system associated with textile production in the Rhode Island mills. Workers were employed for an average of 12 hours a day, 6 days a week, 309 days a year. Only three regular holidays, Fast Day in the spring, the Fourth of July, and Thanksgiving, provided breaks in the normal work routine, though occasionally high water closed the mills for brief periods. Contracts with workers further reinforced this regularity by requiring operatives to work a year in the mills and to give two weeks' notice before quitting. Workers who complied with these regulations were entitled to an honorable discharge, which they needed to secure future employment in any of the Lowell mills. As early as 1829 three firms—the Hamilton, Appleton, and Merrimack companies—agreed not to hire operatives who had left the others' employ without receiving an honorable discharge. In this early intercompany agreement we see the origins of a system of blacklisting aimed at controlling and disciplining members of the mill work force.[3]

The overriding concern of management, then, was control—control of the manufacturing process through the use of laborsaving machinery and control also of the work force through supervision and regulation. Although this control was rarely challenged outright, managerial power was not absolute. The balance of power was not entirely one-sided. A number of factors limited the ability of the managers of the corporations to impose their authority as fully as they might have liked. Throughout the 1830s, as the mills expanded at a rapid rate, there was a constant shortage of labor. Although the regulations required that operatives work at least a year and give two weeks' notice before quitting, companies generally did not enforce these provisions. Hamilton operatives routinely worked shorter periods or left without proper notice, only to be rehired a few months later. If Hamilton did not enforce its regulations systematically on its own workers, there is little likelihood that it did so when experienced operatives from other firms sought employment. [4]

The scarcity of experienced hands led Lowell firms to modify their written regulations in actual practice; there were similar obstacles to their efforts to increase labor discipline and productivity. Innovations in the technology and organization of production in Lowell led to dramatic advances in comparison to the smaller spinning mills of southern New England, but they still left management dependent on the intelligence, skill, and organization of workers. In fact the innovations led to a socialization of work and a high degree of interaction and interdependence among workers, which resulted in the growth of solidarity among women operatives—a result certainly not intended by management.

The concern for control so apparent in innovations in technology and the organization of production was evident even in the arrangement and architecture of mill buildings. Each corporation laid out its mills, outbuildings, and housing to create a unified whole. [5] The buildings generally formed a closed group about a central millyard, and entrance into the complex was restricted. At the beginning of the working day and after breaks for meals, operatives entered the complex through the open mill gates. At other times, however, tardy workers or visitors had to enter through the counting room. One contemporary described the layout of the mills in language suggesting purposeful planning:

> Between the boarding houses and the mills is a line of one story brick buildings, containing the counting room, superintendent's room, clerk's room, and store rooms. The mill yard is so surrounded

by enclosures, that the only access is through the counting room in full view of those whose business it is to see that no improper persons intrude themselves upon the premises.[6]

Workers were isolated from the larger world while on the job; outside influences were not allowed to "intrude" and disturb the work. The arrangement of buildings thus reinforced the control that machine technology and an inflexible work timetable gave management over the work process and the worker.

This development represented a significant departure from common practice in other industries at this time. Consider, in contrast, a contemporary description of the work routine of a New York City shipyard. Work there was neither unrelenting nor isolated from the world around. The first break in the routine came with cake-time at 8:30 A.M. when an Irishwoman peddled cakes and pastries throughout the yard. An English candyman followed on her heels, and at 11:00 "there was a general sailing out of the yard and into convenient grog-shops after whiskey." In the afternoon, a cake-lunch and another candy-break provided diversions before work finally drew to a close at sundown. This was hardly a routine or setting that would have satisfied mill managers in early Lowell.[7]

The order and regularity so essential to the process of manufacturing in the mills was reflected in the physical appearance of the mill buildings themselves. Each corporation generally erected several large mills, each a complete and standardized unit of production (see frontispiece). In the mid-1830s the mills were four to six stories in height, 45 feet wide by 150 feet long. They were constructed of red brick, with regular rows of windows extending along their length and breadth. An outside, enclosed stairway stood along one side, and a bell tower often rose above the roof of the central mill in a given complex (see figure 3). The bell tower stood as a visible and audible symbol of the new time-discipline ushered in by the Lowell factory system.[8]

As with the outward appearance of the mills, so too the interior design and organization of the factories were uniform. The basement housed the waterwheel, purposefully placed below ground level to maximize the power generated and to protect water in the millrace from freezing temperatures. Successive stories housed the carding, spinning, weaving, and dressing steps, each operation occupying a single large room on a floor.

An elevator connected the different floors, moving materials from one step in the production process to the next.[9]

The organization of work was aimed at speeding the flow of materials. The carding room's location on the ground floor, determined primarily by the heavy weight of machinery, also facilitated entry from a separate picking house where machinery opened and cleaned the baled cotton. The initial carding and drawing operations transformed the loose cotton into a coarse roving that spinning frames on the second floor drew down and twisted into yarn. On the upper stories of the mill, warping and dressing machines prepared warp yarn for the weaving process and power looms produced the finished cloth. A single cloth room serviced all the mills of a company, and there operatives measured, folded, and batched the fabric for subsequent bleaching, dying, or printing and eventual shipment to selling agencies in Boston.

The arrangement of machinery within each room minimized the handling of intermediate products by operatives. The initial opening of bales and cleaning of raw cotton took place in a picking house adjacent to the mills. There, separated from the mills by a fireproof wall, male workers tended pickers.[10] Picking opened the compressed cotton lint and separated the fibers somewhat. The combing action of a rapidly rotating spiked picker shaft removed impurities from the cotton. As the shaft turned, heavy particles of dirt or stone fell down through a coarse wire mesh while air currents blew the lighter cotton into a collection box. A lapping machine picked up the loosened cotton fibers and formed them into a wide sheet, or lap, that was wound upon a cylindrical drum for input into the carding step.[11]

In the carding room a series of operations further cleaned the cotton and began drawing out and combining the fibers into a filament. Carding machines, drawing frames, and double speeders transformed the yardwide cotton lap into a continuous strand or sliver.

Basically the carding machine consisted of a large central cylinder revolving beneath a series of stationary "top flats" that ringed its circumference. Cylinder and flats were covered with thousands of fine wire teeth set in opposing directions. Male operatives placed the cotton lap on a conveyor belt that fed it onto a small revolving cylinder (at the right in figure 4a), the lickerin, which plucked small tufts of cotton from the lap.

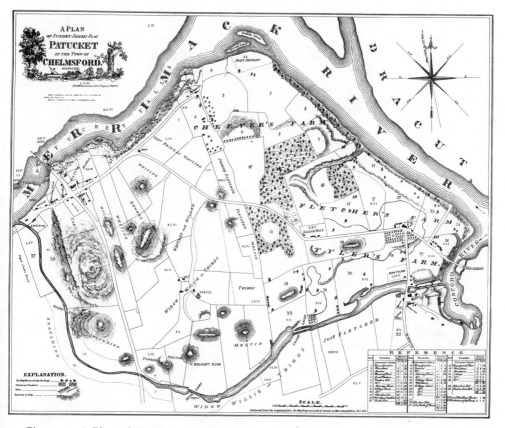

Figure 1 A Plan of Sundry Farms &c. of Patucket in the Town of Chelmsford, 1821.
COURTESY OF THE LOWELL HISTORICAL SOCIETY.

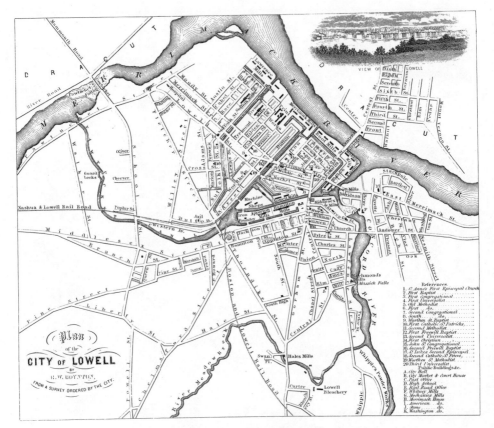

Figure 2 Plan of the City of Lowell, 1845.
COURTESY OF THE LOWELL HISTORICAL SOCIETY.

Figure 3   Middlesex Manufacturing Company, Lowell, c. 1840.
COURTESY OF THE MERRIMACK VALLEY TEXTILE MUSEUM.

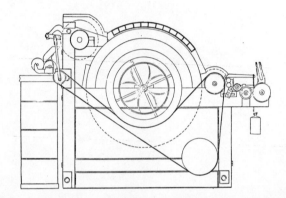

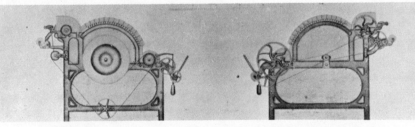

Figure 4 Lowell Carding Machine. (a) Top view: from the *Proceedings of the New England Cotton Manufacturers' Association* (October 1880). (b) Bottom view: from a lithograph in an 1898 Lowell Machine Shop trade catalog.
COURTESY OF THE MERRIMACK VALLEY TEXTILE MUSEUM.

Figure 5   Warp Spinning Throstle, c. 1830.
COURTESY OF THE LOWELL HISTORICAL SOCIETY.

Figure 6 Drawing In. From *A History of Wonderful Inventions*
(New York: Harper, n.d.).
COURTESY OF THE MERRIMACK VALLEY TEXTILE MUSEUM.

Figure 7 Lowell Power Loom, c. 1848. From a lithograph in an 1898 Lowell
Machine Shop trade catalog.

Figure 8 Women Weavers, c. 1860. From an early tintype.
COURTESY OF THE MERRIMACK VALLEY TEXTILE MUSEUM.

After this opening action, the lickerin passed the tufts to the main cylinder, while heavier seed particles and leaf trash remained caught in the wire points. As the main cylinder rotated upward, the opposing sets of wire points on the cylinder and top flats brushed the cotton, further opening and straightening the fibers. Finally, a second small cylinder, the doffer, removed the carded cotton, which was then condensed into a thick strand, or sliver, and coiled into a tall cylindrical can. To produce well cleaned and carded cotton, the process was generally repeated a second time. Two sets of carding machines, designated breakers and finishers, were employed, with the wire points of the second group set closer together to achieve a finer carding action. [12]

Drawing followed carding. Drawing frames, tended entirely by women, stretched four or more strands of sliver and then recombined them into a single strand of the original size. Gears regulated the speed of successive pairs of rollers so that the slivers were stretched slightly between the first pair of rollers and still more between later pairs. [13] This drawing down and recombining was usually repeated three times in succession, thus producing a sliver which was much more even and uniform than that produced in the earlier carding step. [14]

The final set of machines in the carding room, the double speeders, further drew down the sliver and gave it a slight twist to enable it to withstand additional reducing in the spinning step. The coarse roving produced, considerably finer than the earlier sliver, was not suitable for coiling, but rather was wound on large bobbins. Here again women tended the machinery, keeping a close watch to make sure that the quality of the coarse roving was satisfactory, and intervening periodically to piece together broken ends. Given the weakness of the roving at this point, the winding on the double speeder proved a delicate step calling for considerable skill and judgment. Women tending these machines were among the most skilled and best paid in the female work force of the 1830s. [15]

Spinning throstles with 128 spindles predominated in the Lowell mills in this period (see figure 5). The throstles took coarse roving and drew it out between successive pairs of rollers and then twisted it by the action of a flyer revolving about a bobbin. Depending on subsequent use, yarn could be drawn out to varying thicknesses and given more or less twist.

Women tended spinning throstles, piecing up yarns when they broke, while boys and girls, usually 10 to 15 years of age, worked as doffers replacing bobbins as they filled up with yarn.

Spinning throstles produced two kinds of yarn to serve different purposes in the subsequent weaving step. Filling yarn, spun directly onto shuttle bobbins, went straight to the weaving room, but warp yarn had to undergo several intermediate steps. In a winding room women tended machinery that wound warp yarn off small bobbins onto larger spools. In the dressing room women workers placed several hundred of these spools onto a rack, or cradle, and a warping machine wound the parallel warp yarns onto a yardwide beam. Dressing frames treated the warp with a starch paste, called sizing, dried the yarns by fan, and rewound them onto a second beam. [16] Finally, in one of the few hand processes in production, women drew the sized warp yarns individually through the loom reed and harnesses in preparation for weaving (see figure 6).

Power looms employed in the Lowell mills in the mid-1830s incorporated numerous advances over the Waltham loom developed two decades earlier. Self-acting temples held the edges of the cloth at a constant width and tension to ensure that they were not pulled in as the reed beat down each row of filling. The front and back beams let off the warp and took up the woven cloth at the same rate ensuring a constant number of rows of filling for a given length of cloth. Trip-hammers, activated by a revolving crank, sent the shuttle, with its filling yarn, across the loom through the shed created between alternate warp yarns. The reed moved back and forth, beating up successive rows of filling one hundred times a minute. By 1836 the looms ran more rapidly and needed less intervention than earlier, enabling each Lowell weaver to tend two looms (see figure 7). [17]

The mechanical capabilities of the machinery determined the specifics of operatives' jobs in the mills, but management choices rather than technology determined the division of labor between men and women. In the mid-1830s men and women performed distinct, sex-specific jobs, and a firm, though unwritten, policy kept their jobs sex-segregated. Men held all the supervisory positions—overseers and second hands, as they were termed—and also held all operative jobs in the picking and carding steps. In addition, men staffed the repair shop, company watch force, and millyard, from all of which women were entirely excluded. Women, on the other hand, held all machine-tending jobs in the production process after carding. They tended the drawing frames, double speeders, throstles, looms, and winding, warping, and dressing machines.

The assignment of men to certain positions stemmed in part from the skill requirements and physical demands of jobs. Men had a monopoly (which, of course, became self-perpetuating) of the sorts of skills needed in machinists' positions in the repair shop. Other jobs—those in carding and picking in particular—although only semiskilled, demanded considerable strength and endurance and exposed workers to risk of personal injury. These factors, undoubtedly coupled with the influence of tradition, determined that these jobs should be viewed as "men's work."

The exclusive employment of women in basic machine-tending jobs resulted from the relatively low levels of wages that women customarily received. While the mills had to attract men away from competing occupations, such was not the case in the hiring of women. An economist, Howard Gitelman, makes just this point in his analysis of employment at the Boston Manufacturing Company:

> The wages offered males at the start of the Waltham system . . . reflected the going rate in New England for each trade or skill group. The rates offered females were not subject to this market constraint, since at the time there was no well-developed market for female industrial workers. Instead, the lower limit to female wages had to be set high enough to attract girls away from farms . . . and away from competing female employments, such as household manufacture and domestic service. [18]

Men or women could tend the machinery equally well, but the comparative wage rates clearly favored the hiring of women. To the extent that jobs did not require special training, strength, or endurance, or expose operatives to the risk of injury, women were employed.

Comparative economics and assumptions regarding strength and skills were the primary, but not the sole, determinants of the division of labor in the mills. Women never held any supervisory positions in the mills. Although they developed skills over their careers and helped to train newcomers in the use of machinery, they never enjoyed the formal responsibility or the higher status and earnings of supervisors. In this respect the attitudes of male millowners and agents played the decisive role. It was one thing to employ women as "hands" but quite another to place women into positions of responsibility. Mill management had to overcome resistance simply to do the former; they apparently never considered and certainly never attempted the latter.

Separate wage scales for men and women resulted from the division of labor along lines of sex. In 1836 men earned a daily wage that ranged between $0.85 and $2.00, while women received varying piece rates that made their wages proportional to the output of the machines they tended. Their daily earnings averaged between $0.40 and $0.80. Table 4.1 presents the mean daily earnings of the most important male and female occupations at the Hamilton Company in July 1836.[19]

Wage figures suggest a wide range in women's earnings at the Hamilton Company in this period. "Sparehands," that is newcomers just beginning work in the mills, earned on the average $0.44 a day during July 1836. At the other end of the wage spectrum, dressers earned $0.78 daily, fully 75 percent above the figure for sparehands. This wide spread in wages reflected the range of skills among women workers.

The work of all women was repetitious, and almost always machines, not women, performed the basic operations of production. Women's work required watching the machinery and intervening periodically to assure its smooth functioning. But some jobs required routine interven-

TABLE 4.1. MEAN DAILY PAY OF MEN AND WOMEN AT THE HAMILTON COMPANY, JULY 1836, BROKEN DOWN BY MAJOR JOBS

Men		Women	
Job	Mean daily pay	Job	Mean daily pay
Overseer	$2.09 (16)	Speeder	$0.66 (44)
Second hand	1.20 (12)	Drawer	0.52 (60)
Operative[a]	0.85 (38)	Spinner	0.58 (134)
Machinist	1.27 (25)	Weaver	0.66 (316)
Watchman	1.10 (6)	Dresser	0.78 (38)
		Warper	0.73 (23)
		Drawing in	0.66 (26)
		Sparehand	0.44 (185)
Overall[b]	$1.05 (149)	Overall[b]	$0.60 (881)

[a] Includes hands in the picking and carding departments.
[b] Overall totals are greater than the sums for specific jobs because only major jobs are listed.

tion, bordering on the mechanical, while others called for considerable skill and judgment. Women tending spinning throstles and drawing frames were the lowest paid of regular adult operatives. Their work consisted of piecing together yarns when they broke. Automatic stop mechanisms halted the machinery, and the worker had to find the break, piece together the two ends of yarn or sliver, and restart the machine. Reflecting the low level of skill required and limited control over production, drawers and spinners received a daily wage independent of their output.

Dressing and weaving departments accounted for the more skilled and better-paid jobs for women. These jobs required more frequent intervention in the production process, and the individual skill of each operative played an important part in her total output. Accordingly, these operatives were paid on a piece-wage basis, with earnings directly proportional to the number of yards of cloth or yarn their machines processed during the payroll period. [20]

A weaver had to repair broken warp yarns and replace the shuttle bobbin when it ran out of filling yarn. Her output depended on the speed with which she performed these tasks. Tending two looms at a time, she had to keep a watchful eye on each in turn. The task of replacing empty bobbins involved seven distinct steps: "[T]aking the shuttle out, putting in another, starting the loom, taking the empty bobbin or cop tube out of the discarded shuttle, putting in a new bobbin or cop, sucking the thread through the eye, and placing the shuttle in a holder." [21] The frequency with which an operative had to intervene to replace empty bobbins or tie broken yarns limited the number of looms she could tend. Throughout this period the thrust of technological innovation was to perfect the automaticity of machines, thus increasing the number of looms assigned to each worker. Despite these efforts, weavers remained skilled and well-paid workers throughout this period and maintained a pride and self-respect that surfaced in the repeated labor struggles of the antebellum years (see figure 8).

Women's highest paid and most desirable jobs were found in the dressing room. Lucy Larcom, a millhand from the age of 10, described the advantages of this room: "It was more airy, and fewer girls were in the room, for the dressing frame itself was a large, clumsy affair which occupied a great deal of space." She liked the room, but the work was demanding. A dresser had to be alert to a variety of difficulties: the temperature of the sizing had to be correct, the level of sizing could not run down too low, broken yarns had to be pieced together, and the sizing had to dry completely before the yarns were wound on the take-up beam. The tasks were too much for Larcom, who described how a dressing frame got the better of her: "It had to be watched in a dozen directions every minute, and even then it was always getting itself and me into trouble. I felt as if the half-live creature with its great, groaning joints, and whizzing fan, was aware of my incapacity to manage it." This particular "creature" proved intractable, and Larcom switched to lower-paid but less taxing work in another room. [22]

The final job in the dressing room, drawing in, was the only entirely hand-operation in the production process. Harriet Robinson described this work:

> I learned . . . to be a drawing-in girl which was considered to be one of the most desirable employments, as about a dozen girls were needed in each mill. We drew in, one by one, the threads of the warp, through the harness and the reed, and so made the beams ready for the weaver's loom. [23]

The work of drawing in was repetitive, but women took pride in the speed and skill they developed. Eliza Adams expressed these feelings well in a letter home: "You would hardly believe me should I tell how expeditiously I draw the little threads through the harness and reed. The past week I drew 22 beams or about 43000 threads. We use a steel hook in drawing both through the reed and harness and it would astonish aunt how nimbly we use it." [24]

The attractions of drawing in to operatives are evident in these passages. First, only a limited number of drawing-in hands were needed in each mill. While there might be 100 weavers or 50 spinners in a mill, there were only 10 or 12 drawing-in hands. Fewer, more experienced operatives worked in the dressing room, sheltered somewhat from the noise and cotton dust of the more mechanized rooms. Secondly, women were able to develop skills in drawing in, and as they improved their speed their wages advanced accordingly. It is indicative of the values of the day that in the Lowell mills, the technologically most advanced factories in the nation, women operatives preferred, and the corporations paid higher wages for, those few jobs in which human skill and judgment still played a part.

In contrast to adults, children worked under intense pressure for short periods broken by intervals of rest. Lapboys tended the carding machines, periodically carrying full cans of carded laps from the breakers to the finishers and from the finishers to the drawing frames. Bobbin boys and girls in the spinning rooms replaced full bobbins of spun yarn with empty ones. Harriet Robinson began her career in the mills as a bobbin girl and described her work:

> I can see myself now, racing down the alley, between the spinning frames, carrying in front of me a bobbin-box bigger than I was. These mites had to be very swift . . . so as not to keep the spinning-frames stopped long, and they worked only about fifteen minutes every hour. The rest of the time was their own, and when the overseer was kind they were allowed to read, knit, or even to go outside the mill-yard to play. [25]

Although children remained in the mills a full twelve-hour day, their work was less monotonous than that of regular operatives. Their schedule of intermittent hard effort and relaxation enabled them to "get away" from their work, a privilege not shared by adults in the mills.

The technology of textile machines and the division of labor obviously influenced the nature of women's work in the early mills, but the physical arrangements within the mills also played an important role. The operatives can be placed in this physical setting by visualizing a typical room in a Lowell mill in the mid-1830s. The room would be a large one, about 45 by 150 feet, occupying an entire floor of the mill. Long rows of machines, in this case power looms, extend the length of the room. In the aisles between the machines are operatives, one woman for each pair of looms. Perhaps two hundred looms and a hundred women occupy the room. At one end, at an elevated desk, sits the overseer. A male second hand moves about the room making sure the looms are operating properly, while two or three boys assist the overseer and operatives. Although each worker is assigned to her particular machinery—two looms for weavers and one side of 128 spindles for spinners at this date—there is considerable evidence of interaction and work sharing. It is a phenomenon deserving of analysis.

Three factors contributed to this sharing of work: the nature of women's work, turnover in the work force, and the organization of work training. Consider the first of these. In a given room, or in some cases section of a room, women working near one another are all performing identical jobs. The work is repetitive and dull and, at least in the 1830s, does not require a woman's complete attention. This is not assembly-line production. Women doing routine, identical work can talk to each other and learn from one another. Several decades pass before the work load of each operative reaches such a level that the physical distance between workers makes communication difficult. [26]

In the second place, turnover in the work force contributed to making work more social. In the mid-1830s turnover among operatives was very high. During the five-week payroll period ending July 23, 1836, more than a fourth—25.7 percent—of the workers listed on the payrolls of the Hamilton Company entered or left employment. The mobility of women was somewhat higher than that of men, for 26.4 percent of females entered or left work compared to 20.8 percent of males. This turnover led women to be much more dependent on one another than they would otherwise have been.

Only a minority of those who entered during the payroll period were total newcomers to the firm. Many had been employed at some earlier date and were now returning, perhaps following vacations in their rural homes, or after periods teaching school or working in another mill. Of the 115 entrants, 80 had "old" or "new" recorded beside their names, and more than half of this group—44 of 80—had worked at Hamilton previously. Overall, probably about 50 of the 1030 workers employed in July 1836 were total newcomers to the company's mills.

New operatives generally found their first work experience difficult, even harrowing, though they may have already done considerable hand spinning or weaving in their own homes. Lucy Davis, a Nashua, New Hampshire, operative, struggled unsuccessfully at first to adjust to the demands of factory work:

I came here to work in the Mill [and] the work was much harder than I expected and quite new to me. After I had been there a number of days I was obliged to stay out sick but I did not mean to give it up so and I tried it again but was obliged to give it up altogether. I have now been out about one week and am some better then when I left but not verry well. I think myself cured of my Mill fever. [27]

While Lucy Davis did not get down to specifics in the discussion of her difficulties, a writer in the *Lowell Offering* gave more details as she described the initiation of a fictional operative:

> The next morning [Susan Miller] went into the Mill; and at first, the sight of so many bands, and wheels, and springs in constant motion, was very frightful. She felt afraid to touch the loom, and she was almost sure that she could never learn to weave. . . . [T]he shuttle flew out, and made a new bump upon her head; and the first time she tried to spring the lathe, she broke out a quarter of the treads.

After her first day in the mill, she retired to her boardinghouse with a "dull pain in her head, and a sharp pain in her ankles; every bone was aching. . . . "[28] While other experiences were somewhat less harrowing, most accounts indicate that women became proficient and felt satisfaction in their work only after some months in the mills.[29]

Accordingly, the textile corporations made provisions to ease the adjustment of new operatives. They were not expected to fit immediately into the mill's regular work routine, but rather were assigned work as sparehands and earned daily wages independent of the quantity of work turned out. As a sparehand, the newcomer worked with an experienced operative who instructed her in the intricacies of the job. She spelled her partner for short stretches of time and occasionally took the place of an absentee. One woman described the learning process in a letter reprinted in the *Offering*:

> Well, I went into the mill, and was put to learn with a very patient girl. . . . You cannot think how odd everything seemed. . . . They set me to threading shuttles, and tying weaver's knots, and such things, and now I have improved so that I can take care of one loom. I could take care of two if I only had eyes in the back part of my head.[30]

After the passage of some weeks or months, when she could handle the normal complement of machinery—two looms for weavers and one side of 128 spindles for spinners—and when a regular operative departed, leaving an opening, the sparehand moved into a regular position.

Through this system of job training, the textile corporations unwittingly contributed to the development of solidarity among female operatives. During the most difficult period in an operative's career, the first months in the mill, she relied on other women workers for training and support. For every sparehand whose adjustment to mill work was aided in this way, there was an experienced operative whose work was equally affected. Women related personally to one another during the work process and did not simply tend their machines as isolated individuals. Given the high rate of turnover, a large proportion of women worked in pairs. In July 1836, for example, more than a fifth of all females at the Hamilton Company worked as sparehands. Consequently, over 40 percent of women worked with one another. Nor was this interaction surreptitious, carried out only when the overseer looked elsewhere; rather it was formally organized and sanctioned by the corporations themselves.

The training of newcomers extended over the course of several months. Female sparehands at Hamilton worked an average of 57 days before becoming regular operatives. Only 3 of 34 newcomers who began work as sparehands between April and July, 1836, held regular positions at the beginning of their second month on the job. At the start of the fourth month, a third of these newcomers still remained in sparehand positions. This period of worksharing and training was a lengthy and formative experience in the careers of women operatives. [31]

In addition to the training of sparehands, informal—and on occasion, formal—sharing of work went on among operatives. From time to time a woman would take off a half or full day from work to enjoy a brief rest, recover from illness, or spend time with a visiting friend or relative. During her absence fellow operatives would each take an extra loom or side of spindles so that she might continue to earn wages. With friends making sure her looms or throstles kept running, an operative could earn almost a full wage even though she was not physically present. [32] This work sharing did not always result from an operative's absence from the mill. On occasion regular operatives appear to have worked in pairs as a matter of course. In an 1830 letter, Wealthy Page described her work and that of two friends, Sarah and Elizabeth Hodgdon: "Sarah has been tending looms alone. Elizabeth and I are tending four." Since no operatives at this early date tended four looms, Wealthy Page and Elizabeth Hodgdon were evidently working together, sharing a double complement of looms. [33] Altogether, the evidence on the formal and informal work sharing points to the importance of the larger work group in the experience of individual women. Work proved to be a social and not simply an individual experience in the early mills.

The social character of work came out in yet another way—in diversions women enjoyed while on the job. Because the routine was so dull and monotonous, a little sport that enlivened an otherwise tedious working day was generally tolerated. One woman, in a collection of stories entitled *Lights and Shadows of Factory Life in New England*, described antics among weavers that she recalled from her own experience in the mills. The central character in this particular vignette, Fanny, observes the listlessness of her fellow operatives and determines to liven things up. Having put her own looms in good order, she first rouses a daydreaming neighbor with a hearty spanking. Next,

> She takes a cord and ties a girl fast to her loom, in spite of strong resistance. She makes a "rag baby" of her handkerchief and bits of cloth; and while a neighbor is busy with one loom, she ties it to some other that is constantly in motion; and when the owner turns about, the puppet is swinging or dancing before her.
>
> Perhaps she retaliates on Fanny by stopping her looms and carrying her shuttles to the farther corner of the room; and while she is in quest of them, by filling her alley with her own and her neighbor's seats. Others are drawn in; and those not actually engaged, look on and laugh.

Even while this play goes on, some nonparticipants keep an eye on their own looms and those of the pranksters. And what does the overseer think of this conduct? It seems to be an unwritten rule "that he shall not witness such sports." These recreations leave the workers refreshed and better able to resume their work and thus are tolerated in spite of the interruptions involved.[34] Whether in the performance of their actual tasks, or in the diversions that lightened their labors, it is clear that the larger work group played a crucial role in the socialization of women workers in the mills.

Before 1840 the Waltham-Lowell mills were at the forefront of innovation and technological change. The introduction of the power loom and the integration of all the steps in the production process led to remarkable increases in labor productivity and declines in the cost of cloth goods. These developments, in turn, led to a significant expansion of the textile industry and brought large numbers of women into the mills. There machine technology and factory discipline imposed new demands on women workers. But these same factors threw women together at the workplace. The organization of work and the division of labor meant that in a given room large numbers of women performed identical tasks. Few men worked with them, and men never held the same jobs. Men and women related to one another across the formal divide separating supervisor and worker.

In constrast, women related to one another in the aisles between rows of machinery. Experienced women taught newcomers the skills they needed in their work, a process that took several months and involved more than 40 percent of the work force at one time. In addition women frequently assisted one another by taking an extra loom or side of spindles, enabling an operative to enjoy a brief, paid absence from work. The training of sparehands and work sharing created a mutual dependence among women and contributed to the growth of a solidarity among women in their daily work lives. These bonds carried over into the lives of women beyond the workplace where further shared experiences reinforced these ties.

CHAPTER FIVE

The Boardinghouse

Each house was a village or community of itself. There fifty or sixty young women from different parts of New England met and lived together. When not at their work . . . they sat in groups in their chambers; or in a corner of the large dining-room, busy at some agreeable employment.[1]

THE WALTHAM-LOWELL textile firms provided extensive company housing, and this feature distinguished northern New England mill towns from those in Rhode Island and Connecticut. The management of the Boston Manufacturing Company, the immediate predecessor of the Lowell firms, built housing for its workers and carried on this tradition with the formation of the Merrimack Manufacturing Company and subsequent firms. The smaller spinning mills of southern New England lacked comparable institutions for the most part. Customarily this contrast between mills in the two regions has been attributed to differences between their work forces—one consisting of single, female workers and the other comprised chiefly of entire families.[2] This explanation, however, can account only for the existence of boardinghouses for single operatives. The Lowell firms also erected housing for married employees—for agents, overseers, printers and dyers, machinists, and skilled operatives. These family tenements comprised more than half of all company housing in Lowell.

The initial scale of operations and geographical isolation led the early

Waltham-Lowell firms to rely almost exclusively on company housing.[3] The Rhode Island mills usually began on a small scale and expanded at a moderate rate, enabling housing to expand gradually to meet the needs of the growing work force.[4] In contrast, the Lowell mills operated from the outset on a scale much larger than that of competing firms. The need for a substantial source of waterpower forced the mills to locate at some distance from existing population centers. East Chelmsford, the rural site that became Lowell, offered little in the way of workers' housing. Prior to the founding of the Merrimack Manufacturing Company, for instance, the population of East Chelmsford stood at only 200. Within three years after production of the first cotton cloth, the mills employed 1,000 workers and the town population had grown to 2,000.[5] The new company had to recruit workers from a distance, and since the surrounding town offered few accommodations, it had to build its own housing.

The construction of extensive housing constituted an initial capital cost in outfitting the mills. Although the corporations had to maintain these buildings, they did not further increase housing facilities as rapidly as they expanded productive capacity. In 1826 the land, buildings, and machinery of the Merrimack Company were assessed at $36,645; almost half of this figure represented the valuation of thirty dwelling houses. By 1830 the value of housing of the three major Lowell firms had declined to 32 percent of their total assessment, and by 1860 housing of the eight largest firms constituted only 10 percent of the assessed valuations of these companies.[6] Over these three decades the corporations had rebuilt and refurbished the mill buildings almost constantly. New mills were constructed, additions covered almost every foot of frontage on the canals and the river, and inside the mills new and improved machinery crowded available floor space. Additions to company housing did not keep up with this overall expansion of productive capacity. Instead the textile firms came to rely increasingly on the stock of private housing that grew up in Lowell.

Adequate housing was necessary if the early mills were to attract workers from the surrounding countryside, but company housing also served other purposes. By providing low-rent accommodations to overseers, machinists, and skilled operatives, the companies could attract skilled men, reduce turnover, and at the same time keep wage levels down. Obviously men with families would not move to Lowell unless there was adequate housing. Once hired, if a worker wanted to change jobs, he would have to find a new home, no easy matter given the scarcity of houses in early Lowell. Company homes, in fact, tied workers to their jobs more effectively than good salaries alone would have done. Workers migrating from Lowell could take their savings, if any, with them; they couldn't take their low rents.

Housing for female workers kept wage levels down, but it was also an instrument of social control. For women company boardinghouses were part of a broader vision of corporate paternalism. Nathan Appleton, one of the original organizers of the Lowell mills, reflecting on the founding of the Waltham-Lowell mills, argued that a self-conscious effort had been made to avoid the "degradation" of operatives associated with "the manufacturing cities of Europe." In order to protect the virtue of American women workers, "[the] most efficient guards were adopted in establishing boarding houses, at the cost of the Company, under the charge of respectable women with every provision for religious worship."[7]

Appleton wrote these lines in 1858, some 44 years after the founding of the Boston Manufacturing Company in Waltham. He had the advantage of hindsight and undoubtedly placed his actions in the most favorable light. Still he made no effort to hide the motivations of the Boston Associates in setting up this system. He indicated clearly that these measures were required for successful recruitment of a labor force: "Under these circumstances, the daughters of respectable farmers were readily induced to come into these mills for a temporary period."[8]

Clearly there was no contradiction in the minds of the Boston Associates between their desire to protect the morals of women workers and their need to recruit a mill labor force. Ensuring the former evidently made the latter possible. Paternalism also served economic purposes in another respect, by helping to mold a tractable, disciplined labor force so vital to the smooth functioning of the productive process. Henry Miles, a Unitarian minister in Lowell in the 1840s and a consistent apologist for the millowners, elaborated on this aspect of what he called the "moral police of the corporations":

The productiveness of these works [the textile factories] depends upon one primary and indispensable condition—the existence of an industrious, sober, orderly, and moral class of operatives. Without this, the mills in Lowell would be worthless. Profits would be absorbed by cases of irregularity, carelessness, and neglect; while the existence of any great moral exposure in Lowell would cut off the supply of help from the virtuous homesteads of the country. Public morals and private interests, identical in all places, are here seen to be linked together in an indissoluble connection. Accordingly, the sagacity of self-interest, as well as more disinterested consider-ations, has led to the adoption of moral police.[9]

Economic motives and "more disinterested considerations" reinforced one another, and both contributed to the rise of corporate paternalism.[10]

Company regulations attempted to enforce what management consid-ered "moral" behavior upon mill operatives. The Suffolk Company regulations noted "A regular attendance on public worship on the Sab-bath is necessary for the preservation of good order," and stated em-phatically "The Company will not employ any person who is habitually absent [from services]." Furthermore, total abstinence was required on company property. As the Lawrence Company regulations noted: "every kind of ardent spirit (except prescribed by a regular Physician) will be banished from the limits of the corporation." All offenders on this ac-count "will be discharged, unless they reform, after due admonition."[11]

In addition to rules that directly affected the work of operatives—and discussed earlier in chapter 4—a number of regulations restrained the conduct of women operatives after working hours. First, they were re-quired to reside in company boardinghouses, unless they secured a spe-cific exception from the mill agent. These were generally granted only when operatives had family residing in Lowell. Second, residents of com-pany boardinghouses were required to observe a 10:00 P.M. curfew and retire to their quarters before that hour.[12] Together these two provisions sought to ensure operatives sufficient rest to enable them to work well at their jobs.

While mill agents established the regulations, enforcement was left in large measure in the hands of boardinghouse keepers. Keepers were instructed to enforce the rules on women under their charge and to report unbecoming conduct to mill agents. Once again company regula-tions made the requirements explicit:

The tenants will consider themselves responsible for the order, punctuality of meals, cleanliness and general arrangements for ren-dering their houses comfortable, tranquil scenes of moral deport-ment, and mutual good will.

They will report, if requested, the names and occupations of their boarders, also give timely warning to the unwary, and report all cases of intemperance, or of dissolute manners.

Basically, boardinghouse keepers were regarded as surrogate parents and operatives as minor children; keepers accordingly were "considered answerable for any improper conduct in their houses." Of course operatives were held accountable as well; the punishment for failure to live up to the required moral standards was dismissal from the mills and possible blacklisting. [13]

As early as 1829 firms in Lowell required that operatives who had worked at other companies bring with them an "honorable discharge" as evidence of good conduct and character. Those workers guilty of moral infractions or who had left work without giving sufficient notice were denied discharge papers, and their names were sent around to other corporations to make sure they would find difficulty in getting work in any of the Waltham-Lowell firms. [14] Although discharge regulations appear to have been enforced consistently only during periods of labor protest, their mere existence must have influenced the behavior of women operatives at other times as well.

There is little evidence, in the 1820s and 1830s at least, that women workers resented regulation of their conduct by the corporations. Their letters and reminiscences are notably free of complaints on this score. Women's lives were strictly regulated, but they do not appear to have been particularly resentful of, or even sensitive to, limitations on their conduct. Mary Paul expressed this contradiction between reality and perception in a letter to her father in 1846: "I will tell you about our rules at the boarding house," she noted. "We have none in particular except. . . . " and then she began to enumerate the rules. [15] Her conduct was regulated, but she was not very conscious of the restrictions, probably because they were rather similar to those she lived under at home. In these early years at least, boardinghouse rules were not felt to be an imposition. Within the bounds set by the companies, women were able to carve out a group life for themselves in the boardinghouses. Just as at work, where experienced operatives helped the newcomers learn their way about the mill, so in the boardinghouse, women helped one another make the adjustment to urban, industrial life.

A number of factors contributed to the importance of the boardinghouse in the socialization of newcomers. First, as we have seen, the vast majority of women workers in the early mills, almost three fourths at the Hamilton Company, for instance, resided in company housing. Boardinghouse residents were more than simply a large group in the overall labor force. For all practical purposes, they *were* the labor force. Furthermore, the hours of labor gave women little opportunity to interact with others not living in company housing. Women worked some 73 hours each week, averaging 13 hours a day Monday through Friday and 8 hours on Saturday. [16] The typical workday began at dawn—or even earlier in the summer—and lasted until 7:00 or 7:30 P.M. with only 30-minute breaks for breakfast and midday dinner. With perhaps an hour and a half between the end of supper and the 10:00 curfew, there was little time to spend with anyone living "off the corporation."

Within the boardinghouses women lived in close quarters. The typical boardinghouse in the mid-1830s was an apartment in a long housing block that contained both family tenements and boardinghouses. Hamilton Company boardinghouses at this date had three stories and an attic with dormer windows. The first floor contained kitchen and dining room and quarters for the boardinghouse keeper and her family. The second, third, and attic stories held bedrooms. Typically, twenty-five women resided in the Hamilton boardinghouses, with four to six in each bedroom. [17] There was little room to spare here, and one description of boardinghouse bedrooms found them "absolutely choked with beds, trunks, bandboxes, clothes, umbrellas and people." There was usually no furniture other than double beds, one for each pair of residents, and it was not uncommon for women to write their correspondence on a bandbox cover for lack of any more suitable writing surface. Clearly, there was little possibility for privacy within the boardinghouse, and pressure to conform to group standards must have been strong. [18]

The boardinghouse was particularly important in the initial integration of newcomers into urban, industrial life. Upon first leaving her rural home for work in Lowell, a woman typically entered a setting very different from anything she had previously known. One account described the feelings of a fictional operative:

[T]he first entrance into a factory boarding house seemed something dreadful. The room looked strange and comfortless, and the women cold and heartless; and when she sat down to the supper table, where among more than twenty girls, all but one were strangers, she could not eat a mouthful. [19]

In the boardinghouse the newcomer took the first steps that transformed her from an "outsider" into an accepted member of the peer group.

Boardinghouses were also the centers for the ongoing social life of operatives. There they ate their meals, rested, talked, sewed, wrote letters, and read books and magazines. From among their fellow workers and boarders, they found friends who accompanied them to shops, to Lyceum lectures, or to church and church-sponsored events. On Sundays or holidays they often took walks into the nearby countryside. The community of women operatives developed in a setting in which women worked and lived together twenty-four hours a day. [20]

Given the all-pervasiveness of this community, one would expect it to exert strong pressures on those who did not conform to group standards. So it did. Women influenced newcomers to adopt group patterns of speech and dress. One operative described how recent recruits to the mills stood out from the larger group, but how they soon mended their ways:

> Their [newcomers'] dialect was also very peculiar. On the broken English and Scotch of their ancestors was ingrafted the nasal Yankee twang; so that many of them when they had just come *daown,* spoke a language almost unintelligible. But the severe discipline and ridicule which met them was as good as a school education, and they were soon taught the "city way of speaking."
>
> Their dress was also peculiar, and was of the plainest homespun, cut in such an old-fashioned style that each young girl looked as if she had borrowed her grandmother's gown. Their only head-covering was a shawl, which was pinned under the chin; but after the first pay-day a 'shaker' (or 'scooter') sunbonnet usually replaced the primitive head-gear of their rural life. [21]

It must have been an unusual and strong-willed individual who could work and live among her fellow workers and not conform, at least outwardly, to the customs and values of this larger community. [22]

Several factors, however, eased the adjustment of the new worker. First, she often had the friendship and support of an older sister, cousin, or friend who had already worked in Lowell. The kin and friendship networks described earlier operated through the boardinghouse system.

The Griffith sisters aided Mary Paul, and Wealthy Page helped Elizabeth and Sarah Hodgdon cope with their difficulties. Most newcomers came to Lowell with someone to help them. They usually resided in the same boardinghouse and often managed to work together in the mills. These networks gave the newcomer ready entree into the already existing community of women in the mills and boardinghouses.

Beyond these individual kin and friendship networks, the broader cultural homogeneity of women workers played a crucial role in the socialization process. It will be recalled that more than 96 percent of women workers were native-born, drawn primarily from rural communities of northern New England. Shared nativity carried with it shared cultural roots as well. An unstated but important element in the initiation of newcomers was the understanding that even the more experienced women workers had been "rusty" when they first came to Lowell. They too had worn "dowdy" clothes and spoken with a nasal "twang." Newcomers and experienced hands shared common cultural traditions and values that undoubtedly eased the adjustment process.

This socialization helped mold the hundreds of individual rural women who came to Lowell into a close-knit community of women workers. They comprised a "community" and not simply a "group" because of the growth of bonds of mutual dependence among them. Women's experiences were not simply similar or parallel to one another, rather they were inextricably intertwined. Women recruited one another into the mills, helped each other adjust to work in the mills and life in Lowell, and came to a consciousness of themselves as a sisterhood. The reminiscences of former operatives express these attitudes clearly. Harriet Robinson described each boardinghouse as a "village or community of itself." Lucy Larcom felt that class distinctions too often were used to divide women. She argued: "It is the first duty of every woman to recognize the mutual bond of universal womanhood." Finally, in the strikes of the 1830s and in the labor movement of the 1840s, women workers repeatedly spoke of themselves as a "band of sisters."[23] In the mill boardinghouses of this period, we see important roots for the concept of sisterhood, of particular significance considering the growth of the women's rights movement in the second half of the century.

The close bonds among women in company boardinghouses paralleled similar ties among wealthier young women in the female boarding schools of the period. Older students apparently adopted younger ones and helped them adjust to the new demands of life away from the parental home. At the Dorchester Female Academy, students formed an organization called appropriately enough the "Band of Sisters." As one of them wrote: "We . . . are all to live in perfect harmony & friendship & no young Lady belonging to the Society is to speak unkindly of a Sister." After surveying the relevant sources, Nancy Cott concluded that "academies promoted sisterhood among women." The growth of a similar sense of sisterhood in company boardinghouses linked the experience of Lowell operatives with that of American women more generally in the first half of the nineteenth century. [24]

The female community in the boardinghouses had a greater influence than simply its impact on the speech and dress of newcomers. It also enforced an unwritten code of moral conduct. Henry Miles described the way women exerted pressure on those who deviated from accepted norms:

> A girl, *suspected* of immoralities, or serious improprieties, at once loses caste. Her fellow boarders will at once leave the house, if the keeper does not dismiss the offender. In self-protection, therefore, the patron is obliged to put the offender away. Nor will her former companions walk with her, or work with her; till at length, finding herself everywhere talked about, and pointed at, and shunned she is obliged to relieve her fellow-operatives of a presence which they feel brings disgrace. [25]

As an apologist for corporate paternalism, Miles was not an altogether disinterested observer, but there is other evidence that corroborates his account. In correspondence between Delia Page, an operative in Manchester, New Hampshire, and her foster parents, we are afforded a rare glimpse into the social life of a woman worker in an early mill town. Only the parents' letters survive, but from them it is apparent that Delia Page was seeing Sylvester Drew, a man regarded by her parents and their friends as one of questionable character. Delia's foster parents, learning of Drew from one of her letters, wrote a Manchester acquaintance inquiring about him. He replied: "Mr. Drew has a wife & one child in Lowell. He has ben trusteed twice by his wife, is also a man that drinks hard and also runing after other woman. [He] is a very unprincibled Man." Her foster parents attempted to persuade Delia to give him up but to no avail. She left her boardinghouse when the keeper would not permit Drew to continue visiting her. Her former boardinghouse keeper and a former roommate spoke to her further about her conduct, though with little evident effect. As the Manchester informant learned by talking with her acquaintances: "She is conducting very improperly and is creating a good deal of talk." Perhaps the combined pressure of boardinghouse keeper, roommates, and parental letters had the desired effect, because the affair ended soon. Two months after the first references to the matter, Delia's foster father wrote her: "We . . . are glad to see you have got over the dreaded trouble with so little dificulty." [26]

A fictional variation on this theme appeared in a story in the *Lowell Offering*. Women in a company boardinghouse begin to harbor suspicions of a fellow boarder, Hannah Felton, who receives repeated evening visits from a man whom she does not introduce to the others. Concern mounts over his identity and the nature of their relatonship. "I will ask her who he is," says the sister-in-law of the boardinghouse keeper. "She shan't receive company here, that she is ashamed of, or who is ashamed of her, and of the house he visits." Hannah replies that he is a relative, but doubts persist. After continued visits two boarders declare that they will leave if she is allowed to remain. Only one operative in the entire household gives her any support. Finally the boardinghouse keeper demands that she "promise to see the gentleman no more, or leave my house at the close of the week." A fellow boarder speaks to Hannah's overseer, who promptly discharges her from the mill. Here the story departs from that of Delia Page, and in true melodramatic style, Hannah Felton becomes seriously ill. As she nears death the identity of her secret visitor is revealed. He is her brother, hiding this fact in an effort to win the hand of a proud Lowell woman who scorned those who worked for a living. [27] It would be too much to demand that a realistic portrayal be carried through to a reasonable conclusion in the pages of the rather stilted and conventional *Lowell Offering*. Still, this glimpse into the workings of the operatives' peer group seems realistic enough. Certainly, it is consistent with other evidence of the pressure the female community could bring upon those who overstepped the bounds of accepted morality.

On the other hand, since the visitor turns out to be Hannah's brother, the tale might be interpreted as an indirect attack on the system of using peer pressure to induce conformity. The author here may be pointing out that such peer pressure could be used against women whom all would agree were behaving morally. However we interpret the point of the story, the reality of group pressure on behavior is confirmed.

Although these examples are conventional enough, women did not always enforce a moral code agreeable to Lowell's clergy, nor to the mill agents and overseers, for that matter. Looking ahead for a moment to the labor struggles that raged in Lowell in these years, one can see that pressure similar to that on Delia Page or Hannah Felton could be brought to bear on women who would not ordinarily have participated in protests. It would have been much harder to go to work as usual when one's roommates were marching about town, attending rallies, and circulating strike resolutions as they did in 1834 and 1836. Similarly, the ten-hour petitions of the 1840s benefited from the existence of a tight-knit community of women workers in the dense boardinghouse neighborhoods. To the extent that women could not have completely private lives in the boardinghouses, they probably had to conform to group norms, whether these involved speech, clothing, relations with men, or attitudes toward the ten-hour day. Group pressure to conform, so important in the daily life of women in early Lowell, played a significant role in shaping their collective protests as well.

CHAPTER SIX

The Early Strikes: The 1830s

The oppressing hand of avarice would enslave us, and to gain their object, they gravely tell us of the pressure of the times, this we are sensible of, and deplore it. If any are in want, the Ladies will be compassionate and assist them; but we prefer to have the disposing of our charities in our own hands; and as we are free, we would remain in possession of what kind Providence has bestowed upon us, and remain daughters of freemen still.[1]

THE NATURE of work and housing in early Lowell helped weld women workers together, but women as a group did not consciously array themselves against millowners or management. Solidarity grew up among women, but it was based on shared experience and culture and mutual dependence rather than upon antagonism toward employers. Mill management exercised considerable control over the lives of women workers through regulations imposed in the mills and boardinghouses, but mill employment fulfilled important needs for women, and they were generally willing to accept these regulations. As long as their expectations were met, women workers did not challenge the power and authority of the corporations. Twice in the 1830s, however, mill management took a course of action that led women workers to rebel. In February 1834 and October 1836, women workers struck to oppose first reductions in wages and then increases in the board rates charged in company housing. These events are important because they reveal the ways that women used the bonds of community forged in their daily lives to mobilize protest in times of crisis. They reveal also the way women workers drew on preindustrial values in responding to changing conditions in the mills and the way these values were transformed within an industrial setting.

The 1830s, the years of the first strikes in Lowell, were a period of profound unrest in the ranks of American labor. A rapid transformation of the social relations of production, particularly in the skilled urban crafts, led to a new proliferation of labor organizations.[2] The rise of the boss manufacturer and the wholesale merchant undermined an earlier system of production based on master craftsmen, journeymen, and apprentices. The apprenticeship system had established links among the ranks of the urban working class, but increasingly an unbridgeable gulf separated employer and worker. The new urban entrepreneur was no longer an artisan but had become an employer of workers who organized the labor process and marketed the finished products. Workers responded to these developments by organizing to defend their wages, hours, and skilled positions. The period saw the rise of local trade societies within individual crafts, urban central labor organizations, or trades' unions, and national organizations that sought to promote the mutual interests of disparate local groups. The new labor organizations grew most rapidly among male workers in the artisan and building trades of the industrializing Northeast where these economic developments were first felt.[3]

As employers sought to expand production and reduce labor costs, workers began to resist. Moving beyond the benevolent societies of an earlier era, journeymen organized trade unions whose chief concerns were wages and hours. Strikes proliferated in the mid-1830s as trade societies fought to reduce the hours of labor and increase wages in prosperous times and to maintain wage levels in periods of depression.[4] Organized activity spilled over into the political arena as well, as workers sought to use the state to promote economic and social reform. In Boston, New York, and Philadelphia, workingmen's parties united articulate labor leaders and reform-minded merchants and professionals in campaigns aimed broadly at a democratization of economic and political life.[5]

The growth of labor organizations on such a variety of levels—within single trades, in citywide councils, and even along national lines—is evidence of both the strength and the weakness of labor in these years. The urban trades' unions—umbrella organizations of several trade unions in a single city—grew out of the initial weakness of organizations within individual trades and the obvious need for solidarity in the face of unified employer opposition. As these citywide movements gained strength, many trades succeeded in obtaining the ten-hour working day, as in Philadelphia in 1835.[6] But the growth of ever larger regional markets undermined the power of unions organized only at the local level. Employers facing united opposition in one city could shift production to unorganized workers elsewhere. In response, attempts were made to establish national trade unions, particularly among shoemakers and printers. Still, the strength of labor lay in its organization at the local level, and the national unions were never much more than paper organizations, which expired with the onset of depression in 1837.[7]

Labor organizations along these lines did not develop among women textile workers in the 1830s. Several factors help to explain the differences between the responses of women operatives and male artisans in the period. Caroline Ware has emphasized the temporary nature of mill employment, arguing that "[only] as the mill population became more permanent was there any real and prolonged interest in mill conditions and any chance for effective organization." In this view, women who planned to work only a short time in the mills before marriage had little incentive to struggle to improve working conditions. One might add also that women operatives lacked the craft skills and traditions that contributed to organization among artisans in the period. Finally, they did not have the same sort of preindustrial craft work experience with which to judge factory production. They were unlikely to use their years of domestic textile production as a foil against which they would find the factory wanting. All of these factors undoubtedly inhibited the growth of permanent trade organizations among women.[8]

Trade unions, however, are not the only mechanism through which workers can express their opposition to the demands of industrial capitalism. Women in the Lowell mills certainly were not immune from the industrial struggles raging all around them. In prosperous times workingmen complained that they were unable to arouse in operatives an opposition to the factory system.[9] In these periods women evidently were able to fulfill their expectations and lay away enough savings to compensate for the long hours and strict regulation of textile production. Women were not entirely complacent, however. Given provocation, women workers did organize themselves, staging Lowell's first strikes in February 1834 and October 1836. The pattern of sporadic outbursts gave way in the 1840s to the growth of permanent labor organizations among women and repeated campaigns aimed at achieving the ten-hour working day. These struggles placed the Lowell women squarely within the evolving labor movement and indicated that craft traditions were not the only legitimating forces in labor protests of the period.

Why women protested and what their struggles revealed about women's values and attitudes during the transition to early industrial capitalism will be the focus of this chapter and the next. The strikes of the 1830s, and then the Ten Hour Movement of the 1840s, are important not only because they indicate the impact of textile factories on women workers, but also because they reveal the interconnections between the experiences of women in Lowell and those of other workers throughout New England and the mid-Atlantic states. The Lowell protests were part of the larger response to the demands imposed by a maturing industrial capitalism on the working class at this time. From Lowell, Manchester, and Fall River to New York, Philadelphia, and Pittsburgh, workers organized to challenge the power and authority of employers. These struggles developed together and reinforced one another. Channels of communication and coordination developed, and workers' organizations shared tactics and strategy. Lowell operatives emulated earlier strikers, and workers in other communities, in turn, copied their actions. This coordination and imitation resulted because, even with evident differences, working men and women alike drew on certain shared traditional social and cultural values to oppose the novel demands of industrial life. Within this wider context, the Lowell struggles are most significant for what they reveal about the broader conflicts generated by the growth of industrial capitalism before the Civil War.

After a decade of rapid expansion and relative tranquility, Lowell saw its first labor protest in February 1834, when 800 women workers "turned out"—quit work—to oppose a proposed reduction in piece wages. Trouble had been brewing for two weeks since the agents of all the major firms had posted identical broadsides announcing a reduction of wages to take effect March 1.[10] A brief chronology of the events leading up to the protest reveals the values and attitudes that prompted women workers to challenge the power and authority of mill management.

The origin of the turn-out—as the work stoppage was called—must be sought in the Boston meeting rooms of the directors of the Lowell textile firms. Faced with falling prices of textile goods, a sluggish market, and rising inventories of unsold cloth, the directors of the mills met and recommended a 25 percent wage reduction. Henry Hall, treasurer of the Lawrence, Tremont, and Suffolk companies, instructed Robert Means, resident agent at Tremont, to "act in concert with the other agents & endeavor to do what is right between the parties." [11] The agents of all the Lowell mills subsequently met and agreed upon a reduction of half the amount initially recommended by the Boston directors. While the more distant directors pressed for greater reductions, agents in Lowell expressed concern that such action would have disastrous consequences. As William Austin, the Lawrence Company agent, wrote: "The tendency will be unfavorable to the procurement of good help in future & reduce the character of those who remain to a lower standard rendering it doubtful in my own mind whether the permanent interest of the manufacturing establishments here will be promoted by so great a reduction." [12] The differences between the resident agents and their Boston employers remained a private matter, however, and at a subsequent meeting the agents voted to impose reductions about midway between the directors' original recommendations and their own.

The agents had good reason for concern about the reaction of women workers. Agitation in the mills began as soon as the broadsides appeared announcing the impending wage cuts. Even before agents fixed on the actual amount of the reduction, petitions circulated among the women. One agent reported to his company treasurer in Boston: "A good deal of excitement exists in all the mills, not excepting ours, in relation to the proposed reduction. Papers are in circulation, & as I am informed, extensively signed, by which the females pledge themselves to leave if the reduction is made." [13] One such petition has survived, signed by fifty weavers at the Suffolk Company and expressing their determination to give notice and quit work if existing wage rates were not maintained. Their petition read in part:

> We the undersigned considering ourselves wronged and our privi-
> leges invaded by the unjust and unreasonable oblidgment of our
> wages, do hereby mutually and cheerfully engage not to enter the
> Factory on the first of March, nor after for the purpose of work,
> unless the paper which causes our dissatisfaction be removed and
> another signed . . . purport[in]g that our wages shall be after the
> same rate as previous to the first of March.

The signers pledged further that if any of them later reneged she would
pay five dollars to one of their number to be used for "some benevolent
object in this Town." To mobilize support in the other mills, the Suffolk
weavers sent their petition to weavers at the Appleton Company, urging
them to take similar action. [14]

Women continued to hold meetings, a number convening within the
mills during the dinner break. Agitation mounted, to the point where it
began to disrupt the work itself. One agent, seeking to squelch the
unrest before it spread, dismissed a leader. Her fellow workers rallied
around her and quit work, and the turn-out had begun. [15] Protesting
operatives paraded through city streets, visiting the various mills and
attempting to induce others to join in. In all, about a sixth of all women
workers in Lowell turned out. The Boston *Evening Transcript* reported the
procession and the mass outdoor rally that followed:

> The number soon increased to nearly *eight hundred*. A procession
> was formed and they marched about town. . . . We are told that one
> of the leaders mounted a pump and made a flaming Mary Wool-
> stonecroft [sic] speech on the rights of women and the iniquities of
> the *"monied* aristocracy," which produced a powerful effect on her
> auditors, and they determined "to have their own way if they died
> for it." [16]

At the rally operatives endorsed a petition calling on fellow workers to
"discontinue their labors until terms of reconciliation are made." The
petition concluded:

> Resolved, That we will not go back into the mills to work unless
> our wages are continued . . . as they have been.
> Resolved, That none of us will go back, unless they receive us all
> as one.
> Resolved, That if any have not money enough to carry them
> home they shall be supplied. [17]

The turn-out, however, proved to be brief, and it failed to reverse the wage reductions. Turning out on a Friday, striking operatives received wages owed them on Saturday, and by the middle of the next week they had returned to work or left town. Within a week of the turn-out, mills were running near capacity.[18]

Though short-lived, the turn-out points to the tensions evoked by the interconnections of sex and power within the mills. Operatives were, after all, *women* workers, and both strikers and mill managers were very conscious of this fact. The "Mary Woolstonecroft [sic] speech," given at the rally, linked together the causes of operatives as women and as workers. Just as the leaders of the turn-out sought to redefine woman's place, mill managers viewed the protest as decidedly unfeminine. William Austin, agent of the Lawrence Company, described the operatives' procession as an "amizonian [sic] display." He repeated his language in a letter to his company treasurer: "This afternoon we have paid off several of these Amazons & presume that they will leave town on Monday."[19] The turn-out was particularly offensive to the mill agents because of the relationship of mutual confidence they thought they had enjoyed with their operatives. Austin probably expressed the feelings of the other agents when he wrote:

> [N]otwithstanding the friendly and disinterested advice which has been on all proper occassions communicated to the girls of the Lawrence Mills a spirit of evil omen . . . has prevailed, and overcome the judgment & discretion of too many, and this morning a general turn-out from most of the rooms has been the consequence.[20]

Mill agents assumed an attitude of benevolent paternalism toward female operatives, and they found it particularly disturbing that women paid such little heed to their advice. Strikers were not simply unfeminine; they were ungrateful as well.

Such attitudes notwithstanding, 800 women chose to go on strike. They did so for two principal reasons. First, the wage cuts undermined the sense of dignity and social equality that was such an important element in their Yankee heritage. Second, the cuts were seen as an attack on their economic independence.

In a statement accompanying the petition circulated among operatives, the strikers expressed well their sense of themselves and their motives for protest.

UNION IS POWER

Our present object is to have union and exertion, and we remain in possession of our unquestionable rights. We circulate this paper wishing to obtain the names of all who imbibe the spirit of our Patriotic Ancestors, who preferred privation to bondage, and parted with all that renders life desirable and even life itself to procure independence for their children. The oppressing hand of avarice would enslave us, and to gain their object, they gravely tell us of the pressure of the times, this we are already sensible of, and deplore it. If any are in want, the Ladies will be compassionate and assist them; but we prefer to have the disposing of our charities in our own hands; and as we are free, we would remain in possession of what kind Providence has bestowed upon us, and remain daughters of freemen still. [21]

In these lines striking women workers expressed their pride and sense of independence as "daughters of freemen." They were identifying themselves not primarily as working women, but rather as daughters of propertied rural farmers. Here we see the ideological implications of the common social origins of women workers discussed earlier.

This rural identification gave the protest strong ties to the preindustrial traditions of the striking women. They linked their action expressly to the tradition of the Revolutionary War, to the efforts of their "Patriotic Ancestors" to secure independence from England. This identification with the traditions of revolutionary republicanism was expressed clearly in a poem that concluded their petition:

> Let oppression shrug her shoulders,
> And a haughty tyrant frown,
> And little upstart Ignorance,
> In mockery look down.
> Yet I value not the feeble threats
> Of Tories in disguise,
> While the flag of Independence
> O'er our noble nation flies. [22]

There is no doubt who were the Whigs and who the Tories in this particular drama.

By harking back to the Revolutionary War, women workers were drawing on the same traditions cited by contemporary workingmen in their trade union struggles. Seth Luther, carpenter and itinerant labor organizer and agitator in New England, made similar allusions in his writings:

> But if *poor* men ask JUSTICE, it is a most HORRIBLE COMBINA-
> TION. The Declaration of Independence was the work of a combi-
> nation, and was as hateful to the TRAITORS and TORIES of those
> days, as combinations among working men are now to the avari-
> cious MONOPOLIST and *purse-proud* ARISTOCRAT.

Organized workingmen took the revolutionary tradition seriously. When Lynn shoemakers published a newspaper, *The Awl*, in the mid-1840s, they reprinted the Declaration of Independence. As Dawley has noted, "some journeymen compared their bosses to King George, and one proposed that workingmen assemble on Lynn Common on the Fourth of July to erect a monument to their forebears who marched to repulse the British at Concord in 1775." Fittingly enough, the great shoe-makers' strike in 1860 began on Washington's Birthday, a date chosen according to Dawley "to demonstrate that they were acting in the best traditions of the Republic." [23] By appropriating revolutionary rhetoric, Seth Luther, the Lynn shoemakers, and Lowell women workers gave their protests legitimacy, for they became, in their own eyes at least, the direct heirs of the revolutionary tradition. For Lowell women, for in-stance, wage cuts were thus not questions of purely economic concern; they were interpreted more broadly, as attempts to "enslave" women workers, to deprive them of their independent status as "daughters of freemen."

Integral to this appropriation of the revolutionary heritage of their fathers was a clear statement of the women's sense of their own worth and dignity. As independent "daughters of freemen," they felt no defer-ence toward their employers; they would certainly *not* call them their masters. Elsewhere they expressed the conviction that they were the social equals of their overseers, indeed of the millowners themselves. [24] The wage reductions, however, struck at their assertion of equality. The cuts made it clear that the workers were subordinate to their employers, or at least so millowners and agents thought, rather than equal partners in a contract binding on both parties. By turning out the women em-phatically denied that they were subordinates. In returning to work the next week, they yielded to the reality that in economic terms they were no match for their corporate employers.

In point of fact the women workers *were* subordinates in Lowell's social and economic order, but they never consciously accepted this status. Their refusal to do so became evident on those occasions when the millowners exercised their power most blatantly, as in their unilateral decision to reduce customary piece-wage rates. This fundamental contradiction between the objective position of operatives and their consciousness of their status was at the root of the 1834 turn-out and of subsequent labor protests in Lowell before 1850. The corporations could build mills, create thousands of jobs, and recruit women to fill them. Nevertheless, they bought only their operatives' labor power, and then for only as long as the workers chose to stay. Virtually all of the women could return to their rural homes, whatever the tangible and psychic costs of such a return, and all maintained a strong sense of their own worth and dignity.[25] The women's economic independence and their strong sense of themselves both limited the actions of management.

When women workers spoke of independence, they referred at once to independence from their families and from their employers. An adequate wage made them largely independent of their families back home and also allowed them to save enough out of their monthly earnings to return to their native homes whenever they so desired. But this independence was based on the relatively high level of wages in the mills. The wage cuts threatened to deny women these savings and the economic and social independence they provided, offering instead the prospect of a total dependence on mill work. No wonder, then, there was alarm that "the oppressing hand of avarice would enslave us." To be forced, out of economic necessity, into lifelong labor in the mills would indeed have seemed like slavery.[26] The Yankee operatives spoke directly to the fear of a dependency based on impoverishment in offering to assist women workers who "have not money enough to carry them home." Wage reductions, however, offered only the *prospect* of a future dependence on mill employment. By striking, the women asserted that their economic independence and their status as "daughters of freemen" remained intact.

While the women's traditional conception of themselves as independent daughters of freemen played a crucial role in the turn-out, this factor alone would not necessarily have triggered a protest; alone it would have led women as individuals to quit work and return to their rural homes. But the turn-out was a collective action, indicating at once both the strength of women's economic motives and the importance of their sense of shared identity and purpose. They turned out in order to maintain existing wage rates and to hold onto their jobs and the economic independence they enjoyed.

The evidence of the planned, collective nature of the protest is clear. The Suffolk weavers' petition described earlier indicates that women workers initially planned to quit work en masse the day the wage cuts were to take effect. To make their pledge stick, women agreed to forfeit 5 dollars if they failed to abide by its terms. In order to secure additional support for their action, Suffolk weavers sent the petition to their counterparts at the Appleton Company and urged them to join the action.[27] Further, leaders of the turn-out organized a run on the local savings bank, the Lowell Institution for Savings, closely allied with the textile corporations. Women withdrew their savings in order to have funds to survive during the strike and to be able to return to their rural homes. This tactic enabled the organized women to offer assistance to workers who did not have "money enough to carry them home." It also seems to have forced the corporations to provide funds to the bank to enable it to meet the demand for specie.[28]

The extent of organization among women is most clearly revealed in the meetings they held within the mills and in the confrontation that eventually precipitated the turn-out. A remarkable letter written by a mill agent, William Austin, to his company treasurer in Boston, in the midst of the events, provides a vivid firsthand account from an interested participant. He first became concerned when he learned that workers were meeting in Spinning Room No.1 during their dinner break. They had excluded the male watchman from their proceedings, evidently considering him an outsider. The agent described his unsuccessful efforts to dissuade the operatives from their course of action:

> It appeared that before I entered the room, they had appointed a dictatress & voted to be governed by her in all cases. This woman . . . retorted upon me with no little vehemence, & declared that there was no cause for any reduction whatever, that the causes

assigned for it were without foundation in fact, that she had to pay as much for a yard of cloth as ever & that there was no truth in the assertions of the Agents.

Austin could get nowhere with his adversary, and "[p]erceiving that this woman had a great sway over the minds of the other females," he tried to persuade her to accept an "honorable discharge" and to leave the mill. She was not interested, and there Austin let matters rest as the women returned to their work. By the end of the day, however, Austin felt he had to take stronger action. This ringleader "continually had a crowd around her" which disrupted work, and Austin decided to discharge her. In response to her dismissal, "She declared that every girl in the room should leave with her, made a signal, and . . . they all marched out & few returned the ensuing morning." [29] The Boston *Evening Transcript* confirmed Austin's account but suggested that operatives in the other Lawrence mills turned out as well. According to this source:

> On Friday evening, the young woman referred to was *dismissed* by the Agent, from her place in the mill where she worked, and on leaving the office, after receiving 'a bill of her time,' . . . waved her calash in the air as a signal to others, who were watching from the windows, when they immediately 'struck,' and assembled around her, in despite of the overseers.

Both accounts indicate that the turn-out was not simply a spontaneous outburst of enraged individuals, but rather an organized, planned protest. [30]

The organized collective nature of the turn-out, however, did not guarantee its success. First, it mobilized only about a sixth of the female labor force, whose absence from the mills disrupted production but did not bring it to a complete halt. [31] Anticipating the possibility of difficulties, mill agents actively sought replacements even before the turn-out. As Austin wrote on the day of the turn-out: "I have now engaged and ready to come in about two hundred girls who will come in during the ensuing month, and fifty more are offered." [32] Even had the mills been forced to reduce production, it is unlikely that the directors would have yielded to the operatives. Given the accumulation of finished cloth unsold, there were directors who felt that it would not hurt to have the mills shut down for a period. These were not good times in which to launch the first labor struggle in Lowell's brief history.

Compounding these difficulties was the fact that mill management found the turn-out virtually incomprehensible. As one treasurer wrote to his company's agent in Lowell: "The conduct of the Female 'operatives' in yours & the neighboring mills is inexplicable unless they suppose of a *show* of resistance that the proprietors will be intimidated & induced to continue *old* prices."[33] The disbelief expressed here stemmed as much from the fact that striking workers were females as from the novelty of their specific demands. The turn-out shocked and amazed the directors, and they took up an unyielding position in response to the women's challenge to their power and authority. With all the mill managers in Lowell acting in unison, and with agents in neighboring mill towns following suit, women found that if they wanted to work at all, they would have to accept reduced wages. Although the strike did not accomplish its immediate objectives, by demonstrating the possibility of collective action it paved the way for more successful struggles in the future.

In October 1836 women again turned out. This action was similar to the first in several respects. It, too, was a defensive action opposing a decision of management that would have reduced women's earnings—a decision to raise the price of room and board in company boarding-houses. The price increase came in response to petitions from boarding-house keepers complaining that they could not make ends meet because of rapid inflation. The problem with management's action was that it placed the entire burden of inflation on the women workers, without increasing their piece wages accordingly. Since women generally quoted their wages exclusive of the cost of room and board, this action was viewed by women as a wage cut, not very different from that of February 1834.[34] Further, the tactics mirrored those employed earlier. Women marched around town and held large-scale outdoor rallies to drum up support. Even the language of strike resolutions had a familiar ring: "As our fathers resisted unto blood the lordly avarice of the British ministry, so we, their daughters, never will wear the yoke which has been prepared for us." Song enlivened the protesters' march, and the lyrics recalled the earlier turn-out:

> Oh! isn't it a pity, such a pretty girl as I—
> Should be sent to the factory to pine away and die?
> Oh! I cannot be a slave,

> I will not be a slave,
> For I'm so fond of liberty,
> That I cannot be a slave. [35]

Once again the spectre of slavery was raised, clearly viewed in contrast to the economic and social independence that was the women's heritage.

Further similarities linked the two turn-outs. As in 1834 there was considerable excitement after mill management announced its decision to raise the price of board. One company treasurer expressed a concern probably shared by others: "[I] shall be anxious to know how the new rate of Board is rec[eive]d by the Ladies of Your Family. I hope there is good sense enough amongst them to see the necessity of the case." [36] Once again women met and talked within the mills, planning their course of action. Harriet Robinson, 11 years old at this date and an active participant in the struggle, recalled events later in her reminiscences:

> I worked in a lower room, where I heard the proposed strike fully, if not vehemently, discussed; I had been an ardent listener . . . and naturally I took sides with the strikers. When the day came on which the girls were to turn out, those in the upper rooms started first, and so many of them left that our mill was at once shut down. Then, when the girls in my room stood irresolute, uncertain what to do . . . I, who began to think they would not go out, after all their talk, became impatient, and started on ahead, saying with childish bravado, "I don't care what you do, *I* am going to turn out, whether any one else does or not;" and I marched out, and was followed by the others. [37]

This account indicates that the women actively discussed the increase in board rates and planned the turn-out, much as they had in 1834.

Despite these continuities, the differences between the two turn-outs were dramatic. First, the economic settings in February 1834 and October 1836 contrasted sharply. At the earlier date, textile sales were sluggish and a number of directors even welcomed the possibility of halting production; in 1836 sales were booming, and the mills could not recruit enough workers to meet demand. In August 1836, two months before the turn-out, one agent complained of shortages of operatives in three of his firm's mills. He wanted to shift workers from one mill to another but noted their resistance: "[It] will not meet the notions of the girls, who have a high sense of their value in the market & must be treated with corresponding delicacy and forbearance." [38] In these prosperous times the prospects of success for the turn-out were considerably greater than they had been two and a half years earlier. In addition to the more favorable economic circumstances, this second turnout involved a higher proportion of operatives than in 1834. Some 1,500 or 2,000 turned out in 1836, comprising between one fourth and one third of the female labor force, compared to only a sixth two years before. [39] Moreover, the second strike lasted much longer than the first. In 1834 operatives stayed out for only a few days; in 1836 the mills ran far below capacity for several months. Two weeks after the beginning of the 1836 turn-out, the Lawrence Company agent reported that only a fifth of striking operatives had returned to work: "The rest manifest *good 'spunk'* as they call it." Several days later he complained further of the impact of the continuing strike on operations in his mills: "We must be feeble for months to come as probably not less than 250 of our former scanty supply of help have left town." At the Hamilton Company about a fourth of the women workers left the mills during October, leaving the firm so short of help that management closed one of the company's three mills and shifted the remaining workers into the two still in operation. [40]

The larger proportion of women workers taking part and the longer duration of the turn-out meant that the strikers had a much more significant impact on the operations of the mills. Estimates of the total number of participants provide one measure of this impact, but examination of individual firms may place this dimension in a clearer light. At the Lawrence Company, with a normal work force of 1,300, the agent reported that 386 women and 3 men were absent from the mills on the second day of the strike. The next day the number had increased to between 400 and 450, fully a third of all the workers, and a considerably larger proportion of the women. At the neighboring Tremont Mills, between 180 and 200 were out, amounting to one half of the normal work force. Clearly the larger number of participants overall was mirrored in the experience of individual Lowell firms. [41]

Numbers alone were only one reason for the greater impact of the turn-out. The increased organization of women workers and the greater sophistication of their tactics also played a part. To coordinate activities, women formed a Factory Girls' Association, which reached a membership of 2,500. The association organized "committees from the several corporations, to make provisions for those who have not the means to pay their board." Although the Association did not outlive the strike that gave it birth, it clearly contributed to the impact of the turn-out. [42]

The increased organization of women was reflected in the tactics they employed. Strikers, according to one mill agent, were able to halt production to a greater extent than numbers alone could explain. He complained that although some operatives were willing to work, "it has been impossible to give employment to many who remained." He attributed the difficulty to the women's tactics:

> This was in many instances no doubt the result of calculation and contrivance. After the original turn-out they [the operatives] would assail a particular room—as for instance, all the warpers, or all the warp spinners, or all the speeder and stretcher girls, and this would close the mill as effectually as if all the girls in the mill had left. [43]

Apparently giving more thought than they had earlier to the specific tactics of the turn-out, women made a deliberate effort to shut down the mills in order to win their demands. These tactics anticipated those of skilled mule spinners and loom fixers in the last decades of the nineteenth century. [44] Learning from the failure of the 1834 turn-out, and building on the experience gained at that time, women brought a more acute awareness of the importance of tactics to the struggle.

Mill agents were not the only contemporaries impressed by the organization and tactics of striking operatives. A local storekeeper and lay preacher, Aaron Lummus, expressed his amazement at the quality of leadership among the operatives: "[It] was remarkable, that a few, probably less than half a dozen young women, should manage this whole affair with so much dexterity and correct judgement, that no power, or skill, could be successfully employed against them." Lummus allied himself with the women and could clearly appreciate their efforts in a way that mill manager adversaries could not. [45]

The increased tactical awareness of the leadership paid off. Several sources indicate that the striking women achieved a measure of success. According to one observer the companies rescinded the increases in the price of room and board for operatives paid on a daily basis. Including sparehands, spinners, and drawers, this group constituted more than 40 percent of women workers at Hamilton Company and probably a similar proportion in other firms. At two companies the women seem to have been completely successful. As a mill agent wrote in the heat of the struggle: "Merr[imack] and Boott houses have discontinued extra allowance to boarding houses." While this line leaves some doubt, it does appear that the Merrimack and Boott companies had rescinded their recent increases in board rates. These sources indicate a degree of success that was unusual for any strike—of workingmen or women—in the period. [46]

Who were these workingwomen who dared to overstep the bounds of female propriety to turn out when they felt their interests were challenged and their independence attacked? Available evidence suggests that the strikers were drawn from the entire range of female mill occupations. Workingmen did not take part in significant numbers because their interests were never affected. In 1834 only the wages of piece workers were reduced, and men working for a daily wage remained on the sidelines. In 1836 only the board rates for women were raised. It would have made no sense for management to cut male earnings when men made up only 15 percent of the work force and such a large proportion were employed in supervisory roles. The labor savings sought were best derived by reductions in the earnings of the vast female majority in the work force.

One textile corporation, the Appleton Company, kept a list of those workers who took part in the turn-out in February 1834. The document records the names and occupations of 125 women—about 30 percent of all females employed at Appleton at the time—who had quit work "on account of the reduction in Wages." The occupations of the strikers reveal that they were rather evenly distributed throughout the various departments of the company's mills. About 40 percent worked in the low-paying carding and spinning rooms and 60 percent in weaving and dressing, both figures approximating the proportions of women operatives typically employed in these rooms. [47]

Strikers at the Hamilton Company in October 1836 showed a similar occupational distribution. Hamilton kept no lists explicitly identifying those who participated in the turn-out, but surviving records enable one to identify workers who left the company during that month. For several reasons it seems reasonable to consider these women strikers. First, 25 percent of women workers departed Hamilton in October, a proportion

more than twice that of the months immediately preceding and following. Second, it is clear that the primary tactic employed in the turn-out
was the wholesale departure of operatives who returned to their native
homes. A contemporary in Lowell, a Methodist minister, Orange Scott,
estimated that 2,000 women had left the city during the strike, intending
to return only when their demands had been met. [48]

As at the Appleton Company strikers at Hamilton were drawn from
all ranks of the female work force. The highest paid women, those employed in the dressing room, were somewhat underrepresented, but
weavers, the next ranking group, were overrepresented. On the whole,
the occupations of strikers and nonstrikers were not radically different
from one another. The daily earnings of the two groups reflected this
fact, with strikers earning an average of $0.61 per day, and nonstrikers a
slightly higher $0.63. Given the broad wage spread described earlier, this
difference is insignificant.

What factors can account for the ability of women textile workers in
Lowell to organize and sustain this kind of collective protest? After all,
women in the mills lacked the craft traditions and scarce skills of male
artisans. Further, they were not lifelong workers, supporting entire families on their earnings in the mills. Despite these dampening influences,
the signal fact that stands out for Lowell in these early years is that
women workers did organize two large-scale turn-outs. The conjunction
of several interrelated factors best explains this reality. First, the growth
of a close-knit community among women in their daily lives provided a
necessary, though not sufficient, precondition of organized protest. As
has been shown, this community grew out of rich kinship and friendship
networks with roots in the surrounding countryside. Work training and
sharing in the mills and a shared life in company boardinghouses reinforced these bonds. A sense of sisterhood developed that functioned for
women workers rather like craft solidarity among skilled male artisans.
While this solidarity was a necessary precondition for organized protest,
women's identification with a revolutionary republican tradition shaped
their actual response to changing conditions in the mills. Viewing themselves primarily as "daughters of freemen," they saw wage cuts as at-
tacks on their economic and social independence and responded by leaving work. Their effective solidarity then transformed individual decisions
to quit into the collective response of turning out. The turn-out can thus

be viewed as evidence for the continuing influence of preindustrial values and traditions that take on new meanings and serve new functions
within an industrial setting. [49]

While important in their own right for what they reveal about cultural
continuity and change in early industrial capitalism, the turn-outs are
also of interest because of the way they fit into the larger picture of labor
protest in New England textiles in the antebellum period. They were not
isolated incidents; rather they grew out of and reflected earlier strike
activity and at the same time contributed to the growth and subsequent
spread of labor struggle. The Lowell strikes were the largest protests of
working women in the period, but they were not the first nor the last.
They drew on the examples of a number of earlier textile strikes and in
turn sparked protest in other mill communities.

The first strike involving women workers in New England textiles
occurred in Pawtucket, Rhode Island, in May 1824, in the mills of Samuel Slater. In a period of depression, much like that a decade later, Slater
found himself in an economic squeeze brought about by a decline in
prices of finished cloth coupled with increases in the cost of raw cotton.
To cope with these difficulties, Slater announced that beginning June 1
there would be an increase of one hour in the length of the working day
and a 25 percent reduction in the piece wages of power-loom weavers.
All workers felt the increase in the hours of labor, but women were
particularly singled out by the wage cuts for weavers. The response of
Pawtucket workers anticipated that in Lowell a decade later. An unsym-
pathetic reporter described the initial events:

> The female weavers assembled in parliament to the number, it is
> stated of one hundred and two—one of the most active, and most
> talkative, was placed in the chair, and the meeting, it is understood,
> was conducted, however strange it may appear, without noise, or
> scarcely a single speech. The result of the meeting was a resolution
> to abandon their looms, unless allowed the old prices. [50]

Unlike the Lowell turn-outs, working men and women were united at
the outset. Furthermore, strikers found considerable sympathy in the
larger community. In contrast to Lowell operatives Pawtucket millhands
were generally longtime local residents with roots in Pawtucket and the
surrounding towns. Nonworkers thus seem to have been drawn into the
struggle. Purposeful militant crowd actions closed the mills for a time,

and an instance of attempted arson may have influenced Slater. In any event by June 3 a compromise was reached, and workers returned to the mills. Slater and the striking workers were more evenly matched than management and workers in Lowell a decade later. Slater lacked the financial resources of the Boston Associates, and the mill workers enjoyed broad community support. Still, in the use of the mass meeting— dubbed a "parliament" in this account—and of the protest march, Pawtucket workers set precedents that Lowell women followed. [51]

Dover, New Hampshire, was the scene of the first textile strike organized entirely by women workers. In December 1828 the Cocheco Manufacturing Company, one of the Waltham-Lowell type firms, introduced restrictive new regulations. These rules limited visiting in the mills, set fines for lateness, prohibited drinking, smoking, or gambling by operatives, and even banned talking by operatives while in the mills unless directly related to their work. Women workers responded with a turn-out and a mass parade about town, complete with flags and banners. Between 300 and 400 joined in, but the turn-out was short-lived and unsuccessful. Although reports on the strike are brief, it appears to have been quite similar to that in Lowell in February 1834. It had more the character of a brief demonstration than of a sustained strike. [52]

Just as the Lowell turn-outs built on the traditions of earlier strikes, they set patterns that were to be repeated on numerous occasions thereafter. These earlier strikes were isolated affairs, but each of the Lowell turn-outs spawned further labor struggles in surrounding mill towns. These subsequent strikes occurred for two basic reasons. First, management in the smaller mill towns looked to Lowell for leadership. In January 1834 Henry Hall, treasurer of the Suffolk Company, wrote that firm's agent, instructing him to meet with other agents to determine a new schedule of wages. In that note he indicated: "The Nashua & Cocheco Companies will meet your view & probably send a 'delegate' on being notified." After the turn-out, Hall indicated that others would follow the Lowell lead: "The Jackson Co[mpany in Nashua, New Hampshire] will reduce *full* as low as your rates—they have been waiting for the Lowell Companies to set the example." [53]

A second factor at work was the influence, both indirect and direct, of the Lowell turn-out on operatives in other mill towns. Following the brief Lowell protest in February 1834, the Cocheco Company in Dover reduced the wages of its women workers, who reacted in a predictable fashion—they turned out. They undoubtedly were aware of the Lowell events and may have been influenced by that example. In addition, several Lowell operatives may have participated in this second turn-out. A contemporary newspaper account placed a Lowell woman at the head of the protest. Furthermore, one Lowell agent wrote his company treasurer about a former operative who had gone to Nashua and was said to be stirring up trouble there. If one went to Nashua, others may have found their way to Dover. [54] In any event, the language of Dover strike resolutions mirrored that used in Lowell only a few weeks earlier:

> We view this attempt to reduce our wages as part of a general plan of the proprietors of the different manufacturing establishments to reduce the Females in their employ to that state of dependence on them in which they openly, as they do now secretly abuse and insult them by calling them their "slaves."

Dover workers rejected the prospect of industrial slavery in no uncertain language: "However freely the epithet of 'factory slaves' may be bestowed upon us, we will never deserve it by a base and cringing submission to proud wealth or haughty insolence." Like their Lowell sisters, Dover workers lost the turn-out, but not their sense of self-respect and independence. [55]

Similarly, events in Lowell in 1836 were repeated elsewhere. As Lowell firms increased the rate of board in company boardinghouses, others in surrounding mill towns planned to follow suit. When mill management in Chicopee, Massachusetts, copied the Lowell example at the end of October, operatives left work "*en masse.*" The outcome of this contest is unknown, but that management and workers were following the Lowell precedents cannot be doubted. [56]

The turn-outs in Lowell and in other New England mill towns provide important evidence of the growth of a new consciousness among working women in the early mills. The first step in this process came when Yankee women chose to leave their rural homes and enter the urban, industrial world of the factory towns. In this new setting women refashioned traditional values—most notably, their view of themselves as "daughters of freemen"—and used them to justify a novel, and very untraditional, form of protest. The turn-out was itself only a tentative

first effort at labor protest, and it yielded in the 1840s to a more coordinated and organized form of struggle—the Ten Hour Movement. The
sporadic strikes of the 1820s and 1830s gave way to continuous and
coordinated efforts throughout New England in repeated campaigns to
petition for reduction of the hours of labor in the mills. Women played
a leading role in this broader labor struggle, and only in this movement
did the full implications of the changing consciousness of women workers become evident.

CHAPTER SEVEN

The Ten Hour Movement: The 1840s

I am heartily glad when any thing is done to elevate that class to which it is my lot to belong. We are a band of sisters—we must have sympathy for each other's woes.[1]

THE ONSET of a serious depression in 1837 signaled the end of the first phase of labor struggle in Lowell. The years between 1837 and 1842 were a period of relative quiescence, although the mills ran on part-time schedules, laying off hundreds of operatives. In 1837 and again in 1840 wages were slashed, but on these occasions no protest ensued.[2] Layoffs and wage reductions seemed inevitable given the national economic scene, and operatives acquiesced.

Between 1843 and 1848 a new labor movement grew up in Lowell, one which in several important respects moved beyond the earlier struggles. Rather than isolated episodes, as in February 1834 and October 1836, the 1840s saw almost continuous agitation.[3] Each year Lowell workers sent petitions to the state legislature asking it to set ten hours as the legal length of the working day in manufacturing corporations. These campaigns led to the growth of a permanent labor organization among women workers, the Lowell Female Labor Reform Association (LFLRA), founded in December 1844. The Association was at the forefront of the labor movement in New England and played an active part in the New England Workingmen's Association and the New England Labor Reform

League, umbrella organizations which united the efforts of numerous local groups. In terms of its organization, its growing tactical sophistication, and its impact throughout New England, the labor movement in Lowell in the 1840s represented a quantum leap beyond that of the preceding decade.

In contrast to the earlier turn-outs, no single event sparked the Ten Hour Movement. It developed as a response to the steady intensification of work that transformed the leisurely atmosphere of the early mills. The prices of cloth declined with increased competition resulting from the expansion of mill capacity in the mid-1830s and the sagging of consumer demand after 1837. As they tried to reduce costs, mill agents relied on three techniques to stimulate labor productivity: the speedup, the stretch-out, and the premium system.[4] These policies were at the heart of workers' grievances.

The speedup and stretch-out were coordinated with one another in order to increase the output of operatives. The first term refers specifically to the practice of increasing the operating speed of machinery. The second denotes the assignment of additional pieces of machinery to each operative. The two processes complemented one another. Frequently a firm would actually slow down machinery and simultaneously increase the number of machines assigned to each worker, thus mitigating somewhat the impact of the stretch-out. Then, after an initial breaking-in period, the speed of the machinery would be increased steadily. As these techniques were employed, the piece-wage rate—the price paid operatives per unit of output—was reduced to ensure that earnings did not increase at the same rate as output. Only in this way could the firm cut unit labor costs and in the face of declining cloth prices maintain profit margins.

The operation of the stretch-out and speedup is best illustrated by a concrete example. A weaver described a series of experiments in which she participated. At the outset, early in 1842, she tended two looms running at 140 beats per minute and earned $14.52 over a four-week period. Over the next two years her workload was steadily increased. First she was assigned two more looms, though the speed was reduced to 100 beats. Steadily the speed was increased until her four looms ran at 120 beats per minute in June 1844. Her earnings reached $16.92, up 16 percent over the two-year interval. The looms she tended now operated at 480 beats per minute (4 × 120) compared to only 280 beats (2 × 140) earlier, an increase of more than 70 percent. She expressed satisfaction with the results: "I affirm that I have not in any of these, or other months, overworked myself. I have kept gaining in ability and skill, and as fast as I did so I was allowed to make more and more money, by the accommodation of the speed of the looms to my capacity." And, of course, the overseer and agent were pleased, seeing that her output increased 71 percent while her earnings showed only a 16 percent gain. Clearly the corporation reaped the lion's share of the savings that resulted from the speedup and stretch-out.[5]

Not all women workers were so enthusiastic about these experiments. The fact that some operatives willingly participated in the speedup made work increasingly more difficult for the rest. In an open letter to operatives who sought a third loom, a writer in the *Voice of Industry*, a local labor newspaper, argued that such action was not in their best interests:

> [S]hould you be successful in doing this extra work, and in working by the "piece," be enabled to lay up a little more lucre in store, are you sure it will be the best policy? Your employers will, as they ever have done, take advantage of this oversight, by and by, "wages will be reduced," and you will be obliged to work harder, and perhaps take a fourth loom . . . to make the same wages that you now do with two.[6]

With the success of individual experiments, management began to increase the normal complement of machinery assigned to the average worker. This more generalized application of the stretch-out led to a new consciousness of the exploitation involved. Another writer in the *Voice* noted:

> It is a subject of comment and general complaint among the operatives, that while they tend three or four looms, where they used to tend but two, making nearly twice the number of yards of cloth, their pay is not increased to them, while the increase to the owners is very great. Is this just?[7]

The increase in the pace of work was more than simply a "perceived" grievance. Analysis of machinery inventories and of payrolls confirms the workers' complaints. Between 1840 and 1854 the workload of spinners and weavers at the Hamilton Company, for instance, more than doubled. The average number of spindles per operative in the spinning department rose from 129 to 294, while the number of looms per weaver increased from 1.3 to 2.9. Over the same time period, wages remained basically unchanged. [8]

On at least one occasion, a group of Lowell workers collectively opposed the stretch-out. When the Massachusetts Corporation attempted to assign a fourth loom to each weaver while lowering the piece rate one cent per yard, operatives refused to work the extra loom and signed the following pledge:

> Resolved, That we will not tend a fourth loom (except to oblige each other) unless we receive the same pay per piece as on three, and that we will use our influence to prevent others from pursuing a course which has *always* had a tendency to reduce our wages.
>
> This we solemnly pledge ourselves to observe, in evidence of which we hereunto affix our names.
>
> Resolved, That any one giving her name and violating the pledge shall be published in the "Voice of Industry," as a traitor, and receive the scorn and reproach of her associates.

The pledge was published two months after the attempted stretch-out, and at that date none of the signers had violated its terms. [9]

Another grievance of workingwomen was the premium system. In order to increase output, corporations paid premiums, or cash bonuses, to overseers whose workers turned out the greatest product. Overseers competed with one another for these prizes, which could amount to as much as $100, compared to annual earnings of about $600. [10] Operatives resented the premium system. It led overseers, they argued, to favor those who came in early and worked most rapidly. It enabled them to use the accomplishments of the most efficient to prod the others. One operative, writing in the *Voice*, must have spoken for others:

> The premium system is a curse to us. . . . I have worked under this plan, and know too well the base treatment of overseers in many instances.—Often have girls been denied of receiving their friends, and been so afraid of the "Old Man" they dare not ask to go out when sick; for they know he would have a great deal to say. "The work must not be stopped, and if you are not able to work you better stay out all the time." [11]

This policy created a relentless pressure to increase production and in the process undermined human relationships within the mill. In a rare admission, an overseer gave support to the operatives' contentions:

> The relation in which an overseer stands with regard to the girls in his room, is often made an unpleasant one, by the system of manufacturing which is pursued in Lowell. The necessity which he is under of producing work, of the quality, and in the quantity his employers desire of him, compels him (even when he has a disposition to do otherwise) frequently to be apparently harsh and unmindful of those employed under him.

These lines reinforced the very point protesting workers were making— that it was the premium system, not the character of individual overseers, that led them to be overbearing and harsh. In the words of one operative, "the premiums are the kindly tokens of oppression to the employed." [12]

The failure of sporadic, isolated opposition to limit the stretch-out, speedup, and premium system led to the growth of the labor reform movement in Lowell. Unable to halt what they perceived as the degradation of work, operatives sought at least to mitigate its ill effects by limiting the hours of labor. The pattern of resistance here was strikingly similar to that described by E. P. Thompson in his discussion of the working-class response in England in the same period:

> The onslaught, from so many directions, upon the people's old working habits was not, of course, uncontested. In the first stage, we find simple resistance. But, in the next stage, as the new time-discipline is imposed, so the workers begin to fight, not against time, but about it. [13]

So too in Lowell in the mid-1840s, workers shifted their attention from the immediate grievances at hand—the speedup, stretch-out, and premium system—and focused their energies instead on the hours of labor.

Women operatives in Lowell were not the first workers in New England to demand a limitation of the hours of labor, and the Ten Hour Movement of the 1840s followed in the footsteps of earlier struggles. As early as 1825 skilled male artisans in Boston attempted to secure the ten-hour working day. Their initial efforts, though unsuccessful, spurred workingmen in other cities, and by 1835 numerous trades in Philadelphia, New York, and elsewhere had achieved the desired reduction in the hours of labor. These gains were made principally by strikes or threats of strikes and resulting collective bargaining between trade unions and employers' associations. These struggles also won governmental support at times, as in 1835 when the Philadelphia common council set 10 hours as the legal working day on local public works. The crowning success of the early movement came in 1840 when President Van Buren issued an Executive Order making ten hours the legal length of the working day for federal employees and workers on government contracts.

Still, in the 1840s, workers in Massachusetts lagged behind their counterparts elsewhere in the country.[14] In very few trades at this date did workers enjoy a ten-hour working day. Given the failure of skilled workingmen relying on economic actions, women operatives in the mills looked to the state legislature for redress of their grievances. Since the legislators had granted charters of incorporation to the textile firms in the first place, it seemed logical enough to address them for further regulation.

Lowell operatives learned from the experiences of trade unionists in the previous decade, but they also benefited from their participation in a broader statewide reform movement. The first petitions came from operatives in Fall River and a number of other smaller mill towns in 1842. The next year a petition signed by 1,600 citizens of Lowell requested limitation of working hours in incorporated businesses. Petitions followed yearly, peaking in 1846, when Lowell organizers secured more than 4,000 signatures to their petitions, out of a statewide total of 10,000.[15] Clearly the labor movement in Massachusetts had come of age, and women workers in the Lowell mills were at the heart of the struggle.

In contrast to the turn-outs of the previous decade, the Ten Hour Movement brought together workingmen and women in united action. Women operatives predominated in both the rank and file and in the leadership of the movement, in the larger mill towns at least. Though outnumbered, workingmen still had the vote and thus played a decisive role in what was ultimately a political movement. The new legislative strategy grew quite naturally out of the defeats of the earlier turn-outs. Having failed in opposing the corporations on the purely economic front, workers moved into the political arena. Although the turn-outs had demonstrated their economic subordination to the millowners, they maintained their belief in political equality and acted accordingly. The petition campaigns of 1845 and 1846 reveal well the attitudes that organized women workers brought to the new struggle.

In 1845 about 1,150 workers signed petitions in Lowell, about three fourths of them women. [16] In response the state legislature appointed an investigating committee, headed by William Schouler of Lowell. Schouler, editor of the procorporation Whig newspaper, the Lowell *Courier*, promptly wrote to the leaders of the petition campaign, J. Q. A. Thayer and Sarah Bagley, indicating that he would soon be hearing testimony with regard to the petitions. Though no advocate of an expanded sphere for women, Schouler noted that women would be expected to be the principal speakers. "I would inform you," he wrote, "that as the greater part of the petitioners are female; it will be necessary for them to make the defence, or we shall be under the necessity of laying it aside." If he had expected that this requirement would discourage the petitioners, he had miscalculated badly. Bagley took it upon herself to reply and informed Schouler "that we hold ourselves in readiness to defend the petitions referred to at any time when you will grant us a hearing." Several days later, eight operatives, six women and two men, received notices of the hearings and were directed to attend and give testimony. It was indicative of his intentions that Schouler chose which petition signers would testify and did not allow the organizers to select their own representatives. [17]

The six women acquitted themselves well in their testimony. They were for the most part experienced operatives; although one had been working only 16 months, the rest had been employed in Lowell between four and eight years. In their testimony the operatives argued for the ten-hour working day, claiming that conditions in the mills were detrimental to their health. They complained particularly about the shortness of breaks allowed for meals and the impurity of air in the mills, polluted by cotton dust and smoke from the oil lamps used to light the rooms. A reduction of the hours of labor, they argued, would improve their health and also benefit their "intellectual, moral and religious habits." [18]

After taking further testimony from men, including several who had not signed the petition, the committee adjourned to Lowell, visited several mills, and gathered material from mill agents. In the end the committee concluded that legislation was not warranted. It argued that any legislation would have to be general in application and not be limited to corporations alone. Yet the committee opposed any general legislation, because it would apply only to Massachusetts, and thus discriminate unfairly against business within the state. Further, hours could not be regulated without affecting the "question of wages [, a subject] which experience has taught us can be much better regulated by the parties themselves than by the Legislature." In this portion of its report, the committee revealed the new "laissez-faire" ideology that had come to limit state intervention on behalf of factory operatives. Although workers were petitioning the legislature for assistance, committee members felt that workers could take care of themselves. They judged conditions in the United States to be different from those in England: "Here labor is on an equality with capital, and indeed controls it, and so it ever will be while free education and free constitutions exist." Finally, although admitting the existence of abuses in the factory system, the committee argued that these were best left to concerned private individuals—i.e., to the employers—for remedy. [19]

Leaders of the LFLRA responded promptly to the committee's report, charging that it had withheld and distorted their testimony. They aimed their strongest fire at the committee chairman, Schouler:

> *Resolved*, That the Female Labor Reform Association deeply deplore the lack of independence, honesty, and humanity in the committee to whom were referred sundry petitions relative to the hours of labor.—especially in the chairman of that committee; and as he is merely a corporation machine, or tool, we will use our best endeavors to keep him in the "city of spindles," where he belongs, and not trouble Boston folks with him.

The association worked to discredit Schouler in the fall election and when he was defeated expressed its thanks to the voters "for consigning William Schouler to the obscurity he so justly deserves." [20]

Following the negative response from the legislature, the LFLRA renewed its efforts and in 1846 submitted another petition, this time with more than 4,000 signatures. When another legislative committee responded equally unfavorably to the petitioners' request, one operative penned an open letter to the legislators: "Your actions are in perfect keeping with the ruling spirit of the *times*. You are no doubt, true to the interests of wealth and monopoly. . . . Your sapient heads are very busy in forming laws to protect, uphold, and upbuild the rich." Here we see evidence of the growing realization among organized workingwomen that the economic power of the millowners was being translated into political dominance as well. [21]

The Female Labor Reform Association was the heart of the Ten Hour Movement in Lowell. The existence of this relatively permanent female labor organization, surviving though in modified form for at least three years, is an important distinguishing element of the period and sets it off from the earlier years. From the start the LFLRA was part of the larger movement for labor reform. Organized in conjunction with the male Mechanics and Laborers' Association in December 1844, the LFLRA used that association's reading room for its first meetings. *The Operative*, a labor paper published in Lowell, welcomed its formation. "Let the work go on," the paper noted. "We greatly need the cooperation of the females in the cause. Their influence is potent and powerful, and with their aid shall we not succeed?" [22]

In fact the LFLRA began slowly. An early organizer recalled that initially the Association had only two more members than its list of officers. Still by June 1845 it had reached a membership of more than 400, and by the following April the number had climbed to 600. [23]

The growing membership reflected the activity and excitement generated by the LFLRA. It drew strength from the fact that it did not operate in isolation. It cooperated with the local Mechanics and Laborers' Association and participated in the regional labor reform agitation that swept New England. Lowell operatives were active in the formation of the New England Workingmen's Association (NEWA), which, despite its name, depended in no small part on the organizing efforts of workingwomen. They participated in the preliminary meeting in Lowell in March 1845 that adopted the constitution of the NEWA and specifically provided for the admission of female labor groups on an equal basis with male organizations. At the first regular meeting of the NEWA in Boston in May 1845, 10 of the 30 delegates present were women. Sarah Bagley, president of the LFLRA, addressed the group and set the tone for future female participation:

> For the last half a century it has been deemed a violation of woman's sphere to appear before the public as a speaker; but when

our rights are trampled upon and we appeal in vain to legislators, what shall we do but appeal to the people? Shall not our voice be heard and our rights acknowledged . . . ?[24]

Bagley and other Lowell operatives continued to play an active role in the NEWA. At a mass Fourth of July meeting in Woburn, Bagley addressed a gathering of some 2,000. At successive association meetings officers of the LFLRA made reports on their progress in organizing. In March 1846 a mill worker, Huldah J. Stone of Lowell, was elected secretary of the NEWA, and in September she served on a committee that prepared a revised constitution. The new constitution renamed the NEWA the New England Labor Reform League. Three of the eight directors of the League were Lowell women. Finally, when the association chose ten delegates to a National Reform Convention in Worcester, Sarah Bagley, Huldah Stone, and Mehitable Eastman, a Manchester operative, were among them.[25]

The energies of the organizers of the LFLRA were not totally focused on the broader labor reform movement. Their chief efforts were expended in stirring up interest among Lowell workers. Toward this aim they held periodic fairs and picnics, combining a blend of music, socializing, and propaganda. The first of these affairs met on the eve of the organizing convention of the NEWA in March 1845. On Saint Valentine's Eve, February 1846, they held a "Social Gathering" and raised $100 for their cause. A notice for the affair extended invitations to workers from surrounding communities and described plans:

> Eminent and distinguished speakers will attend from abroad to interest and instruct—a band of music, together with singing, will be there to gratify the lovers of harmony, and a rich treat of fruits and other *eatables* will not be wanting; making in all a "feast of fat things," for the sum of 25 cts. only; the proceeds of which will be appropriated to the cause of *Labor Reform*.[26]

A final May party topped off the schedule of major fundraisers. The association invited the Rhode Island democrat, Thomas Dorr, hoping to engage him as the principal speaker. He declined, for reasons of health, and the LFLRA secured two noted reformers, the Reverend William Channing and John Allen, in his stead.[27] The Rogers Family and Bond's

Brass Band provided musical entertainment. As one of the organizers described it: "We intend to have the greatest time that old Lowell ever saw." [28]

The activities of the association went beyond these gala social events. From the start they met weekly to promote labor reform. A newspaper notice advertised meetings every Tuesday evening in the reading room of the Mechanics and Laborers' Association, "All females interested in the reform of the present system of labor . . . respectfully invited to attend." These meetings were supplemented in 1846 with an Industrial Reform Lyceum, a lecture series aimed at countering the traditional, apolitical lyceum lectures. The first series of six lectures, with an admission price of 25 cents for the set, featured such well-known reformers as William H. Channing, Robert Rantoul, William Lloyd Garrison, George Ripley, William White, and Horace Greeley. [29]

Probably the signal contribution of the LFLRA was the support it gave to the *Voice of Industry*, a labor newspaper. Initially the *Voice* was published in Fitchburg, Massachusetts, and from the start Huldah J. Stone, secretary of the association, served as a correspondent to the paper. When, in October 1845, the New England Workingmen's Association made the *Voice* its official organ, the paper moved its office to Lowell, and Sarah Bagley, president of the LFLRA, joined its three-person publishing committee. Early in 1846 the LFLRA purchased the paper's press and type. Through the fundraising activities described earlier it sought to raise money to make the periodic payments necessary to complete this purchase. Several officers of the association served as traveling agents and correspondents for the paper, selling subscriptions in and submitting articles from other industrial communities throughout New England. [30]

In addition to supporting the paper, women workers used it to further their own cause. In its pages they announced their meetings and fundraising activities. When weavers at the Massachusetts Corporation refused to take an extra loom, the *Voice* publicized their pledge. When the association sought to defeat state representative William Schouler, its leaders turned to the *Voice* to get their message to the voting public. Besides its full coverage of the activities of workingwomen throughout New England, the *Voice* had a separate "Female Department" with articles by and about women workers. The stance of this department, shaped by its editor, Sarah Bagley, was strongly feminist:

> Our department devoted to woman's thought will also defend woman's rights, and while it contends for physical improvement, it will not forget that she is a social, moral and religious being. It will not be neutral because it is female, but it will claim to be heard on all subjects that effect her intelligence, social or religious condition.

Clearly this was a department of, by, and for women, and the editor acknowledged this aspect from the outset. Thus the *Voice of Industry* became a powerful organizing tool for women in the Ten Hour Movement. [31]

The *Voice* publicized the activities of the LFLRA and enabled its leaders to reach a broad constituency throughout New England. Soon women workers in other communities requested assistance from the LFLRA in local organizing. A letter from Fitchburg, Massachusetts, described the visit and speech of John Cluer, an Englishman on tour on behalf of the NEWA. According to the letter, the operatives held a meeting, and "they turned out about twenty of them and went, although it was a very bad night, half a mile to hear him. . . . And now they may if Miss Bagley or some of the Society in Lowell, will come up with Mr. Cluer next time he comes, they will form a Society." [32]

This is precisely what Sarah Bagley had done a month before, when she was instrumental in the formation of a Female Labor Reform Association in Manchester, New Hampshire. Early in December 1845, at a spirited meeting in the Manchester town hall—an assembly that was actually presided over by Lowell operatives—more than a thousand workers, two thirds of them women, passed resolutions calling for the ten-hour day. Later the meeting divided, and men and women met separately to set up parallel organizations—a Mechanics and Laborers' Association and a Female Labor Reform Association. Sarah Bagley presented a constitution for the new association, which the women present readily adopted. Sixty women joined the Manchester FLRA that evening, and by the following summer it claimed over three hundred members. [33]

Having helped to found the Manchester association, Lowell operatives continued to express interest and offer support. The secretary of the LFLRA wrote an open letter to Manchester operatives. It began: "Sisters in the cause of human improvement and human rights" and went on to offer the new group support in working toward their common goals:

> Operatives of Manchester, you have begun well, may God grant that you persevere united, faithfully, triumphantly! You have now an Association organized and consisting of a goodly number already, and hundreds more are ready to join your ranks. . . . We shall be extremely happy to correspond with you and meet with you . . . as often as possible. Let us seek to encourage and strengthen each other in every good word and work.

The two associations and their leaders provided mutual support. At a Manchester gathering in June 1846, Lowell operatives attended and the Lowell Brass Band provided entertainment. A Manchester operative, Mehitable Eastman, in turn, became a frequent contributor to the *Voice of Industry* and an active participant in the numerous regional conventions held in the period. [34]

Manchester was the site of the first and most successful of the organizing efforts of the LFLRA. Soon additional associations had been established in Dover and Nashua as well. The *Voice* gave publicity to the activities of these branches and encouraged them to work further for the cause of labor reform. Several Lowell operatives, in their roles as traveling agents for the paper, were instrumental in developing support for the Ten Hour Movement in the smaller satellite mill towns. [35]

In the course of their organizing, women workers repeatedly came up against the power of the corporations. In numerous ways mill management attempted to thwart the labor reform movement. In both Lowell and Manchester, reformers on occasion were denied use of city hall for their meetings. Overseers were said to have discharged workers found to be subscribing to the *Voice of Industry*. Activists also had to be careful about the corporate blacklist, for if they missed work by attending a labor meeting they might well be discharged. Lowell workers planning to attend a NEWA meeting in Nashua were advised to "[play] the hypocrite, and go into the country sick, that you may attend the Convention, without having your name sent to the counting room 'black lists.'" Women workers thus had to accommodate their actions to the ongoing struggle with the corporations. [36]

Management's opposition to the labor reform movement was just as intense as its resistance to the earlier turn-outs had been. Mill agents expressed clearly their attitudes toward the new labor movement. When the new mill town of Lawrence was established several miles down-stream from Lowell, the agent of the Middlesex Company in Lowell wrote to warn his counterpart at the Essex Company in Lawrence about Huldah J. Stone, the prominent Lowell activist. His brief note went straight to the point: "Huldah J. Stone a radical of the worst sort & late Editress of the Voice of Industry intends to get a Boarding House at the New City. I write this to warn you 'to keep hands off of her.'"[37] If his information was correct, perhaps Stone intended to use her position as a boardinghouse keeper to spread the Ten Hour Movement to "New City." In any event the note expressed well the attitudes of mill agents toward the labor organizers in their midst.

The enthusiasm and excitement generated by the ten-hour campaigns and by the movement of reform activity from Lowell to other mill towns inevitably outgrew the confines of the single-issue focus that had prompted the initial organizing. Furthermore, the contact that leaders of the LFLRA had with a wide range of working-class activists influenced their thinking in new directions. Early in 1847 when the New England Workingmen's Association rewrote its bylaws and reemerged as the New England Labor Reform League, women operatives revised the con-stitution of the LFLRA and created in its stead the Lowell Female Indus-trial Reform and Mutual Aid Society. Maintaining the initial concern with labor reform, the new society added sickness insurance provisions. For an initiation fee of 50 cents and weekly dues of 6 cents, operatives became eligible, after a three-month waiting period, to receive sick fund benefits of $2 to $5 weekly for a period of four weeks. Organizers were attempting to attract new members and thought that they should offer prospective recruits something more concrete than speakers and educa-tional activities.[38]

In addition, women activists in the Ten Hour Movement found their way into related causes. Sarah Bagley, for instance, represented the Low-ell Union of Associationists—a group of American advocates of Fourier's utopian schemes—at a national convention in Boston in 1846. Eliza Hemingway, one of the operatives who testified before the state legisla-tive committee in 1845, later became involved in consumer cooperatives. In the second half of the 1840s and in the 1850s, the New England Protective Union grew up with hundreds of local branches in cities and villages throughout the region. Each branch consisted of a local store where a variety of products, chiefly food goods, were sold to members at or near wholesale prices. These consumer cooperatives enabled organized working people and farmers to bypass middlemen in making necessary purchases. Lowell was a major center of the movement with eight cooperative stores and 984 members at its height. Two of the local branches "were made up entirely of women," and ten-hour advocate Eliza Hemingway served as an officer of one of these divisions in 1849. [39]

It must be said that although the Ten Hour Movement of the 1840s involved a greater proportion of women operatives than the earlier turn-outs, it never commanded the loyalties of a majority of the women. At the height of the petition campaigns in 1846 some 2,500 women signed the massive petition forwarded by the LFLRA to the General Court in Boston. If all female signers had been operatives, they would have comprised about 36 percent of the female work force in the mills. [40] At this point in the discussion, it may be helpful to view the petition signers in a somewhat broader context.

In a recent study Alan Dawley and Paul Faler have formulated a tripartite typology of workers in this period, based on their responses to the demands of early industrial capitalism, and the categories they present prove useful in looking at the reactions of women textile workers as well. Dawley and Faler have divided workers into three groups—traditionalists, loyalists, and rebels—according first to their rejection or acceptance of industrial morality and second to their views on "political economy." Traditionalists, in this perspective, were those workers who rejected the demands of the new industrial morality, who "refused to give up their casual attitudes toward work, their pursuit of happiness in gaming and drinking, and the raucous revelry that accompanied fire and militia musters." Loyalists and rebels, on the other hand, were "modernists"; both groups accepted the morality of their employers and spurned the preindustrial values and attitudes of an earlier era. They differed primarily in terms of their view of class relations. Loyalists saw the interests of worker and employer as joined and thus "held aloof from the labor movement." Rebels, on the other hand, viewed the interests of workers and employers as opposed and saw collective action as the only means to secure their accustomed living standard and independence. Both of these latter groups accepted the injunctions of the nineteenth-century work ethic, but the loyalists also accepted its invocation of in-dividualism and social mobility, while the rebels saw collective action as the only means to success and independence. [41]

Although Faler and Dawley evolved their analysis with particular ref-erence to Lynn shoemakers, the basic framework makes clearer the divi-sions among women operatives as well. The fit is not perfect but does contribute to an understanding of women's responses to the novel de-mands imposed by mill employment. One would have to look far and wide for many strict "traditionalists" among women textile operatives. This is true for a number of reasons. First, the very language that Faler and Dawley employ suggests a masculine definition of traditionalist cul-ture. Few women in the preindustrial setting would have found their happiness in gaming and drinking, for instance. Even if we broaden the definition somewhat to allow that women might be "traditionalist" in other ways, we would expect few of this group in the mills. The disci-pline and work routine of the new factories discouraged women who had "casual attitudes toward work." Overseers generally discharged any who in the first weeks showed themselves incapable of adjusting to the demands of factory production. Furthermore, the very fact that women had to move to the new factory towns meant that only those who con-sciously sought out the mills would find employment. More likely than not, traditionalist women simply rejected mill employment from the start and would not have even entered the mills.

Loyalists and rebels there were aplenty, however, in the Lowell mills in the 1840s. In fact the more articulate members of the two groups engaged in a spirited debate over the impact of industrial capitalism while they worked in the mills. In the pages of the *Lowell Offering* and the *Voice of Industry*, the two opposing camps addressed each other and any-one else who may have followed the debate.

The *Offering* sought to counter "the prejudice, which has long existed against the manufacturing females of New England." By publishing the writings of women workers, it tried to show "what factory girls had power to do." The magazine's audience was thus viewed primarily as men and women in urban circles who had formerly looked down on mill operatives, though the *Offering's* editors expressed satisfaction that the attitudes of their fellow workers had changed as well: "The involuntary blush does not so often tinge the faces of any operatives, when mingling with strangers, as when they claimed no place among the worthy, the educated." [42]

While demonstrating "what factory girls had power to do," the *Offering* self-consciously eschewed criticism of conditions in the mills and dissociated itself from the reform efforts of the decade. As one editorial pointedly expressed it: "With wages, board, &c., we have nothing to do—these depend upon circumstances over which we have no control." The decision to avoid controversial issues was more than an acknowledgment of the limited power of mill operatives, however. Harriet Farley, one of the editors of the *Offering* and its most articulate writer, expressed positive satisfaction that the magazine's authors had not displayed a tone of "captious discontent." She noted,

> [T]hey have done thus honor to their heads and hearts. They have shown that their first and absorbing thought was not for an advance of wages or a reduction of labor hours. They have implied that it was quite as important to be good as to have good. They have striven for improvement of head and heart before that of situation.

Farley and her cowriters were Lowell's loyalists, more interested in demonstrating their own upstanding morality than in pointing out the shortcomings of millowners and agents. The fact that the *Offering* received substantial support from the textile corporations helps account for the contemporary and subsequent visibility of the literary mill girls, but in no way undercuts the authenticity of the loyalist beliefs they expressed. [43]

The *Offering* writers were not the only women opposed to or uninterested in the Ten Hour Movement. One organizer writing in the *Voice of Industry* noted that there were "some who never heard of Labor Reform." She described the difficulties she faced: "On asking one of them if she would not join the Association, 'Oh,' said she, 'I belong to no religious society.' Some would ridicule, censure and oppose me and ask what necessity there could be in establishing the ten-hour system." Another supporter of reform testified that many operatives "get back to the gate before the bell rings," apparently to be ready to start work the moment the power was turned on. The *Offering* noted this practice but argued that it was not "evidence of a general desire to work even more hours than at present." According to Harriet Farley this conduct stemmed from a general competition among some of the operatives to be considered "the smartest girl in the room," i.e., to be the most productive worker. Whatever the reason, these workers seem to have had little interest in shortening the working day. Since most women came to Lowell for only a brief period of time, in hope often of laying up savings, it is understandable that some would oppose any reduction in the hours of labor that might undercut their earnings. [44]

Sarah Bagley, Huldah J. Stone, and other leaders in the Lowell Female Labor Reform Association comprised the most articulate element of the rebels at this date. They felt no need to demonstrate their own morality and dignity but took these qualities for granted. Rather they acted upon their beliefs and sought to oppose changes in mill employment that they felt tended to degrade operatives.

A decade earlier similar rebels had challenged the economic power of millowners and agents by turning out, and in the 1840s they assailed corporate political power by bringing their cause into the halls of the state legislature. While the Ten Hour Movement was essentially a labor struggle, it also reminded operatives that they were women workers, as opponents regularly held their femaleness against them. The negative report of the 1845 state investigating committee argued that operatives should rely on the good will of their employers, rather than on legislative intervention. The implication of this argument was that women could count on the benevolent paternalism of the millowners for protection of their interests. [45] Operatives developed a skepticism, tinged with bitterness, toward this supposed benevolence. That they regarded paternalism as a tool of sexual as well as economic discrimination is revealed by the response of one worker in an open letter to a state legislator reprinted in the *Voice of Industry*:

Bad as is the condition of so many women, it would be much worse if they had nothing but your boasted protection to rely upon; but they have at last learnt the lesson which a bitter experience teaches, that not to those who style themselves their "natural protectors" are they to look for the needful help, but to the strong and resolute of their own sex. [46]

From an opposition to the paternalism of mill agents and legislators it was only one step to a questioning of accepted standards of women's conduct and of the limits of "women's sphere." In the course of the labor struggles of the 1840s, women activists came to a new sense of the "sisterhood" of working women and developed a critique of the "cult of true womanhood," that ideology of women's sphere that evolved in the period and was expressed in popular women's magazines and domestic advice books. [47]

The very language that women organizers used reflected these developments. Correspondence from the secretary of the LFLRA with her Manchester counterparts began: "Sisters in the cause of human improvement and human rights." Somewhat later a Manchester operative wrote: "I am heartily glad when any thing is done to elevate that class to which it is my lot to belong. We are a band of sisters—we must have sympathy for each other's woes." It is interesting and revealing that this worker equated her class and sex in these lines. She evidently identified herself as a member of a specifically *female* working class. [48]

Sex was an issue in the campaigns, and activists had to work to legitimize their own roles in order to further the cause of reform. Thus the prospectus for the Female Department of the *Voice of Industry* indicated one direction that department would follow: "It will make an effort to soften down the prejudices that exist against [woman] as a reformer, and show those who read candidly, that she has a great duty to perform to herself and her race." The secretary of the LFLRA addressed this concern by posing and answering a rhetorical question:

> Why should not woman seek to improve, elevate and raise higher her standard of moral and intellectual worth, in order to keep pace with the age in which she lives? We surely can see no impropriety in such aspirations and exertions. And until we are convinced that it is unfeminine and out of place to labor and toil for the *best good* of all our race, we shall devote a portion of the time which heaven may allot us here, to this great—this all important work. [49]

Huldah Stone addressed her audience in mild, questioning tones in an effort to persuade and change minds. Others were more pointed, accusing society, and men in particular, of determining a narrow sphere for women and forcing them through law and ridicule to toe the line. One woman complained in a letter:

> Marriage is almost the only *business* in which there is any chance of success, that the world (to its shame be it told) willingly leaves to women. . . .
> It may be, that most women are so dwarfed and weakened, that

they believe that dressing, cooking, and loving . . . make up the whole of life; but Nature still asserts her rights, and there will always be those too strong to be satisfied, with a dress, a pudding, or a beau, though they may take each in its turn, as a portion of life.

"An Operative" wrote similarly that men determined the customs, laws, and opinions that defined women. She went on to complain of the narrowness of this perspective:

Woman is never thought to be out of her *sphere*, at home; in the nursery, in the kitchen, over a hot stove cooking from morning till evening—over a wash-tub, or toiling in a cotton factory 14 hours per day. But let her once step out, plead the cause of right and humanity, plead the wrongs of her slave sister of the South or of the operative of the North, or even attempt to teach the science of Physiology, and a cry is raised against her, *"of out of her sphere."*[50]

In arguing in favor of women's participation in reform movements and for a broadening of women's sphere, these activists joined the Grimke sisters and others who championed women's rights prior to the organization of an institutionally based women's rights movement. Their initial commitment was, of course, to the broad movement for labor reform, but as women they developed and expressed a sense of sisterhood in their organizing. In turn they developed an antagonism toward male opponents of reform and toward the dominant ideology that defined women's sphere in entirely domestic and subordinate terms. In this experience women labor activists shared much with other women reformers in the antebellum years.[51]

Carroll Smith-Rosenberg has described the activities of the New York Female Moral Reform Society in the 1830s and 1840s in terms that may easily apply to the LFLRA as well. The society, a middle-class reform organization, sought to reform prostitutes and bridle male licentiousness. Like the Lowell association the society sent organizers out to establish additional local branches. Although the paramount purpose of the societies was to combat the double standard of sexuality evident in the spread of prostitution, Smith-Rosenberg also sees evidence of a growing "feeling of sisterhood" among reformers. A thorough reading of the society's journal, *The Advocate of Moral Reform*, led her to conclude: "A growing sense of solidarity and emotional affiliation permeated the correspondence between rural members and the executive committee. Letters and even official reports inevitably began with the salutation, 'Sisters,' 'Dear Sisters,' or 'Beloved Sisters.'" The basic similarity of language and sensibility of moral reformers and labor reformers suggests a broader, distinctly female culture in this period uniting women reformers of varying interests. All of these women shared the "bonds of womanhood" that Nancy Cott has analyzed so well, and their reform efforts expressed repeatedly the sense of sisterhood that united them. [52]

In asserting their identity as women, activists in the Ten Hour Movement also challenged the dominant cultural ideal that Barbara Welter has called the "cult of true womanhood." Based on an extensive study of women's magazines, domestic advice and gift books, religious tracts and sermons, and popular novels in the period between 1820 and 1860, Welter argued that there appeared in these years a new formulation of the characteristics of the "true" woman. Some aspects of the cult were not new and would have seemed familiar enough in an earlier period, but considered as a whole this ideal marked a significant departure from that of the late eighteenth century. With the increasing commercialization and industrialization of the New England economy we can see a new devaluation of women's work and a new emphasis on women's noneconomic activities. A woman's "dependence" on her husband took on a new meaning in this changed social and economic setting. [53]

The textile mills played a crucial role in inducing women to question the basic tenets of the cult because they permitted women to support themselves outside of the family setting. In following the traditional ideal that everyone should work and contribute to self-support, Lowell women found themselves in conflict with the newer notion that women should be "supported" by men, that economic dependence and subordination were hallmarks of "true womanhood." [54] When they saw these ideals being used against them under the guise of "protection" and paternalism, they expressed opposition to these standards as well as to their proponents. Thus they saw the sphere of home and family as being too limited and accused men of fostering confining definitions of womanhood. They felt a particular animus toward male writers who offered gratuitous advice to women. One woman wrote, with more than a touch of sarcasm: "I have observed that it is a common practice, among Editors, to fill their papers with advice to women, and not infrequently with ill conceived taunts of woman's weakness. It is a pity that they should so neglect their own sex." Some made a less direct attack on the cult, carrying its precepts to their logical conclusions and thereby demanding more power for women than the cult's advocates had ever intended. One writer gently poked fun at the assertion that women had a peculiar capacity for instructing the young:

> But if woman is well adapted to teach, so beautifully calculated and gifted by the author of her existence, to instruct the youthful mind, as has been represented—qualified to impress the great lessons of truth and morality, and give a right tone to sentiments—in short, capable of making man a noble being, but a litle below the angels, I wish to inquire why in the name of common sense she is not permitted to finish the work she may have begun? Why are all the offices in public institutions of learning filled by men? Why is the child taken from under the maternal care and placed under the teachings of man? Why is every professorship usurped by man? Why not confer them upon woman, and permit her to go on with the good work?

This writer did not need anyone to answer her questions, and she concluded in a more certain tone: "I think I have proved that the 'power behind the throne' is powerless." The daily lives of women in the mills and the experience of the labor reform movement made women organizers sensitive to questions of power, and they could see through claims that viewed woman's position through rose-colored glasses. [55]

It would be inaccurate to conclude that all working women rejected the "cult of true womanhood" and joined in a demand for women's equality. If some of the rebels in the LFLRA did, the traditionalists of the *Lowell Offering* certainly did not. Just as the *Offering* writers tended not to question the actions of millowners and agents, so they most frequently accepted a subordinate place for women. Thus Ella wrote in an essay entitled "Woman":

> He is made more strong, that he may protect and defend; she more lovely, that he may be willing to shield and guard her; and that physical difference which, in one state of society, makes woman the slave of man, in another makes him her worshiper. . . . Woman must be the mother and that fount of "deep, strong, deathless love," has been implanted in her breast, which can turn a mother's cares to pleasures. In that station where woman is most herself, where her predominating qualities have the fullest scope, there she is most

influential, and most truly worthy of respect. But when she steps from her allotted path into that of the other sex, she betrays her inferiority, and in the struggle would be inevitably subdued. [56]

There is no way to determine whether the attitudes expressed in the *Offering* or those found in the *Voice of Industry* were more representative of the values and beliefs of women operatives in Lowell. Both the rebels and the traditionalists presented authentic voices, and undoubtedly each group found sympathetic audiences. Although activists and apologists differed in their attitudes toward collective action, they did not argue from profoundly different assumptions about woman's role in life. While labor reformers rejected those who argued for the strict obedience and total submission of women to men, the kind of independence they sought was compatible with marriage. They called for a broadened, not a revolutionized, sphere for women. And, as indicated in chapter 3 above, women operatives married in numbers not unlike others around them.

Fully 85 percent of women workers in the New Hampshire sample did marry after they completed their mill careers. Mill employment offered women a degree of independence in the years before marriage, but few women chose independence over marriage in the long run. Mill women may have questioned the narrowest interpretation of their sphere and the strictest view of their subordination, but they did not question the basic structures that defined their life roles. They were more likely to work un-self-consciously to modify their roles before and during marriage than to attack the institution directly.

In fact, traditional and nontraditional views often coexisted in the writings of the same operative. One article in the *Voice of Industry*, entitled "The Rights of Women," began conventionally enough: "Let her as she has to be, remain the woman; and let her appropriate and specified duties be domestic, or to engage in any line of action in any calling which shall not interfere with their discharge." Having made this reservation, the author went on to affirm that women had a right to education, to respect from men, and to full participation in economic activities. Then in her conclusion she addressed her female readers in tones that contrasted sharply with her opening lines:

You have been degraded long enough. You have sufficiently long been considered "the inferior"—a kind of "upper servant," to obey and reverence, and be in subjection to your equal. . . . Enter at once upon your privileges. Cultivate a clear, strong, matter of fact way of thinking, and a natural and therefore, conclusive mode of reasoning. [57]

While there was no unanimity on questions concerning woman's sphere and the "cult of true womanhood," there was certainly a strong tendency that opposed confining views of womanhood and demanded for women a right to participate fully in reform movements and to develop themselves as complete human beings. The women's labor movement, which began in the 1830s as a defensive effort to maintain existing levels of wages, had by the middle of the next decade moved, in part at least, to the aggressive expression of much more fundamental demands. For many the hours of labor were simply the starting point for reform and they demanded much more of American society. As Huldah J. Stone—that "radical of the worst sort"—described the attitudes of members of the LFLRA toward reduction of the hours of labor:

> They do not regard this measure as an end, but only as one step toward the end to be attained. They deeply feel that their work will never be accomplished until slavery and oppression, mental, physical, and religious, shall have been done away with and Christianity in its original simplicity, and pristine beauty shall be re-established and practiced among men. [58]

Even allowing for some element of hyperbole, Stone makes clear that the labor movement of the 1840s was no single-minded, narrow lobbying effort. It was a broad reform movement that repeatedly overflowed its banks and stimulated interest in wide-ranging issues. For Lowell operatives woman's proper sphere was certainly one of those issues.

CHAPTER EIGHT

The Transformation of Lowell, 1836-1850, and the New Mill Work Force

THE LABOR protests of workingwomen in Lowell in the 1830s and 1840s were attempts to oppose deteriorating working conditions and declining piece-wage rates. On occasion, as in 1836, the struggles resulted in some gains for women, and overall the existence of protest undoubtedly limited the actions of management. Still, in the long run, the protests failed to halt the deterioration of earlier standards. The wage cuts, the speed-ups, and the stretch-outs were symptoms of a broader transformation of work in Lowell over these years. The forces behind this transformation were beyond the control of organized workers, and at times even of mill management itself.

The almost continuous expansion of textile manufacturing in Lowell and in New England as a whole resulted in a number of interrelated changes in Lowell in the period. The increasing size and purchasing power of Western, Southern, and urban markets stimulated demand for coarse textile goods. [1] Operating as they did on a large scale and utilizing the latest technology, the Lowell firms were in a particularly strong position to benefit from this growing demand. Table 8.1 reveals the tremendous growth of textile production in Lowell between 1836 and 1850. These figures show the doubling of both the number and the capitalization of mills over the period and an even greater increase in the number of looms and spindles in operation.

TABLE 8.1. GROWTH OF TEXTILE MANUFACTURES
IN LOWELL, 1836–1850

Measures of Growth	1836	1850
Number of mills	20	40
Assets of textile firms	$6.1 million	$12.0 million
Number of spindles	130,000	320,000
Number of looms	4,200	9,900
Number of workers	6,800	10,100

SOURCE: *Statistics of Lowell Manufactures*, 1836 and 1850.

The expansion of textile production in Lowell was part of a broader process at work throughout New England in these decades. In fact the textile industry of Massachusetts expanded at a rate considerably higher than that of Lowell. In the 1840s, for instance, capital invested in the Lowell cotton mills increased by about 25 percent; for the state as a whole, capitalization increased by more than 60 percent over the same decade.[2] The most dramatic expansion resulted from the founding of two new mill towns, Lawrence and Holyoke.[3] Both communities were conceived in the Lowell tradition, planned by enterprising Boston capitalists, including not a few who had done well by their investments in Lowell. Neither proved so profitable as Lowell had been, but they stood as testimony to the almost unbounded optimism of millowners in the buoyant years of the mid-1840s.

With the steady expansion of textile manufacturing in Lowell, the size and productive capacity of individual mills increased as well. The first mills in Lowell typically had about 5,000 spindles each. The Appleton Company's two mills, constructed in 1828 and 1829, had together 10,240 spindles. Thereafter the initial size of new mills rose steadily. The Lawrence Company mills, erected 5 years later, were equipped with just over 6,000 spindles each, while the Prescott Mills, completed in the mid-1840s, had over 8,000 spindles apiece. The greatest increases were still to come, as the fourth Hamilton mill in 1847 added over 11,000 spindles to that firm's capacity, and the sixth Merrimack mill (1848) added a whopping 26,000 spindles to production.[4]

Along with the construction of larger mills, additions to existing buildings augmented productive capacity. Commonly, two small mills were physically joined together, as occurred at the Hamilton Company in

1846, resulting in an increase of more than 3,500 spindles.[5] In this manner the textile firms tended to encroach on the green space that had made their millyards so attractive in the early years. Just as all the frontage on the river and the canals was occupied, so too virtually all the square footage on mill sites was utilized. The demand for expansion of productive capacity took precedence over aesthetic considerations.[6]

The rapid growth of capacity called forth improvements in other areas. The added looms and spindles required additional waterpower. Construction of new power canals, the Western and Eastern canals, provided a steady flow of water to the new firms established in Lowell in these decades. Digging of a massive feeder canal, the Northern Canal, completed in 1847, enabled the Locks and Canals company to supply adequate waterpower for the continuing growth. In addition, the Lowell firms, acting in unison, purchased the outlets of several New Hampshire lakes at the headwaters of the Merrimack River. With this purchase, Lowell management could control the flow of water not simply in its network of power canals, but in the Merrimack River itself. Dams erected far upstream held back flood waters in the spring for release in the drier months of the year.[7]

The rapid expansion of the mills had broader consequences for the city of Lowell. The population of the city grew feverishly, from 17,000 in 1836 to more than 33,000 in 1850. At the same time, the rising population coupled with a decline in the construction of new company housing led to a steady shift in residence patterns in Lowell. Increasing numbers of mill workers resided in private houses and tenements, and the importance of company housing shrank accordingly.

Corporate policies contributed to this shift in housing. The new firms founded after 1836 did build boardinghouses and tenements, but with the increased scale of the new mills, company housing simply did not keep up with rising employment. Furthermore, established companies built new mills and added to existing ones without corresponding increases in their housing facilities. Of the older firms only the Merrimack Company increased capacity when in 1848 it replaced a row of early two-story double houses with a massive block of brick boardinghouses. "New Block," as it was called, proved to be the last major addition ever made to company housing in Lowell.[8]

Private development had to provide the bulk of housing for the expanding mill labor force of these years. Initially, opportunities were quite limited as the predominant share of unoccupied land was held by the Proprietors of Locks and Canals, the development company set up by mill management to regulate use of waterpower and the growth of Lowell. In 1845, however, when all of the major power sites in the city had been occupied, the Locks and Canals company began selling its remaining lands at auction.[9] New streets were laid out and housing erected. Increases in the supply of private housing brought to an end the uniformity of residence among operatives that had prevailed earlier. No longer did three fourths of women workers reside "on the corporation." Some continued to do so, but increasing proportions lived in private boardinghouses or with their families in private tenements.

Even the expansion of private housing, however, could not keep pace with the ever-increasing population, and observers were shocked at the overcrowding that resulted. Lowell boardinghouses had always been densely populated, but high standards in their construction and maintenance had afforded some protection to residents. Company housing was invariably made of brick, whitewashed regularly, and had its sanitation needs well attended to. The mills had to maintain standards in order to attract a steady stream of operatives from the surrounding countryside. Such considerations played no part in the construction of the expanding tenement neighborhoods in Lowell in the late 1840s and 1850s. One observer described the resulting overcrowding evident in a 3.5 acre section in 1849:

> At this date . . .in a central district . . . we find the City Hall . . . the post office, city library, two churches, three banks, one grammar and three primary schools, . . . ninety stores . . . two smithies, several machine shops, a foundry, coal and wood yard, three livery stables, and two hundred and fifty-four tenements, inhabited by one thousand and forty-five individuals.

"[F]ew cities are so crowded as Lowell," judged another commentator.[10] Indeed the careful planning and order of the factory town at its founding were swamped by the uncontrolled and chaotic growth of succeeding years. Corporate policies—the decline in construction of new boardinghouses and the decision to sell undeveloped lands at auction—contributed to this process.

The expansion of production followed conscious decisions by mill management, but it was not always possible to anticipate or control the consequences of expansion. Earlier the Lowell firms had possessed a monopoly of much of the most advanced technology employed in the mass production of cotton cloth. The competitive advantage these companies enjoyed made for high profits but at the same time stimulated the growth of textile manufacturing throughout New England. The expiration of Waltham-Lowell patents and continued technological advance elsewhere narrowed the gap between the productivity of Lowell firms and that of their competitors. Initially, southern New England firms had abandoned the production of cheap goods and concentrated instead on higher quality yarns and cloths. The new firms of the 1840s, however, met the established Lowell mills head-on, producing a line of goods basically competitive with that of the older companies. The result was a sharp decline in the prices of staple goods for the mass market. Between 1830 and 1849, for instance, the price of brown shirting on the New York market declined from 7.5 to 4 cents per yard. Prices received by the Boston Manufacturing Company for an equivalent coarse cloth decreased by a similar proportion, as did those for coarse sheeting produced by the Suffolk Manufacturing Company.[11] While the Lowell firms were able to regulate wages and working conditions and standardize the basic provisions of the labor contract, they were unsuccessful in their attempts to exert control over total output or over prices in their product markets. According to one historian, "the crowding of the industry from the inside" caused the decline in prices for staple cotton textile products in this period.[12]

These developments put a squeeze on the profits of Lowell firms. The high profits of the pre-1836 years could not be maintained in the face of this new competition. Accordingly, the high level of dividends gave way. Annual dividends of the Waltham-Lowell firms listed on the Boston Stock Exchange averaged 11.4 percent before 1836 but declined to less than 6 percent between 1847 and 1859.[13]

Increased competition and the resulting pressure on profits led Lowell companies to search for ways to reduce costs in order to keep pace with declining prices. The cost of raw cotton was dependent largely on the size of the annual crop and the extent of British demand. Therefore the only major variable that firms could control with any real effectiveness was the cost of labor. Mill management thus made a concerted effort to increase productivity and thereby reduce the labor cost per unit of output. The response of women workers to the resulting speedup and stretch-out has been considered, but it remains to examine the impact of these measures on the production process itself.

Of the various efforts undertaken by management, the stretch-out and improvements in technology proved most important in raising productivity. With the stretch-out, firms assigned additional looms or spindles to workers and reduced prevailing piece rates in order to keep overall earnings more or less constant. As the output per worker increased, the cost of labor per yard of finished cloth declined, offering the possibility of maintaining profit levels even in the face of declining prices.

The clearest evidence for the stretch-out comes from the records of individual firms. At the Hamilton Company, for instance, the workload of spinners and weavers more than doubled between 1840 and 1854, two years for which particularly accurate figures can be calculated. The average number of spindles per operative in the spinning department increased from 129 to 294 over this period, while the number of looms per weaver rose from 1.3 to 2.9. This increase in the workload was not accompanied by any similar advance in the wages of women workers.[14]

The Hamilton Company was not an isolated case on this score. Between 1840 and 1854 the spindle capacity of the eight major cotton textile firms in Lowell more than doubled, increasing from 155,000 to 330,000. The size of the work force, however, rose by only about 30 percent over the same period. The average number of spindles per millhand increased by almost 64 percent.[15] In its drive for efficiency the Hamilton Company was simply keeping in step with the other Lowell firms.

Needless to say the speedup and stretch-out were not confined to the Lowell mills but affected textile manufacturing throughout New England. An economist, Robert Layer, has examined wages and output of textile workers in four representative mills of Waltham-Lowell firms in northern New England. His data demonstrate that output per worker averaged across these firms rose by almost 49 percent between 1836 and 1850, while daily wages increased only 4 percent. Clearly, the forces at work transforming production in the Lowell mills were operating broadly throughout the New England textile industry in these years.[16]

The simple assignment of additional machinery to workers was only one of the means employed to raise productivity. Technological change played a contributing role as well, as evidenced in the partial substitution of mule spinning for throstle spinning in the period. Once again the experience of the Hamilton Company illustrates well the larger patterns at work in Lowell. In 1836 all spinning at Hamilton had been performed by throstles. In 1847, however, when the company completed construction of a fourth mill, it installed mule spinning frames in one of the two new spinning rooms. In 1850 a second mule spinning room was set up in another mill. [17]

Motivations other than simply a desire to increase productivity led to the introduction of spinning mules in the late 1840s. Mules produced a soft yarn particularly well suited for use as filling, and considerations of quality figured in the increasing reliance on mule spinning. Still, the fact that mule spinners on average tended 730 spindles each, or about 2.5 times the normal workload for throstle spinners, must have helped mill agents make the decision to switch to mule spinning. [18]

The changes described thus far—the expansion of productive capacity and the implementation of the stretch-out and technological innovation—had a profound impact on the Lowell mills in the years after 1836. Steadily these developments brought about a transformation of the mill work force, eliminating the high degree of homogeneity that prevailed in the earlier period. In both its composition and residence, the mill work force of the 1850s differed significantly from its predecessor two decades before.

The most dramatic change in the mill work force over this period was the substantial increase in the proportion of immigrants. In 1836 only 3.7 percent of those employed at Hamilton had been foreign-born. This proportion rose to 38.6 percent in 1850 and to 61.8 percent a decade later, as table 8.2 shows clearly. [19]

The rapid increase in the proportion of immigrants in the Lowell mills resulted from the simultaneous decline in the numbers of Yankee women coming to Lowell and increase in the numbers of Irish, beginning with their mass immigration after 1845. The falling off in the recruitment of Yankee women is evident in their actual numbers in the mill work force. At the Hamilton Company, for instance, the number of identifiable native-born females in the work force declined from 737 in 1836 to 539 in 1850 and finally to 324 in 1860, even though overall

TABLE 8.2. ETHNIC MAKEUP OF THE HAMILTON COMPANY WORK FORCE,
AUGUST 1850 AND JUNE 1860

Nativity	August 1850	June 1860
Native-born	61.4%	38.2%
Irish	29.4	46.9
English	4.9	8.3
Canadian	3.4	4.5
Other foreign	1.0	2.1
Total cases	1175	1195
Missing cases	46	63

NOTE: See appendix 3 for discussion of linkage methods.

female employment remained unchanged.[20] This decline occurred even though the mills began active recruiting in the rural countryside. One mill agent, John Clark, employed a recruiter whom he instructed to "engage for the Merrimack Company any smart, active & healthy girls whom you happen to meet who would like to come to Lowell." He indicated that the company could use "from 50 to 100 girls."[21] Even this active effort did not suffice, however, as the mills expanded in the prosperous mid-1840s. Into this gap stepped the immigrant Irish.

Three major factors can account for the declining recruitment of Yankee women in these years. First, there was a decline in the number of young, single women living in the rural communities that sent large numbers into the mills. In Boscawen, Canterbury, and Sutton, the three New Hampshire towns studied earlier, the population of women between the ages of 15 and 29 declined by 7.5 percent between 1830 and 1840.[22] The increasing movement of the young to urban centers and to the West reduced the population from which the expanding mills could draw. Second, and more importantly, increasing opportunities in alternative occupations gave rural young women a greater variety of wage-earning options. Teaching, for instance, expanded at a rate considerably higher than mill employment between the mid-1830s and 1850, and, relative to wages in the mills, teachers' earnings showed marked improvement. Between 1834 and 1850 the number of female teachers employed in Massachusetts increased from about 3,000 to 5,500, a gain of more than 80 percent, while in the nation as a whole, the proportional increase was even greater. Furthermore, the wages of Massachusetts teachers relative to those of textile workers rose significantly in these years. [23] Finally, the cumulative impact of the speedup, stretch-out, and wage cuts undoubtedly led many rural Yankee women to view mill employment as less desirable in the mid- and late 1840s than they had earlier. More demanding work and stagnant, even declining, earnings discouraged women who were not compelled by economic necessity from entering the mills.

Just as recruitment among Yankee women slowed down, the stepped up migration of the Irish offered mill agents a way out of their dilemma. As tens of thousands of immigrants arrived in Boston, or came south from Quebec, mill agents once again had a ready supply of willing workers. The Irish, of course, were often in dire economic need. They were in no position to complain about wage reductions or the increasing pace of work. The mills offered steady, and in comparison to domestic service or outdoor labor, relatively well-paid jobs. Mill employment was particularly attractive to the Irish as it offered work to children, enabling them to benefit from the earnings of several family members.

In the transition period after 1845 it is particularly difficult to unravel these two factors—the declining recruitment of Yankees and the greater availability of the Irish—and determine which was primarily responsible for the changing composition of the mill work force. Did the Yankees leave because the Irish were coming, or did the vacancies caused by Yankee departures attract the Irish to Lowell? And similarly, did deteriorating conditions lead the Yankee women to leave, or with the departure of the Yankees did mill agents simply take advantage of the Irish newcomers who had no real options but to accept mill employment whatever the conditions? Simply to pose these questions is to indicate the ambiguity of the situation. There must be a certain "sponginess" in the analysis here because all of the factors described were closely intertwined. The overall impact of these developments is evident, although we cannot clearly distinguish cause and effect.

With the increase in the number of immigrants in the mills, the proportion of children grew also. The proportion recorded in the Hamilton Company register books bringing certificates of school attendance rose from 2.3 percent of the work force in 1836 to 6.5 percent in 1860. Furthermore, the proportion of specifically "children's" jobs in the mills— lap boys, doffers, and back and front boys in mule spinning—increased from 3 to 6 percent over the period. On both scores the proportion of children at Hamilton grew significantly. [24]

Not only were increasing numbers of children working at the Hamilton Company, but the proportion of older men and women in the work force rose as well. Hamilton records lack age data, but efforts at tracing workers in the 1850 federal manuscript census partially fill this void. Table 8.3 presents findings on the age distribution of operatives successfully linked to the census. [25]

TABLE 8.3. AGE DISTRIBUTION OF THE CENSUS-LINKED GROUP OF HAMILTON OPERATIVES, AUGUST 1850, BROKEN DOWN BY SEX

Age Group	Males	Females	Overall
Under 15	15.4%	2.7%	6.6%
15–19	11.7	31.7	25.6
20–29	46.9	43.4	44.4
30–39	15.4	14.4	14.7
40 and over	10.5	7.9	8.7
Total cases	162	369	531
Missing cases	129	561	690

Several findings emerge from an examination of these data. First, the proportion of women over 30 years of age rose from 12.5 percent in 1830 to 22.3 percent in 1850, a gain of almost 80 percent. [26] These figures also corroborate the estimate of the proportion of children in the Hamilton work force derived from the register books. Finally, they demonstrate that the increase in the proportion of children resulted entirely from a rise in the number of boys employed in the mills. Girls under 15 continued to comprise less than 3 percent of the female work force, while the proportion of boys rose to more than 15 percent, a development due entirely to the introduction of mule spinning in the period.

Along with this evident decline in the earlier age-homogeneity of the mill work force, there was a decline in the sex-homogeneity; this period saw a steadily increasing proportion of males at work in the Lowell mills. At the Hamilton Company in 1836 males had comprised only 14 percent of all workers. By 1850, however, men made up 24 percent of the company work force, and by 1860 this figure had reached almost 30 percent. The same trend was evident in all the Lowell mills. Between 1836 and

1860, the proportion of males employed in the Lowell cotton textile mills increased from 13.5 to 25.2 percent.[27]

Increasingly men and boys performed work previously done entirely by women. The substitution of mule for throstle spinning accounts for a part of this trend, but a similar pattern is evident in weaving as well, although unaccompanied by any significant technological change.[28] In 1836 women had done all the weaving at Hamilton. By 1850 men held 4 percent of all weaving jobs, and by 1860 they comprised almost 9 percent of weavers. Here we see evidence of a new development in the mills, the apparent easing of the formerly rigid division between men's and women's work in the mills.

It is a telling fact that with the increase of immigrants in the mills, the once clear line between men's and women's occupations began to blur. With the entry of male immigrants at wage levels considerably below those of native-born men, the wages of the lowest-paid men and the highest-paid women overlapped for the first time. There existed in the 1850s a body of unskilled men (mostly Irish) willing to work at wages comparable to those of women. It was specifically from this group that the Hamilton Company recruited its male weavers. In 1850 all 15 of the male weavers were foreign-born; in 1860, 30 of 32 were immigrants.[29]

The entry of immigrant men into the ranks of weavers was not simply the result of any sudden availability, however. There had always been immigrants who would have traded the insecurity and irregularity of outdoor common labor for steady work in the mills. The male-female division of labor in the mills was based only in part on the economics of supply and demand. The proscription of men in the early years was an element in the larger system of paternalism adopted by the corporations in order to recruit a female work force. The division of labor by sex in the mills, like the boardinghouse system and the regulation of operatives' conduct outside the workplace, was established nominally to protect the virtue and morality of female operatives. Both at work and in the boardinghouses, women were to be shielded from the potentially "corrupting" influences of factory life—particularly from encounters with unscrupulous workingmen. This system of paternalism had undoubtedly been important in easing the fears of parents who otherwise might not have allowed their daughters to work in Lowell.

By the 1850s, however, under the combined pressure of economic and social change, the Lowell mills had abandoned the major elements of their former paternalism. Women no longer had to live in company housing, nor did corporations insist upon weekly church attendance by operatives. [30] The earlier concern for separating men and women at work declined as well, leaving the corporations free to follow more strictly economic considerations in job placement. If men could do a job as well as women, and at no greater expense, then there was no reason why they should not be employed. Moreover, as the Irish came to form the largest ethnic group within the mills, the earlier compulsion to "protect" the morals of women workers disappeared. Like the boardinghouse system, corporate paternalism had been necessary to attract a labor force in an earlier era. With the influx of the Irish, labor was in abundant supply, and so the boardinghouse system and corporate paternalism rapidly became secondary elements in the new Lowell.

This pattern of male movement into formerly all-female jobs is revealing about management's attitudes toward both women and immigrants. The hiring of Irish men to do women's work simply reinforced the lower status both of the Irish and of women. To have hired women, on the other hand, to perform work formerly reserved for men would have placed them on an equal footing with native-born men. Given the attitudes of mill agents toward their "girls" evident in the early turn-outs, such action was highly unlikely. Only in the 1880s and after, when male immigrant mule spinners organized in trade unions, and when virtually all native-born men had left the mills, did management seek to displace male operatives with females. [31]

Just as the ethnic, age, and sex composition of the Hamilton work force changed over these years, so too did the pattern of residence for operatives. We have seen how corporate policy shifted and dependence on private housing increased after 1845. For the workers themselves, this shift can be seen in figures on residence between 1836 and 1860 (see table 8.4).

By 1850 a substantial majority of the work force resided in private housing. This development reflected in part the entry of immigrants into the labor force, but it also reflected a change in residence patterns among native-born workers. In 1836 more than 70 percent of Yankee workers at Hamilton had resided in company housing; by 1850 this proportion had declined to 55 percent.

TABLE 8.4. RESIDENCE OF THE HAMILTON COMPANY WORK FORCE,
JULY 1836, AUGUST 1850, AND JUNE 1860

Type of Housing	1836	1850	1860
Company[a]	73.7%	39.0%	33.0%
Private	26.3	61.0	67.0
Total cases	945	1168	1183
Missing cases	85	63	75

NOTE: For a discussion of linkage methods, see appendixes 1, 3.
[a] Includes housing of the Hamilton and Appleton companies.

The changing patterns of residence resulted from a steady movement away from the earlier labor force of young, single women toward a family labor system. Increasingly entire families, Yankee and immigrant, were coming to Lowell and sending several family members into the mills.[32] The expansion of the mill work force, coupled with its new makeup, resulted in a dispersal of workers' residences throughout Lowell. No longer did they all reside "on the corporation," as they had in the 1830s. The full significance of this new dispersal will become apparent as the analysis of work and protest in Lowell in the 1850s proceeds.

CHAPTER NINE

Immigrants in the Mills, 1850-1860

FROM ITS INCEPTION Lowell attracted immigrant workers. In 1822 thirty Irish laborers trekked from Boston to East Chelmsford and began work widening the Pawtucket Canal to provide waterpower for future mill sites. By the mid-1820s skilled English artisans—printers, engravers and dyers—found employment in the print works of the Merrimack and Hamilton Companies. Scottish handloom weavers came to work in the carpet factory established in 1829. Whether unskilled or skilled, immigrants found ready employment in early Lowell. [1]

Among the first immigrants, unskilled male construction workers and day laborers predominated. The Locks and Canals company engaged contractors who took responsibility for employing itinerant workers for specific undertakings. These workers, in turn, were housed in makeshift tents erected on what was known derisively as "Paddy Camp Lands." After the initial construction a more permanent arrangement was sought, and as one contemporary reported "the barracks of the men were removed to two large barns on the Fletcher farm, near the hosiery mill, fitted up with bunks for sleeping, and rough tables for eating." [2] Men outnumbered women in Lowell's immigrant population for a considerable period, in striking contrast to the composition of the Yankee community. Males comprised 61.3 percent of residents in immigrant households in Lowell in 1830 but only 34.0 percent in Yankee homes. [3]

Even as they became more settled, immigrants resided in distinct, segregated neighborhoods. An 1831 visitor, for example, remarked on the residences of the Irish:

> [W]ithin a few rods of the canals is a settlement, called by some, *New Dublin*, which occupies rather more than an acre of ground. It contains a population of not far from 500 Irish, who dwell in about 100 cabins, from 7 to 10 feet in height, built of slabs and rough boards; a fireplace made of stone, in one end, topped out with two or three flour barrels or lime casks.[4]

The Irish in their wooden shanties were evidently outside of the paternalistic system of corporate housing in this period. Skilled English and Scottish workers did enjoy housing provided by the textile companies, but even that tended to be confined to distinct ethnic neighborhoods. "John Bull's Row" and "Scotch Block" denominated the blocks that housed these two groups.[5]

The segregation of immigrants evident in their housing patterns was reflected in their occupational concentration as well. The 1830 federal manuscript census of Lowell recorded fifty-two households in the Irish neighborhood. Of the twenty heads of these households who can be traced in the *Lowell Directory*, sixteen worked as laborers or were employed by the Proprietors of Locks and Canals.[6] These figures reflect a dominant fact of life in early Lowell—that the Irish were largely excluded from mill employment, just as they were excluded from company housing.

Similar occupational concentration is evident for English and Scottish immigrants, although these groups were more fully integrated in textile production. Of the sixteen household heads enumerated in the English neighborhood in the 1830 census, at least ten were employed at the Merrimack Print Works. Similarly, ten of fourteen alien household heads concentrated in "Scotch Block" worked at the carpet factory.[7] Residential and occupational concentration clearly characterized each of the immigrant groups in Lowell in 1830.

In cultural terms the Irish were decidedly the most "alien" of the immigrants in early Lowell. Their Catholicism set them apart from the Protestant majority—in their own eyes and those of their Yankee neighbors. Throughout the 1820s visiting priests from Boston ministered to the needs of the growing Irish community, until in 1831 the completion of St. Patrick's Church provided the basis for a local parish and resident priest. Separate Irish Catholic schools developed as well and reinforced the social distance between native-born and Irish.[8] This distance is evident in the reminiscences of Harriet Robinson recorded in her autobiography, *Loom and Spindle*:

> Before 1840, the foreign element in the factory population was almost an unknown quantity. . . . [T]he Irish came as "hewers of wood and drawers of water." The first Irish-women to work in the Lowell mills were usually scrubbers and waste-pickers. They were always good-natured, and when excited used their own language. . . . These women, as a rule, wore peasant cloaks, red or blue, made with hoods and several capes, in summer (as they told the children) to "kape cool," and in winter to "kape warm."[9]

The social distance between Yankees and Irish is apparent; differences in dress, language, and culture reinforced the occupational and residential segregation. The Irish appear in the writings of Yankee operatives as something of a curiosity, as one of the features that set the big city apart from the country.[10]

The tremendous influx of the Irish associated with the famine migration after 1845 transformed the Irish from a curiosity into a dominant feature of Lowell life. Just as thousands of Irish were landing in nearby Boston, the Lowell mills enjoyed expanding markets and steady profits that had been absent for almost a decade.[11] With the end of the 1837-1843 depression and the passage of a higher tariff in 1844, production in the mills expanded rapidly and generated a new demand for labor. The inability of mill agents to secure enough Yankee women to meet these new needs led to the recruitment for the first time of Irish women for regular positions in the mills.[12] Immigrant representation in the mills rose dramatically. From a mere 8 percent in 1845, their proportion in the Hamilton Company work force increased to one third in 1850 and to more than 60 percent in 1860.[13] About three fourths of immigrants were Irish, who by 1860 comprised 47 percent of Hamilton workers, thus becoming the largest single ethnic group in the mills.

Earlier attitudes that had relegated the Irish to the least skilled and lowest-paying occupations did not fade overnight, and even as they moved into the mills, the Irish faced discrimination. Foreign-born men and women at Hamilton earned consistently less than their native-born

TABLE 9.1. MEAN DAILY PAY OF HAMILTON WORKERS,
AUGUST 1850, BROKEN DOWN BY NATIVITY AND SEX

Nativity	Males	Females
Native-born	$1.08 (183)	$0.63 (539)
Foreign-born	0.78 (83)	0.54 (370)
Missing cases	25	21

counterparts. During August 1850, for instance, immigrant women on average earned 17 percent less than native-born women. For immigrant men the wage differential was even greater as table 9.1 reveals.

The substantial native-immigrant wage differential was not the result of outright wage discrimination, but grew out of patterns of job placement. When native-born and immigrant women worked in the same jobs, they were paid identical piece rates and earned virtually identical wages. The differences between the earnings of Yankee and immigrant spinners and weavers, for instance, amounted to less than 2 percent of their average daily earnings. Among spinners, immigrants earned slightly more; among weavers, the native-born. Most immigrant workers, however, worked in the low-paying carding and spinning departments, their Yankee counterparts in the high-paying weaving and dressing rooms. Table 9.2 presents the distribution of immigrant and native-born women in the major departments of the Hamilton Company in 1850.

TABLE 9.2. DISTRIBUTION OF NATIVE-BORN AND IMMIGRANT WOMEN
IN THE MAJOR DEPARTMENTS OF THE
HAMILTON COMPANY, AUGUST 1850

Department	Mean Daily Pay (cents)	Native	Immigrant	Total Cases
Spinning	48.3	21.6%	78.4%	185
Carding	52.7	43.1	56.9	109
Weaving	64.8	76.3	23.7	413
Dressing	64.9	84.3	15.7	140
Overall[a]	59.2	59.3	40.7	909

[a] Overall mean daily pay based on all women workers. Sum of total cases is less than 909 due to exclusion of minor departments.

The proportions of native-born were highest in the dressing and weaving departments, the two best-paying rooms at the company. Immigrants, in contrast, were concentrated in the lowest-paying rooms in the mills.[14] Fifty-six percent of all Irish women at Hamilton in 1850 worked in carding and spinning, compared to only 16 percent of the native-born. At the other end of the wage spectrum, 22 percent of native-born women but only 4 percent of immigrants worked in dressing rooms. These patterns of job placement account for the 17 percent wage differential between native and immigrant women workers at Hamilton.

That the jobs of immigrant women were different from those of the native-born is clear; it remains to explain why. Various explanations seem possible. The higher educational levels of native-born women might have led mill management to assign them to the more skilled jobs in the female work force. Most of the native-born had worked longer at the company—a residue in part of the earlier exclusion of the Irish from mill work—and their added experience might account for their advantages in job placement. Finally, the Irish may simply have been placed in the lowest-paying jobs because they were Irish. The question comes down to this: which of the three variables—education, experience, or ethnicity—best accounts for differences in job placement of native-born and immigrant women at Hamilton in 1850?

There is no evidence that the level of education of operatives had a significant impact on their productivity or daily earnings. It is not possible to measure education per se using company records, but these sources do indicate literacy. Taken as a group, women who were able to sign their names in company payroll volumes were probably more educated than those who could not, suggesting that literacy may be a reasonable proxy for education. Evidence in the payrolls, presented in table 9.3, makes clear that the earnings, and hence the productivity, of literate and illiterate piece workers were virtually identical.

Where women earned piece wages, and where significant numbers of literate and illiterate women were employed, the differences in their earnings were insignificant. For two jobs—spinning and weaving—literate operatives earned slightly more than illiterates. For warp winders, however, the pattern was just the reverse. And in all three cases, the wage differential was far too small—2 percent at the most—to account for the native-immigrant differential of 17 percent.

TABLE 9.3. MEAN DAILY PAY OF FEMALE PIECE WORKERS AT HAMILTON, AUGUST 1850, BROKEN DOWN BY JOB AND LITERACY

| | Mean Daily Pay | | Total |
Job	Literate	Illiterate	Cases
Spinning	$0.50 (76)	$0.49 (70)	146
Weaving	0.67 (341)	0.66 (40)	381
Warp winding	0.54 (12)	0.55 (18)	30
Total cases	429	128	557

Although literacy played no part in determining the productivity of women workers, job placement patterns were strongly correlated with literacy. Almost half of spinners—70 of 146—were illiterate, and fully 60 percent of warp winders were as well. In the high-paying weaving room, by contrast, only 10.5 percent—40 of 381—were illiterate. Clearly illiterate workers were far more likely than literate ones to work in spinning and winding. From these patterns alone we cannot judge whether or not management consciously considered literacy in making decisions concerning job placement. We need more direct evidence on the attitudes of mill agents.

There is no doubt that mill managers considered literate, educated workers more productive. In 1841 Horace Mann, Secretary of the Massachusetts State Board of Education, sought to substantiate the economic value of education. He drafted a circular letter to employers and in his *Fifth Annual Report* published a number of their replies. James K. Mills, Boston commission merchant and director of several Waltham-Lowell firms, reported that on average illiterate operatives earned 27 percent less than the "better educated." John Clark, superintendent at the Merrimack Company, examined the earnings of illiterate piece workers, and found them to be 18.5 percent below the general average of others employed in the same departments. Focusing on the earnings of ex-teachers in the work force, Clark found them to be almost 18 percent above the general average for all female operatives. [15]

This testimony stands in sharp contrast to the actual findings for earnings at the Hamilton Company in 1850. In fact there is no contradiction between the two sets of evidence. The Hamilton findings suggest that within occupations there were no significant differences in the earnings of literate and illiterate workers. The employers' letters to Horace Mann provide data reflecting prevailing patterns of job placement. Clearly, literate workers, and more especially former teachers, were placed in the most skilled positions in the female work force, and thus they earned higher than average wages. Mills's 27 percent wage differential does not control for job placement, while Clark controls for department rather than job. Even within a given department, differences in earnings among jobs could be quite substantial. The letters to Mann speak much more about the attitudes of mill management (and of Mann, who chose to publish them) than they do about differences in productivity based on education. Still they are crucial because they clarify the attitudes of management toward the Irish. Clearly, mill agents and overseers thought more of the educated Yankee worker than of the Irish newcomer, and their preferences were reflected in the patterns of job placement that emerged.

The contentions of management on this score are further undermined by the continuous increase in productivity in the mills during the period in which immigrants replaced Yankee operatives. Although the newcomers were undoubtedly less educated than their native-born predecessors, there is no evidence that their entry into the work force halted the impressive productivity gains of these years. Recent studies by McGouldrick and Davis and Stettler have demonstrated this point conclusively. [16]

Work experience remains the final variable to consider in analyzing the job placement patterns of native-born and immigrant workers at Hamilton. The length of time an operative had been employed at the company clearly affected job placement. Generally speaking newcomers in the mill work force were likely to be employed at first in the carding and spinning rooms. When job openings developed in the high-paying dressing room, the company most frequently filled the positions with experienced operatives. In August 1850 women working in the dressing rooms of the company had been employed an average of 4.50 years, a figure more than double that for women in any of the other major departments.

In comparing the job placement patterns of native-born and immigrant women it is important then to control for any differences in the length of time each group had been employed at Hamilton. Even when this is done, however, it is evident that immigrant operatives were still more likely to be placed in the low-paying rooms than were native-born. More than 56 percent of immigrant newcomers at Hamilton—those with less than a year's employment at the company—worked in the carding and spinning rooms in August 1850. Less than a third of this proportion—17.6 percent—of native-born newcomers were so employed. At the upper end of the wage scale, more than 20 percent of native-born newcomers worked in the dressing room, compared to only 5 percent among immigrants. These differences persisted in all ranges of experience in the female work force. Table 9.4 isolates women with less than one year's experience and those with six or more years at the company. The ethnic differences in job placement patterns are striking at both levels of experience.

Both native and immigrant operatives tended to move into higher-paying jobs as they gained experience. Nevertheless, the gap between the placement patterns of the two groups remained substantial even among the most experienced women workers. Immigrant women with

TABLE 9.4. ROOM PLACEMENT OF NATIVE- AND FOREIGN-BORN FEMALES
AT THE HAMILTON COMPANY, AUGUST 1850,
BROKEN DOWN BY EXPERIENCE

Women with less than one year's experience		
Room	Native-born	Immigrant
Carding	9.0%	23.8%
Spinning	8.6	32.7
Weaving	62.2	38.5
Dressing	20.1	5.0
Total cases	209	122
Women with six or more years' experience		
Room	Native-born	Immigrant
Carding	8.3%	18.2%
Spinning	8.3	36.4
Weaving	47.9	27.3
Dressing	35.4	18.2
Total cases	48	11

NOTE: Females not working in main rooms and those with missing data on nativity or experience excluded. Columns may not add up to 100.0% due to rounding.

six or more years of employment at Hamilton were still three times as likely as their native-born counterparts to be working in the low-paying carding and spinning rooms. Experienced immigrants had only half the chance of the native-born to work in the high-paying dressing rooms. There was a slight narrowing of the gap as a few immigrants moved into the dressing room with experience, but the differences in job placement, and thus in daily earnings, remained substantial even among experienced workers.

These conclusions hold even if one controls for experience and literacy at the same time. For each level of experience, literate immigrant women were at least three times as likely as their native-born counterparts to be employed in the low-paying carding and spinning rooms; they worked in the dressing room in proportions only half of those for the native-born (see table 9.5).

It is clear that ultimately nativity, rather than experience or education, was the primary factor making for the overall differential between the earnings of native-born and immigrant women workers. Unstated company policy reserved the highest-paying jobs for Yankee women and channeled immigrant newcomers into the most disagreeable and low-paying work. The firm discriminated against the Irish because they were Irish. It did so even though immigrants were evidently as productive as the native-born. In purely economic terms such a policy appears to have been irrational.

What functions, however, did the separation of Irish and Yankee in the mills serve? It is unlikely that mill managers were acting simply to satisfy personal whims; they must have had some larger purposes in mind. Unfortunately the correspondence of mill agents and treasurers is rather thin on this issue; still, enough material of interest has survived to support a number of reasonable inferences. It is evident that Yankee women resented the increasing proportion of immigrants employed in the mills at this date. Harriet Farley, editor of the *Lowell Offering*, noted that "the greatest dissatisfaction, among American operatives is caused by the introduction of foreign laborers into manufacturing establishments."[17] Mill managers were concerned about the growing resentment among Yankee operatives because the departure of these women deprived the mills of skilled, experienced workers. In an effort to reduce turnover among native-born women, mill agents seem to have tried to

TABLE 9.5. PROPORTIONS OF LITERATE FEMALE OPERATIVES EMPLOYED IN
THE MAJOR DEPARTMENTS OF THE HAMILTON COMPANY, AUGUST 1850,
BROKEN DOWN BY NATIVITY AND EXPERIENCE

Literate Females with less than one year's experience

Department	Native-born	Immigrant
Carding	6.8%	21.7%
Spinning	7.8	23.3
Weaving	64.6	46.7
Dressing	20.8	8.3
Total cases[a]	192	62

Literate Females with one to three years' experience

Department	Native-born	Immigrant
Carding	7.4%	13.0%
Spinning	5.8	40.6
Weaving	62.0	37.7
Dressing	24.8	8.7
Total cases[a]	121	69

Literate Females with three to six years' experience

Department	Native-born	Immigrant
Carding	9.2%	15.0%
Spinning	8.3	55.0
Weaving	61.7	20.0
Dressing	20.8	10.0
Total cases[a]	12	20

NOTE: No table was prepared for operatives with six or more years' experience
because 46 of 48 literate females with that level of experience were native-born.
[a] Excludes females with missing data on experience or nativity, and those not
employed in major departments.

concentrate the immigrant newcomers into a limited number of rooms
within the mills, thereby cushioning somewhat their impact on Yankee
operatives.

The changing makeup of the mill work force over time demonstrates
that there was a pattern of introducing the Irish into the mills one room
at a time. Table 9.6 provides evidence on immigrant job placement at
Hamilton between 1845 and 1850, those years when the Irish first entered the mills in large numbers.

All departments in the Hamilton Company felt the influx of immi-

TABLE 9.6. PROPORTIONS OF IMMIGRANTS AMONG WOMEN WORKERS
IN THE MAJOR DEPARTMENTS AT HAMILTON, 1845–1850

Department	1845	1847	1850
Spinning	16.1%	45.8%	78.4%
Carding	4.6	19.8	56.9
Weaving	4.6	9.7	23.7
Dressing	3.8	8.3	15.7

SOURCES: 1845, Layer, "Wages, Earnings, and Output," p. 186, combines males and females; 1847, Luft, "New England Textile Labor," p. 37; 1850, payroll analysis.

grant workers in this period, but the spinning department led all others in this regard. Consistently in these years the proportion of immigrants in spinning was about four times that of the high-paid weaving and dressing departments. Carding had a sizable proportion of immigrants after 1845, but it always trailed spinning by a significant margin.

The logical result of this job placement process was that native and immigrant workers were concentrated in different rooms within the mills. By 1850, for instance, more than 75 percent of immigrant workers at Hamilton were employed in rooms that were predominantly foreign-born. In contrast, more than 80 percent of native-born women worked in departments in which they comprised more than three fourths of the female work force.

The separation of immigrant and Yankee was even more pronounced in housing beyond the mills. In the boardinghouses of the Hamilton Company in 1850 only about 8 percent of female residents were foreign-born, while immigrants made up more than 40 percent of the female work force as a whole.[18] The boardinghouses provided subsidized accommodations for workers; they never earned returns comparable to overall profits of production.[19] The fact that immigrants were largely excluded from these facilities meant that the lion's share of this subsidy went to native-born workers. Thus the discrimination against the Irish was compounded: not only did they earn lower wages through job placement in the mills; they were largely denied subsidized housing as well.[20]

The patterns of job placement and housing described here simply could not have developed unconsciously. While none of the records of the Lowell firms provide evidence of self-conscious planning in this regard, a memorandum of the Salmon Falls Manufacturing Company, in New Hampshire, one of the Waltham-Lowell type firms, provides insight on this issue. The particular document survives in the papers of Amos A. Lawrence, a director of the Salmon Falls Company, and also of numerous Lowell firms. The 1854 memorandum discussed the difficulties of recruiting satisfactory operatives. The problems that resulted from the interaction of Yankee and Irish led the author of this memorandum to urge the strict segregation of the two groups:

> The difficulty of keeping the Irish and Americans together in an isolated village like ours appears to be much greater than in the large manufacturing towns. *It may be that one group will supplant the other.* If the Irish sh[oul]d predominate so as to disgust the American operatives, the character of the village must be very much changed *for the worse.* Every care must be taken to keep them in separate boarding houses, & to separate them in the mills.

Among the actions taken by the firm to meet this concern was the purchase of a large boardinghouse, suitable for a hundred residents, for the Irish, located "at some distance from the others," so that Irish and Yankee would not mix with one another. [21]

The separation of Yankee and Irish may have avoided outbreaks of unrest outside the mills; it also served to reinforce the dual nature of the mill labor market. It is clear that Yankee and Irish came to the mills for different reasons, had differing expectations about mill employment, and responded differently to the pressures of wage reductions, speedups, and stretch-outs. Yankee women with rural homes to which they might return could afford to be considerably more sensitive to these company actions and were more likely to respond by leaving the mills. The Irish, fleeing famine and starvation, appreciated the steady, certain employment of the mills even at low wages. Even in the New England context, the mills offered surer income than uncertain day labor in Boston, for instance. Finally, by separating Irish and native-born in the mills, management to a certain extent was able to apply the techniques of speedup and stretch-out selectively, undermining working conditions in predominantly Irish departments, while protecting standards in the largely native-born rooms.

Harold Luft has examined the production and employment records of the Hamilton Company with just this question in mind: did the speedup and stretch-out policies of the company affect immigrant and native-born workers equally? He found that between November 1847 and May 1849 total output rose 13 percent, although the number of women employed increased by only 5 percent. The growth of female employment, moreover, was not distributed evenly among all departments. Total employment in dressing and weaving grew by 7 and 11 percent respectively. The work forces in spinning and carding, on the other hand, declined by 5 and 10 percent over the same period. Clearly the increased productivity was concentrated in departments employing larger numbers of immigrant women. The figures suggest increases in productivity on the order of 5 percent in predominantly Yankee departments and of 20 percent in those with larger numbers of immigrants. [22]

There is also some evidence of a conscious effort to protect the wage levels of native-born women workers at the expense of the immigrants. In September 1850 George Motley, agent of the Appleton Company, wrote to his firm's treasurer with regard to an impending wage reduction. Apparently his directors had proposed a wage cut somewhat in advance of the other Lowell firms, and Motley expressed his concern: "The effect to this company will be, in my judgment, unless immediately followed by a similar reduction in other mills, that we shall loose [sic] our best hands and their places will be filled by inferior ones." [23] A week later, in a second letter, Motley revealed the means he had taken to reduce wages and yet keep from losing his "best" (i.e. native-born) hands. He had reduced the piece wages of female operatives selectively,

bringing the speeder and S[trecher] tenders down to $1.75 per wk Drawing Tenders $1 a week, the reduction to take effect this morning—also the spinners to about [$]1.00. This is reducing all the female help in the carding and spinning Rooms about the am[oun]t you directed.
Unless otherwise directed by you I would rather not reduce the weavers till the other mills have come to some conclusion as to what they intend to do. The weavers are what I am fearful of loosing [sic]. [24]

The exact composition of the various departments at Appleton in 1850 is uncertain, but if it followed the pattern evident at the neighboring Hamilton Company, the carding and spinning departments were probably predominantly immigrant at this date. Motley's action thus undermined the earnings of immigrant women for the most part, while for the time being, at least, maintaining the wage rates of the predominantly Yankee weavers. Even if after consultation with the agents of other Lowell companies Motley did reduce weavers' piece rates, there was no need to enforce a strict equality in the wage cuts. Relatively speaking, he appears to have treated the preferred native-born women with kid gloves. The separation of native-born and immigrant women within the mills made this distinction possible.

Initially Irish newcomers in the Lowell mills faced considerable discrimination; in the long run, over the decade of the 1850s, their position in the mills improved significantly. Over the period the gap between the earnings of native-born and immigrant women declined substantially as immigrants moved into the higher-paying jobs from which they had been initially excluded. Throughout these years the growing shortage of native-born women entering mill employment resulted in a demand for labor that created opportunities for the Irish to move up the occupational hierarchy.

Between 1850 and 1860 the native-immigrant wage differential for women declined by more than 80 percent.[25] In 1850 native-born women had earned on average 9.6 cents more per day than immigrants; by 1860, this difference had declined to only 1.4 cents (see table 9.7).

The narrowing of the difference between the daily earnings of native and immigrant women resulted from two distinct developments. First, the pay differential between what had been low- and high-paying jobs in the mills began to disappear. Second, immigrant women moved up into the higher-paying jobs. By 1860 immigrant women were more evenly

TABLE 9.7. MEAN DAILY PAY OF NATIVE- AND FOREIGN-BORN FEMALES
AT THE HAMILTON COMPANY, AUGUST 1850 AND JUNE 1860

Ethnicity	Mean Daily Pay (in cents)	
	1850	1860
Native-born	63.2 (539)	57.5 (324)
Foreign-born	53.6 (370)	56.1 (524)
Missing cases	21	38

spread out among all the major departments in the mills than in 1850, and the wage differences among departments had declined. Together, the two developments brought immigrant female operatives almost up to parity in wages with native women.

To demonstrate the narrowing of the wage gap between high- and low-paying departments at Hamilton, it may be helpful to examine the change in the mean daily pay of women workers in various departments over the period 1850-1860. Table 9.8 presents these findings.

TABLE 9.8. MEAN DAILY PAY OF FEMALE OPERATIVES AT THE HAMILTON COMPANY, AUGUST 1850 AND JUNE 1860, BROKEN DOWN BY DEPARTMENT

Department	Mean Daily Pay (in cents)	
	1850	1860
Carding	52.7 (112)	52.3 (117)
Spinning	48.3 (186)	48.0 (161)
Weaving	64.8 (421)	60.5 (442)
Dressing	64.9 (147)	58.6 (136)

NOTE: Excludes minor departments—winding and cloth room.

At both dates dressing and weaving room operatives were paid at significantly higher wage rates than less skilled hands in carding and spinning. Over the decade, however, the differences in wages among departments declined. In 1850 dressing room operatives earned 16.6 cents per day more than spinners, a differential of 34 percent. By 1860, however, the gap between the highest-paid department, weaving, and the lowest-paid one, spinning again, was only 12.5 cents, a margin of about 25 percent. Both the absolute and the relative wage differentials declined over the decade.[26] Even had immigrant operatives remained in the lowest-paying rooms in the same proportions as in 1850, the native-immigrant wage differential would have been reduced because of the narrowing spread of wages among female jobs.

In the abstract, at least, the narrowing in the wage differential between high- and low-paid jobs could have come about in either of two ways: by the elevating of low-paying jobs up to the skill and wage levels of the more skilled occupations, or by the degradation of previously well-paid jobs to the skill and wage levels of the less skilled ones. Both developments would result in a more homogeneous work force, but in the first case it would be relatively more skilled and well-paid, while in the latter it would be less skilled and less well-paid than the earlier work force had been.

The latter tendency prevailed in the Hamilton mills during the 1850s. The steady improvement of looms, and of warping and dressing machines, reduced the intervention required by operatives during production. These developments led to what might be termed the "proletarianization" of the female labor force at the Hamilton Company. Women's work became more homogeneous (in wage and skill terms), less skilled, and lower paid. As overall women's wages declined, wage differences among women workers narrowed and the distinctive job placement patterns of workers with different levels of experience tended to disappear. Despite claims by millowners and managers that conditions in the American mills were better than those prevailing in the English textile industry, developments in the late 1840s and 1850s in fact appreciably narrowed the gap between the two systems. The wide range of skills and earnings that had prevailed in the earlier Yankee work force narrowed, and overall wage levels declined to the point where the more "independent" Yankee women no longer entered the mills in such large numbers. In the face of increasing competition, mill management chose to maintain high levels of profit rather than maintain the earlier labor system. With the speedup and stretch-out and with technological change, mill management overcame its early dependence on a relatively skilled and well-paid female work force. And with the entry of large numbers of immigrant Irish eager to work in the mills, management was able to reduce piece wages without undercutting the overall supply of workers. Periodically the correspondence of managers reveals a preference for the more experienced and educated Yankee women workers, but the preference was never strong enough to halt the basic trends. The almost nostalgic view of the superiority of old-stock Yankee workers could not compete with considerations of profit and loss. Thus millowners opted for technological improvement and the accompanying proletarianization of the work force. Even as these developments transformed conditions within the mills, agents and owners continued to boast of the superior conditions in the American textile factories. They acted as if by making these claims they could maintain the earlier standards. However, they deceived only themselves; workers knew better and acted accordingly. Still, the rhetoric of the millowners is important, for it reveals that they did not consciously welcome the coming of the new industrial order in the mills. But although they tried to deny the changes that were occurring, their very decisions fostered the process of change.

The reduction of the mean daily pay of women workers at Hamilton between 1836 and 1860 was substantial, with the greatest share of the decline concentrated in the decade of the 1850s (see table 9.9). While the overall reduction amounted to 5 percent, the wage cut for regular operatives, as opposed to sparehands, was almost twice that figure.[27]

TABLE 9.9. MEAN DAILY PAY OF FEMALE OPERATIVES AT THE HAMILTON COMPANY, 1836–1860

	Mean Daily Pay (in cents)	
Payroll Date	Overall	Regular operatives
July 1836	59.5 (881)	63.6 (694)
August 1850	59.2 (930)	61.0 (822)
June 1860	56.6 (886)	57.6 (793)

The decline in average earnings cannot be accounted for by changes in either the age or experience of the female work force. The proportion under 15 years old in the female work force at Hamilton held steady at about 3 percent. The general level of experience among women operatives actually increased over the period. The proportion of sparehands, a good indicator of the number of newcomers in the work force, declined from 20 to 10 percent between 1836 and 1860. The mean length of time women had been employed at the company increased from 1.75 to 3.20 years over this interval. Clearly the decrease in women's wages resulted from decisions by the Hamilton management to lower piece-wage rates.

This long-term reduction in women's earnings did not affect all women's jobs equally. Two women's occupations, sparehands and spinners, among the lowest-paid jobs in the 1850s, experienced wage gains over the decade. Six other female occupations—including all of the best-paid positions in the weaving and dressing departments—suffered declines in

TABLE 9.10. MEAN DAILY PAY OF MAJOR FEMALE JOBS AT
THE HAMILTON COMPANY, AUGUST 1850 AND JUNE 1860

Job	1850	1860	Trend
Sparehands	$0.45 (108)	$0.48 (93)	+
Drawers	0.47 (29)	0.45 (28)	−
Spinners	0.50 (148)	0.52 (126)	+
Speeders	0.57 (71)	0.54 (27)	−
Drawing in	0.57 (39)	0.54 (34)	−
Weavers	0.67 (377)	0.63 (354)	−
Warpers	0.67 (43)	0.55 (50)	−
Dressers	0.83 (31)	0.79 (32)	−

wages. The result of these contrasting developments was a narrowing of
the spread of female wages at Hamilton that is apparent in table 9.10.

The textile corporations reduced wages and narrowed the range between high- and low-paying women's jobs by manipulating piece-wage
rates. Throughout this period the pace of work in the mills increased,
while average daily earnings declined. This result could be achieved in
only one way: by reducing piece rates more than productivity increased.
This was precisely the approach taken by mill agents, who could do so
because the steady influx of immigrants brought in ready replacements
for workers who chose to leave rather than work at lower rates. The new
immigrant operatives had limited knowledge of previous working conditions and therefore little reason to question their wage rates or work-
loads.

The fact that the proletarianization of the female work force occurred
at the same time that immigrants came to predominate in the mills could
not have escaped native-born workers. With some justice Yankee
women probably attributed the reduction of their wages and the deterioration of working conditions to the entry of immigrants into the mills.
The causes of the wage cuts and speedup lay in the declining prices of
finished cloth and in the consequent squeeze on profits; however, the
influx of the Irish, by creating an abundant reservoir of unskilled operatives, doubtless contributed to the deteriorating situation. Native-born
and immigrant alike were exploited by the changing conditions in the
mills, but the fact that the native-born were likely to blame the newcomers for their plight made the prospect of united protest unlikely.

At the same time that the overall wage spread of female jobs narrowed, immigrant women began to move up into the higher-paying departments of the Hamilton mills. The proportion of foreign-born rose most dramatically in the weaving and dressing departments of the company, as table 9.11 demonstrates.

TABLE 9.11. PROPORTIONS OF FOREIGN-BORN AMONG ALL FEMALES IN
THE MAJOR DEPARTMENTS OF THE HAMILTON COMPANY,
AUGUST 1850 AND JUNE 1860

	Proportion of Foreign-Born			
Department	1850		1860	
Carding	56.9%	(109)	80.4%	(112)
Spinning	78.4	(185)	79.1	(158)
Weaving	23.7	(413)	60.1	(429)
Dressing	15.7	(140)	27.4	(124)

Although the proportions of immigrants in each of the major departments were not identical in 1860, it is clear that the differences in the composition of the female work force across departments narrowed over the decade. The proportion of immigrants who worked in the higher-paying weaving and dressing rooms rose from 32 to 56 percent over the decade. Most of this increase resulted from a shift of immigrants from the spinning to the weaving room. By 1860 almost half of the foreign-born women employed at Hamilton worked in the weaving room, only slightly below the comparable figure for Yankee women. On the eve of the Civil War, only the dressing room remained something of a bastion of Yankee supremacy, but even in that department more than a fourth of women workers were foreign-born. [28]

The improvement of job placement patterns of immigrants raises an interesting question about their native-born co-workers. Were the immigrant gains made at the expense of Yankee operatives? As immigrants moved into better-paying departments, were native-born women displaced? Evidence from the Hamilton records suggests that they were not. In 1850 just over 80 percent of all native-born women at Hamilton worked in the weaving and dressing rooms. In 1860 the proportion remained virtually unchanged. The upward job mobility of immigrants did not result in a downward movement of native women. Rather immigrants moved into the better-paying jobs simply because there were no longer enough new native-born females entering employment to replace all those who left. The absolute number of Yankee women at Hamilton declined from 539 to 324 over the decade, and immigrant women moved into the void their departures created. The evident decline in discrimination against immigrants at Hamilton was brought about by a shift in the ethnic makeup of those entering the work force. The corporations had no choice but to place immigrants in the more skilled positions. Economic necessity, rather than any change in attitudes toward immigrants, is sufficient to explain this change in corporate policy.

CHAPTER TEN

Housing and Families of Women Operatives

THE YEARS between 1836 and 1860 saw a dramatic shift in the ethnic makeup of the Hamilton Company work force and in the wage structure within the mills. Important as these changes were in the transformation of work in Lowell, they were only aspects of a pervasive pattern of change in the entire social setting. Residence patterns of operatives showed similarly dramatic shifts, as declining proportions of mill workers resided in company housing and the numbers living at home with their families increased sharply. In 1836 almost three fourths of Hamilton operatives had boarded in company housing; by 1860 this proportion had declined to a third. The decay of the earlier boardinghouse system, and of the peer-group culture it had supported, was the final element in the transformation of work and community for women operatives in antebellum Lowell.

Hamilton records alone do not enable us to penetrate the households and family lives of women workers. To examine this dimension of workers' lives, the federal manuscript census proves most valuable. In 1860 the census for the first time recorded women's occupations, making it possible to examine the housing and families of women operatives without relying on uncertain record linkage of payrolls with the census. To facilitate this study I drew a systematic sample of millhands from the census. For every tenth millhand enumerated in the census, I recorded a broad range of personal, family, and household data. The discussion that follows examines the housing and family patterns of the 761 women in the millhand sample. [1]

Almost half of the women workers in the sample—49 percent—resided in noncompany housing, up considerably from the 25 percent figure at Hamilton in 1836. Even more dramatic was the increase in the proportion of women residing at home with their families. This figure reached 35 percent for 1860 millhands, more than triple the 11 percent recorded for Hamilton operatives in 1836. [2]

The overall residence figures for women only summarize what in fact were two distinct patterns. Native-born and immigrant operatives lived in very different sorts of settings in Lowell in 1860. First, native-born women were much more likely than immigrants to reside in company housing; more than 70 percent did so, compared to less than 30 percent among immigrants. Since company housing consisted primarily of boardinghouses, a much higher proportion of native-born than immigrant—74 percent in contrast to 39 percent—lived in boardinghouses. By contrast, more than twice the proportion of immigrants as native-born—48 as opposed to 23 percent—lived at home with their families.

What is most striking about housing patterns of women workers in 1860 is the variety of available options. The homogeneity of the housing arrangements of women at Hamilton in 1836 had largely disappeared. Among native-born women, almost 66 percent still boarded in company housing, while fully 18 percent lived at home with families in private tenements and another 7 percent resided in private boardinghouses. The growing dispersal of housing is even more evident among immigrants. More than 45 percent of female immigrant millhands resided at home with their families in private tenements, while 28 percent boarded in company housing, and another 24 percent boarded in private households. Table 10.1 summarizes available evidence on residence patterns for women mill workers in Lowell in 1860.

As more women came to live in private housing, they moved outside the compact residential neighborhoods of the early boardinghouses. In 1836 fully three fourths of women employed at Hamilton had resided in four parallel blocks of houses adjacent to the mills. Each boardinghouse held some 25 women who worked and lived together. Even if two operatives did not live in the same household, it was likely that they resided

TABLE 10.1. RESIDENCE PATTERNS OF 1860 FEMALE MILLHANDS
BROKEN DOWN BY ETHNICITY

Type of Residence	Native	Immigrant	Overall[a]
Company, boarding, boarder	65.8%	27.7%	47.8%
Company, boarding, fam. mem.	0.7	0.3	0.5
Company, tenement, boarder	0.2	0.2	0.2
Company, tenement, fam. mem.	4.0	1.4	2.8
Company housing	70.7%	29.6%	51.3%
Private, boarding, boarder	7.2%	9.8%	8.4%
Private, boarding, fam. mem.	0.5	1.4	0.9
Private, tenement, boarder	3.5	14.0	8.4
Private, tenement, fam. mem.	18.0	45.3	30.8
Private housing	29.2%	70.5%	48.5%
Total cases	401	358	759

[a] Sums of columns may not total 100.0% due to rounding.

within a minute's walk of each other. This proximity meant that relationships that developed in the mills could be maintained after working hours.

The growing residential dispersal, however, led to a disjuncture of work and home life for operatives. Some women lived in company boardinghouses, others in private ones, and still others in private tenements. In private boardinghouses, operatives lived with women who worked at other mills or were employed in jobs outside of textiles. Women who lived with their families were even more isolated from the peer group of their fellow operatives. The new residential diversity removed an important element in the shared experience of women workers.

Women workers living at home with their families were particularly cut off from the larger body of female operatives. This separation was in part physical, based on residence in a family, rather than a boardinghouse, setting. In addition, familial emotional and economic ties distanced these women workers from their peer-group community. Mill employment must have served rather different purposes for them than it did for single women workers who supported only themselves. The fuller significance of these new residence patterns becomes apparent as we place female millhands more specifically within their family setting.

More than a third of female millhands in the 1860 census sample—35 percent—lived at home with their families. About four fifths of these operatives were children living with their parents, while the remainder were heads of households, or wives or sisters of household heads (see table 10.2).[3]

TABLE 10.2. RELÀTIONSHIPS OF 1860 FEMALE MILLHANDS LIVING AT HOME TO HOUSEHOLD HEAD, BROKEN DOWN BY ETHNICITY

Relationship	Native-Born	Immigrant	Overall
Household head	2.3%	8.4%	6.3%
Spouse	2.3	9.6	7.1
Child	92.0	74.7	80.6
Sibling	3.4	7.2	5.9
Total cases	87	166	253[a]

[a] Excludes 12 millhands living in single-person households.

There were substantial differences between native-born and immigrant operatives living at home. Almost 10 percent of immigrant millhands at home were married and living with their husbands, whereas only 2 percent of the native-born were of comparable status.[4] Similarly, the proportion of immigrant female millhands heading households was much greater than that for native women in the sample group—almost four times as large. On the other hand, a much larger proportion of native-born than of immigrants—92 in contrast to 75 percent—resided in their parents' homes. Judging from these figures it would be reasonable to conclude that immigrant women working in the Lowell mills were drawn from a wider range of life-cycle statuses than were Yankee women. In all, the proportion of employed nondependents among immigrant millhands living at home was about three times that for Yankees.

Of female millhands living at home, children, comprising four-fifths of the group, merit particular attention. I use the term "children" deliberately. The ages of operatives living with their families were not strikingly low; their mean age was 20, for instance. Still they were younger than women operatives residing in boardinghouses, who were 24 years old on average. More importantly, living in their parents' households, they were more subject to parental discipline and control than co-workers in boardinghouses. This final element, rather than chronological age, leads me to consider them children. There were undoubtedly constraints on the decisions they could make regarding the use of free time and the spending of their earnings—constraints that stemmed from residence with their parents.

The changing residence patterns of women operatives in Lowell over this period lend support to Michael Katz's contention that autonomy declined for adolescents in the nineteenth century.[5] The cause is not so much industrialization, however, as the changing nature of the Lowell labor system. In the 1830s, when the mills relied entirely upon a Yankee work force recruited from the surrounding countryside, mill employment offered young women increased independence and autonomy. Only when large numbers of Yankee and Irish families migrated to Lowell in the 1850s do we find large numbers of working children living at home contributing their earnings to the family till. Even though it is clear that increasing numbers of working women are living with their families in 1860, we should exercise some caution in interpreting the qualitative nature of relations among family members. Autonomy and subordination are best viewed as extremes on a continuum. Wage-earning children probably enjoyed a measure of autonomy, even though they lived under direct parental supervision. Conversely, boardinghouse operatives, though distant from their families, were not totally isolated from their families or immune from demands of the family economy. While the change between the 1830s and the 1850s is dramatic, the contrast in the family relations of women workers should not be posed too starkly.

If the broader meaning of family residence remains somewhat uncertain, the basic outlines of residence patterns are clear. Immigrant millhands were much more likely to be living at home with their parents than were the native-born. Although immigrants comprised less than half of the entire sample of female millhands—358 of 759, or about 46 percent—they made up a much larger proportion of sample members living at home with their parents. About 61 percent of millhand children living at home were foreign-born. Even this figure somewhat understates the immigrant component, as half of the native-born were in fact the children of immigrants (see table 10.3).

Although more than 39 percent of female millhand daughters were native-born, only half of the heads of their households were also. Mill-

TABLE 10.3. NATIVITY OF 1860 FEMALE MILLHANDS LIVING AT HOME
WITH PARENTS AND OF THE PARENT HOUSEHOLD HEADS

Nativity	Female Millhands	Parent Household Heads
United States	39.2%	19.6%
Ireland	51.0	70.1
Great Britain	6.4	7.4
Canada	3.4	2.9
Total cases	204	204

hand children thus consisted of three distinct groups: the largest, almost
61 percent, being first-generation immigrants, primarily Irish; the second, 19.6 percent, consisting of second-generation children of immigrants, again largely Irish in extraction; and finally, a third contingent,
19.6 percent, comprised of native-born daughters of native-born parents.

The most striking fact about the households with daughters in the
mills is that about half—101 of 204—were headed by women. Female-
headed households were almost invariably single-parent households,
while male-headed ones usually included two parents. The proportion of
female-headed households was the same among native-born and immigrants, suggesting that class, rather than ethnicity, was primarily responsible for the observed family patterns.

A number of factors may account for the high proportion of families
headed by women. First, it is possible that widows moved to Lowell to
take advantage of a labor system that offered employment primarily to
women and children. Certainly in the 1830s numerous widows came to
Lowell with their children to manage company boardinghouses. Daniel
Walkowitz found a similar pattern in Cohoes, New York, where in 1880,
26 per cent of Irish mill families were female-headed. The large proportion of female household heads over 40 led Walkowitz to suggest that
the inmigration of widows with their families may have been responsible for this pattern.[6] Or perhaps, as Handlin has pointed out for Boston's Irish, large numbers of fathers in millhand families may have been
working on construction projects that took them out of Lowell for extended periods in the summer.[7] Finally, a labor system offering steadier
employment to women and children than to men may well have undermined the economic position and authority of males in working-class
families, thus leading to high rates of desertion. Although not addressing

the question of desertion directly, Dubnoff argues that the power and authority of male Irish household heads in Lowell were undermined by the structure of economic opportunities. He stresses, in particular, the contrast between conditions obtaining in Lowell and those likely to have prevailed in Ireland before the famine migration.[8] Whatever the specific causes, the pattern is evident, for the proportion of female-headed households among Irish mill families in Lowell was far higher than similar figures reported for Irish in other communities in this period.[9] Only by tracing families over time through the manuscript census—a procedure not attempted here—might it be possible to determine which of these factors proved most important.

Whether female- or male-headed, the families of female millhands were dependent on the employment of several family members for their subsistence. In these mill families—all with at least one employed daughter—more than 72 percent of all family members had occupations recorded by census enumerators in 1860. There were few young children and few elderly in the families. Children tended to be in their teens and twenties, with parents in the thirties and forties. That the employment of children was viewed as a necessity is evident from family occupational patterns. The employment of children varied inversely with the earnings of parents. In female-headed households, more than 80 percent of children worked, while in male-headed ones, the comparable proportion was only 67 percent. Despite this difference, both groups of families relied heavily on the earnings of children.

An examination of the composition of these households and families underscores the extent of family dependence on the earnings of children. Excluding those families residing in boardinghouses—only 9 in number—leaves 195 tenement families with at least one daughter employed in the mills.[10] Table 10.4 presents data on the household and family composition of these families.

Children in these families were well integrated into the Lowell labor system. Three fourths of the children worked, 91 percent of them in the mills, while only 24 percent attended school. In a majority of the families, no children reported school attendance during the year. Furthermore, there were few children of preschool age. The ages of children clustered in the teens and twenties. The median age of the oldest child in these families was about 21; of the youngest child employed in the mills,

TABLE 10.4. STATISTICS ON FAMILIES AND HOUSEHOLDS OF 1860 FEMALE
MILLHANDS LIVING WITH PARENTS IN PRIVATE TENEMENTS

Variable[a]	Mean
Number in household	6.2
Number in family	5.6
Number of children in family	3.9
Number in family working	4.1
Number of children working	3.0
Number of children working in mills	2.7
Number of children in school	0.9
Number of households	195

[a] For a fuller discussion of the definition of each variable and of assumptions in
the analysis, see appendix 4.

16. These statistics suggest that the mills relied on families at a particular
point in the family cycle—on families with children concentrated in their
late teens and early twenties. The corporations benefited from a healthy
supply of workers, while the families were able to combine the earnings
of several wage earners.[11]

Employed children in these families were secondary wage earners in
the sense that most were not sole, or even primary, breadwinners. Yet
their wages were of crucial importance to their families' living standards.[12] Two factors point to this conclusion: the ages of working children and the occupations of parents. From the ages of working children—clustered between 16 and 22—one can reasonably infer that most
held regular adult jobs in the mills. Only twelve percent were under 15
and thus likely to have held low-paid jobs as doffers, lap boys, or back or
front boys in mule spinning. Most employed children probably earned
wages comparable to the $3.40 per week paid to adult women operatives
at the Hamilton Company in June 1860.

The parents of these millhands, moreover, worked in low-paying, un-
steady occupations outside of the mills. Only 20 percent of male and 16
percent of female household heads worked in textiles. The majority of
male heads were employed as day laborers; 80 percent of female heads
were recorded as housekeepers. The best recent estimates of the wages
of unskilled outdoor laborers in Massachusetts suggest that average daily wages amounted to about $1.00 at this time.[13] The Massachusetts

Bureau of Statistics of Labor reported in 1873 that laborers typically worked about 250 days per year. [14] If this figure also holds for the earlier date, unskilled laborers probably earned about $250 annually in 1860. [15] Given an average of 3 employed children in these families, and our knowledge of their ages and typical earnings, a reasonable estimate for the combined children's annual earnings would be $470, or about 65 percent of family income. [16]

This figure represents the minimum contribution of children to the family income because fully half of mill families were female-headed. A mother working in the mills earned about the same wages as her children and considerably less than an unskilled male laborer. Housekeepers undoubtedly earned still less, and in many cases probably were not actually earning wages but simply keeping their own homes. Children's earnings must have amounted to more than 80 percent of family income in female-headed households. Millhand daughters in 1860 clearly had a far different role in the family economy than Yankee women had had two or three decades earlier. Mill families needed the earnings of their daughters for immediate subsistence as most of the farming families of earlier Yankee operatives had not.

The dependence of mill families on the earnings of their children varied across the family life cycle. Examination of the employment patterns of families according to the age of their oldest child (see table 10.5) provides interesting data on this score.

Over the family cycle two sorts of changes led to an increase in chil-

TABLE   10.5. CHILDREN'S   SCHOOL   AND   EMPLOYMENT   PATTERNS   IN FAMILIES OF 1860 MILLHAND DAUGHTERS

	Age of Oldest Child Living at Home		
Variable	14–17	18–22	23+
Number of children	3.70	3.81	4.34
Children employed	1.80	2.81	3.67
Children in school[a]	1.93	1.07	0.64
Mean age, oldest child	16.0	20.2	26.4
Mean age, youngest in mills	14.4	16.1	18.8
Number of families	30	75	92

[a] The sum of children employed and in school may exceed the number of children as some children both worked and attended school within the year.

dren's contributions to family income. First, more children came of age to work in the mills, and second, those working in the mills became older, and thus were more likely to bring in adult wages for their work. Families in which the oldest child living at home was between 14 and 17 years old had on average only 3.70 children, about half of whom were employed. As the age of the oldest child increased, the number and proportion of employed children increased, until for families with the oldest over 22 years of age, there were on average 4.34 children living at home with more than 80 percent of them working. [17]

For each of these groups of families one can estimate the children's contribution to family income. Assuming that children under 15 earned on average $2.00 per week—i.e., children's wages as doffers or back or front boys—and that older children earned regular adult wages of $3.40 weekly, one can estimate likely annual earnings for children in each group. To set a lower limit on the children's contribution, I assume that all the families were male-headed and that all fathers worked as day laborers. These last assumptions undoubtedly overstate parents' earnings, but are useful in establishing a base line for children's contributions. For families with the oldest child 14-17 years of age, I estimate that children earned on average $260 out of a family income of $510, or almost 51 percent. This figure climbs steadily as the age of the oldest child increases, until for families with the oldest child over 22, children would be expected to earn $606 out of $856, or 71 percent of family income. [18]

If, on average, millhand children earned about 65 percent of family income, the proportion was considerably higher in female-headed households. Children's contributions ranging from 67 to 83 percent, depending on children's ages, were likely in these households, figures reflecting the restricted earning power of adult women compared to men in Lowell. [19]

This analysis is based on the important assumption that children did in fact turn over their wages to their parents. Payroll records and operatives' letters strongly support this assumption. Hamilton payroll records for 1850 and 1860 provide repeated instances in which fathers signed for and probably picked up their children's pay envelopes. These children, then, did not even receive their wages, which went directly into the family till.

While surviving Lowell letters reveal little on this point, the correspondence of operatives in other mill towns indicates that parents thought of their children's earnings as part of family income. In the spring of 1843, after 6 years of depression, Jemima Sanborn moved to Nashua, New Hampshire. In an unusually detailed letter she described her motivation and the strategy she had adopted to help make ends meet:

> You will probely want to know the cause of our moveing here which are many. I will menshion afew of them. One of them is the hard times to get a liveing off the farm for so large a famely. So we have devided our famely for the year. We have left Plummer and Luther to care for the farm with granmarm and Aunt Polly. The rest of us have moved to Nashvill [a part of Nashua] thinking the girls and Charles they would probely worke in the Mill. But we have had bad luck in giting them in. Only Jane has got in yet. Ann has the promis of going to the mill next week. Hannah is going to school. We are in hopes to take a few borders but have not got any yet. [20]

Here, then, is an example of a Yankee mother moving to a mill town with three daughters and a son for the expressed purpose of improving the *family* economic situation. Jemima Sanborn expected to send her children into the mills and hoped to find boarders to bring in additional income. The children's wages were clearly an integral part of her economic thinking. It does not appear that she ever considered working in the mills herself.

The family economic planning evident in the Sanborn move was a logical response to economic depression. Mill towns also proved attractive in periods of prosperity. In 1847 Gardner Plimpton moved with his family to Whitinsville, Massachusetts. He wrote home and tried to persuade a friend in Fayettesville, Vermont, to bring his whole family and give the mill a chance. "I do no[t] know how you are situated," he wrote, "but I think you can live here eas[i]er and make more money here then up thare." His enthusiasm mounted as he listed his new opportunities:

> You take some Borders, the children work in the mill, you can have steady work all the time and good wages if you are all well. You[r] incum will at least bee six hundred Dollars a year. . . . I wish you to come down this winter and see me and look around an see if it is not best. Fore it is hard bisness for a poor man up thare.

He went on to describe the labors of his children—or rather their earnings:

> The girls like working in the mill vary well. They have two Dollars a week apiece. James have one fifty a week. Webarwe [?] has worked some; he will have the same as James after school is done. So you see my children earn something. The children have earnt about one hundred and thirty Dollars.

Gardner Plimpton was sold on the family labor system. As he noted in his letter, "I would not go back to vermont and live as I did the last two or three years." [21]

If the family labor system seemed particularly well suited to the needs of parents, children were not always so satisfied with its operation. For the additions to family income made possible by the employment of children could also be viewed as so much lost income by the children themselves. Joseph Hollingworth, an English-born operative in a woolen mill in South Leicester, Massachusetts, expressed this complaint in a letter to relatives. His letter, written in 1829, began dramatically enough: "I write this letter INCOGNITO, I therfore desire you to keep it to your selves. I shall state a few of my grieveances in a brief manner." His principal complaint concerned his wages:

> Last winter, I had to work a good deal of overtime at Nights; had I refused the whole Family might have lost their work; so I calculated to have the overtime wages for myself. It amounted to nearly five Dollars. I have succeeded in getting 2 dolrs ONLY! which is all the pocket money I have had in this country!

At the time Joseph Hollingworth had lived in this country about a year and a half. He had been working almost continuously and was earning more than $15 a month. Yet out of these earnings he had secured only two dollars for himself. And his complaint was not that he was denied his wages, but that he had not been allowed to keep his overtime earnings—a mere five dollars out of a much larger income. Interestingly, Joseph was unwilling to confront his father directly on this score but wrote instead to an aunt and uncle. He carefully instructed them— pleaded with them—to write his father and suggest that he permit Joseph to go to Poughkeepsie to work. He wanted to get out from under his father's domination but was unable to confront parental authority directly. [22]

The picture of the family labor system that emerges from both the census data and operatives' letters is one in which family members function as a unit to provide for family needs, as defined by parents. Children were the crucial supplementary wage earners in working-class families. Where married women worked, there were generally no or few children in the family.[23] As soon as the first child reached the early teens, his or her contribution to the family economy began. Thereafter, the earnings of children increased steadily relative to overall family income until, at their height, children's earnings accounted for more than 70 percent of all family income. The low wages and irregularity of work for adult males made the earnings of children crucial to the standard of living of Lowell's mill families.

Just as the surviving letters of operatives in the family system in the mills can be read from the perspective of either the parents or the children, so too the census sample data can be interpreted in various ways. The discussion thus far has focused on the family as an economic unit and on the role of children in providing for the family subsistence. The census also permits us, however, to consider the place of mill employment in the individual life course.[24] Moving from the familial to the individual perspective, we may ask at what age did boys and girls first begin working in the mills? To what extent did they continue to attend school while working? How long did they tend to remain at home contributing to the support of parents and siblings? By placing mill work within the context of the individual life course, we can better appreciate the role of mill employment in the lives of children growing up within the shadow of the mills.

The limitations of Lowell censuses dictate the use of a snapshot, cross-sectional view of the life cycle. In the best of all possible worlds, one would want to examine life patterns by tracing individuals over time through successive census enumerations. Only in this manner could one provide a truly dynamic view of aging. As indicated earlier, however, not until 1860 did the manuscript census record the occupations of females, a crucial dimension of data for a textile mill town. Neither the 1850 federal manuscript census nor the 1855 state census provides such information. In addition, the closing of the mills during the Civil War marks a discontinuity that limits the possibility of tracing 1860 mill operatives in later years. Thus it has not been feasible to follow individuals over time. Rather, the approach used here depends on cross-sectional data from the 1860 census. By analyzing the work and school experiences of different age groups of children in the families of female millhands, it is possible to depict the experience of individuals over time. Given the limitations of the sources, this method provides the closest possible approach to a longitudinal analysis. [25]

School had a limited place in the lives of children growing up in mill families in Lowell. Between the ages of 6 and 9 a large proportion--about 84 percent of both boys and girls—attended school but thereafter attendance dropped off rapidly. Girls, in particular, exchanged work for school at an early age; by 13, more than half of the girls in millhand families worked in the mills. Not until the age of 15 did a majority of boys work in the mills. Tables 10.6 and 10.7 provide data on the employment and school attendance of children in the families of female millhands. [26]

Boys and girls differed in the ages at which they typically left school and began work. The vast majority of boys in the 10-13 year old age group remained in school and did not work, in contrast to girls of the same age. About 74 percent of boys of this age attended school and did not work, compared to only 52 percent among girls. Conversely, almost 42 percent of girls worked, while only 13 percent of boys of this age did so. Between 14 and 17 the gap in employment rates between boys and girls narrowed until by age 18 the work patterns of the two groups were roughly the same. [27]

The school and work patterns suggest that working-class families sent daughters into the mills as soon as possible. The patterns here are particularly striking because the mills actually offered less work for girls than

TABLE 10.6. SCHOOL ATTENDANCE AND EMPLOYMENT PATTERNS OF
MALE CHILDREN IN THE FAMILIES OF FEMALE MILLHANDS, 1860

School/Work Status	Age Group (years)				
	6–9	10–13	14–17	18–22	23+
Neither	16.2%	13.1%	7.6%	3.6%	2.8%
School only	83.8	73.8	12.1	1.8	0
School and work	0	8.2	7.6	1.8	0
Work only	0	4.9	72.7	92.9	97.2
Total cases	37	61	66	56	36

TABLE 10.7. SCHOOL ATTENDANCE AND EMPLOYMENT PATTERNS OF
FEMALE CHILDREN IN THE FAMILIES OF FEMALE MILLHANDS, 1860

School/Work Status	Age Group (years)				
	6–9	10–13	14–17	18–22	23+
Neither	13.2%	6.0%	1.4%	1.6%	0.9%
School only	84.2	52.2	5.7	0.5	0
School and work	0	19.4	10.6	1.0	0
Work only	2.6	22.4	82.3	96.9	99.1
Total cases	38	67	141	191	117

boys. The proportion of females under 15 employed at Hamilton, it will
be recalled, was only 3 percent in 1860, compared to the figure of 15
percent for males. Two jobs of increasing importance, back and front
boys in mule spinning, were both exclusively male jobs, while boys and
girls shared positions as doffers in throstle spinning.

Why did parents send their daughters into the mills so soon, while
keeping their sons in school? They probably expected their daughters
would marry and sought to maximize their earnings in the meantime. In
contrast, they may have been willing to keep boys in school somewhat
longer because they took a longer-range view of male careers. Although
we are sorely lacking in documentation on this point, we may speculate
that parents accepted reformers' claims that education paid economic
returns and hoped that greater education might eventually help their
sons acquire better-paid employment outside the mills.

Boys began work later than girls and tended to move into nonmill
occupations while girls remained concentrated almost entirely in textiles.
Boys between 14 and 17 were most likely to be working in the mills. In
that age group more than 68 percent of boys in mill families did so.
Among older male children, however, while the proportion working increased, the proportion employed in the mills declined. For the 18-22
year old group, more than 40 percent of employed males worked in
nonmill occupations. For sons over 23 and still living at home, this proportion increased to 60 percent. For daughters, in contrast, the proportion of the employed working in the mills held steady at more than 90
percent in all age groups over 13. The data suggest that boys found their
first jobs in the mills but as soon as possible switched into occupations

which offered greater long-range opportunity than dead-end mill jobs. For girls, however, the only alternatives to work in the mills appear to have been marriage and motherhood.

The stark picture sketched out thus far for girls in mill families in their teenage years did not apply equally to native-born and immigrants in Lowell. Daughters in native mill families, for instance, were much more likely to attend school than were daughters of immigrants. More than 42 percent of native daughters between the ages of 10 and 17 attended school and did not work, compared to only 17 percent of daughters in immigrant families. In native families daughters were more likely to attend school than sons, just the reverse of the situation in immigrant families. In addition, daughters in native families were not so tied to mill employment as their immigrant counterparts. More than 18 percent of native females over 13 years old and living at home worked in nonmill occupations, compared to only 3.5 percent among daughters of immigrants in this age group.[28] Evidence from this sample suggests that girls in native mill families had greater opportunities to attend school and to work in better-paying jobs outside the mills than the daughters of immigrants. The lower income of immigrant males probably resulted in a greater pressure on girls to make immediate contributions to family income. This pressure led girls to quit school sooner and their lesser education may well have confined them to the unskilled and low-paid jobs within the mills.

Patterns of growing up for boys differed from those for girls in still another respect. Boys left their parents' homes at a much earlier age than did girls. The earlier departures of boys led to a growing surplus of girls in mill families, a fact evident in the changing proportions of males and females in the various age groups of children shown in table 10.8.

TABLE 10.8. PROPORTIONS OF MALES AND FEMALES AMONG CHILDREN IN THE FAMILIES OF 1860 FEMALE MILLHANDS, BROKEN DOWN BY AGE

| Age Group | Proportions | | N |
	Male	Female	
9 and under	44.3%	55.7%	150
10–13	47.7	52.3	128
14–17	31.9	68.1	207
18–22	22.7	77.3	247
23 and over	23.5	76.5	153

This distribution of children in mill families suggests that boys were leaving home to support themselves before girls. [29]

Alternative interpretations do not seem very plausible. Earlier marriage for males than females cannot explain their earlier departures from home, for all the evidence suggests that males married at a later age than females. [30] Differential mortality undoubtedly affected the age distribution of males and females over 50, but was unlikely to have had any significant impact on young people in their teens and twenties. One might also postulate that families with large numbers of daughters moved to Lowell to take advantage of the mill labor market. If this were true, however, one would expect to find females outnumbering males throughout all age groups among children in mill families, and the evidence suggests that this was not so. Children under 13 were relatively evenly divided between boys and girls. The steady decline in the proportion of males among those 14 and over must have been due to the different rates at which boys and girls left the home. What probably happened, although single snapshot data from one census do not prove it, was that large numbers of boys were leaving their homes and taking up residence in boardinghouses in Lowell or were leaving to work for a period of time in other cities. [31] Whatever the explanation, it is clear that daughters were much more integrated into the family economy than sons. They left school before boys; they began work sooner and remained in mill occupations more steadily; finally, they continued to live at home with their parents considerably longer than did their brothers.

This view of the family labor system in Lowell in 1860 suggests a transformation of the relationship of women's work to the family economy between the 1830s and 1860. In 1860 girls went to work at much earlier ages than they had earlier. Fully half of daughters living in the families of female millhands were working in the mills by the age of 13, whereas 19 had been the median age at which Boscawen, Canterbury, and Sutton daughters had begun employment at Hamilton in the earlier period. This age shift reflected in large measure the different place that children's employment had in the two family economies—that of Yankee families in the New England countryside in the 1830s and that of immigrant mill families in Lowell two decades later. Yankee women in the earlier period had been motivated, as has been shown, largely by the possibilities of individual economic gain. Certainly their employment did free families of the obligation to feed them and perhaps to provide them with a dowry. This gain, however, represented more a reduction of demands placed on the family economy than a positive contribution. On the whole, the evidence suggests that Yankee women kept their own earnings and spent them as they pleased. Certainly Mary Paul (and there must have been others like her) felt the pull of familial obligation, but for the most part her earnings went for self-support. By contrast, immigrant (and native-born) millhand daughters in 1860 played a much more crucial role providing for their families' immediate subsistence. Children's earnings provided a minimum of 65 percent of income in the families of millhand daughters. Daughters began working at 13 or so, and all the evidence suggests that they kept on working well into their twenties. On average, they contributed to the support of their families for a good ten years before marrying and starting families of their own. Economic necessity coupled with a different conception of familial duty, rather than visions of individual economic gain or social independence, motivated millhands within the new family labor system. The new motivations of women workers in Lowell in 1860 flowed from the new economic needs of mill families and in turn must have shaped new expectations on women's part. The new needs and expectations of operatives were particularly evident in the changing career patterns of women workers in the 1850s, a topic to which we now turn.

CHAPTER ELEVEN

Careers of Operatives, 1836-1860

DOROTHY AND MARY TILTON lived together in Number 7 Hamilton in the summer of 1850 and worked in the Hamilton Company's mills. Mary, 24, worked as a warper; Dorothy, 23, was employed in Weaving Room B. Both from Epping, New Hampshire, and probably sisters, the Tiltons between them worked at Hamilton for more than two decades. Mary started in Spinning Room A in April 1836, and in July she earned $0.58 a day as a warp spinner. Fourteen years later her earnings had inched up to $0.62 a day. Dorothy began work at Hamilton as a weaver in May 1846, at the age of 19, and over the next four years her earnings rose from $0.58 to $0.75 per day. A decade later she had become a dresser. Thirty-three years old by then, still unmarried and residing in the same company boardinghouse, Dorothy now earned about $0.80 a day, a wage that placed her at the very top of the female occupational structure in the mills.[1]

The longevity of the Tiltons' employment at the Hamilton Company sets them apart somewhat from the majority of women workers in the early mills. Nevertheless, their experience raises interesting questions. Now that we have analyzed the proletarianization of the female work force at Hamilton and the growth of a family labor system by 1860, it is appropriate to examine the impact of these developments on patterns of careers for women workers. What was the nature of these patterns and how, if at all, did they change over the course of time?

Contemporary observers were interested in these questions and attempted to collect data concerning them.[2] Time and again, supporters of the Waltham-Lowell system argued that the noteworthy feature of the mills was the fact that they were not dependent on a permanent factory population as was the case in England. Indeed, the high level of turnover in the work force was often praised as a safeguard against the degradation of operatives thought to be a consequence of the English factory system.[3] The extensive payroll and register records of the Hamilton Company offer the possibility of verifying these claims, and also of carrying the study of operatives' careers to a level far beyond that of the contemporary debate. At first, cross-sectional evidence drawn from Hamilton payroll records for July 1836 provides a basis for examining women's careers; later, the tracing of individuals' careers over time will reinforce the initial findings.

Operatives in the early mills had, as observers noted, very brief careers in the mills. In Mill A of the Hamilton Company in 1836, for instance, male workers had been employed on average only 2.17 years; for females, the comparable figure was only 1.75 years. Table 11.1 presents grouped data on the previous work experience of men and women employed at Hamilton during the payroll period including July 1836.[4] Fully half of the Mill A work force had been working less than a year at the company prior to July 1836, while only 7.5 percent—20 out of 266— had been working six years or more.[5]

Although the lengths of men and women's careers at Hamilton were similar, the work patterns of the two groups were markedly different. Men tended to work continuously at Hamilton, while women frequently took breaks, returning for rests in their rural homes. Mary Hall, of Con-

TABLE 11.1. PREVIOUS WORK EXPERIENCE OF HAMILTON MILL
A SAMPLE, JULY 1836

Years at Company	Males	Females
0.00–0.99	45.5%	56.2%
1.00–2.99	21.2	21.0
3.00–5.99	27.3	15.0
6.00+	6.1	7.7
Total cases	33	233
Missing cases	1	4

cord, New Hampshire, was probably typical in this respect. Between 1831 and 1837 she worked on and off at the Lawrence and Tremont companies, for periods of 7, 4, 10, and 12 months, alternating with visits to her family in Concord.[6] Women who worked at Hamilton in July 1836 averaged fourteen months between entrance and departure from the work force. Men, in contrast, worked steadily for more than three and a half years on average.[7]

Although few men or women had lengthy careers at the Hamilton Company in the mid-1830s, those who stayed in the mills for several years enjoyed significant gains in wages. Earnings increased steadily with work experience, as indicated in table 11.2.

TABLE 11.2. MEAN DAILY PAY OF HAMILTON MILL A SAMPLE, JULY 1836, BROKEN DOWN BY SEX AND BY PREVIOUS WORK

Previous Work	Mean Daily Pay	
(in years)	Males	Females
0.00–0.99	$0.69 (15)	$0.53 (131)
1.00–2.99	0.94 (7)	0.62 (49)
3.00–5.99	1.39 (9)	0.69 (35)
6.00+	2.08 (2)	0.74 (18)
Total cases	33	233
Missing cases	1	4

For both men and women, mean daily pay increased in proportion to the length of employment at the company. However, the differential between the pay of experienced workers and newcomers was much greater for men than women. The most experienced men earned 200 percent more than male newcomers, while for women the comparable differential was only 40 percent.[8] The wider range in male earnings resulted from the fact that only men could move into supervisory positions. The exclusion of overseers and second hands would narrow the range of male earnings to a point comparable to that of women.

The range of female earnings—from $0.53 per day for beginners to $0.74 per day for experienced hands—reflected the existence of a graded series of jobs into which women were placed according to experience. At the bottom of the job ladder were sparehands, women who spelled regular operatives in various departments and who served something akin to an apprenticeship while they learned the necessary skills. Among regular workers, carding and spinning room operatives occupied the bottom rungs of the job ladder, while weavers and dressing room hands stood at the top.[9] The existence of this job ladder offered women the prospect of occupational mobility and an accompanying increase in wages over the course of their careers. This mobility was real, as evidenced by the fact that at Hamilton in 1836 women in the lowest-paying jobs were invariably less experienced than those employed in the highest-paying positions. Table 11.3 presents data on the work experience and earnings of women operatives according to the jobs they held.

TABLE 11.3. MAJOR JOBS OF FEMALES IN THE HAMILTON MILL
A SAMPLE, JULY 1836, BROKEN DOWN BY PREVIOUS WORK

Job	Mean Daily Pay[a]	Previous Work (in years)				
		0.00–0.99	1.00–2.99	3.00–3.99	6.00+	Totals
Sparehands	0.44	41	6	0	2	49
Drawing	0.52	10	7	0	0	17
Spinning	0.58	20	7	6	1	34
Weaving	0.66	44	18	19	8	89
Dressing[b]	0.73	8	6	3	4	21
Total cases[c]		123	44	28	15	210

[a] Figures are drawn from table 4.2 above and are based on all women workers at Hamilton.
[b] Includes dressers, warpers, and drawing in hands.
[c] Excludes females in minor jobs with too few individuals for comparison.

The contrasting levels of experience of women employed in various occupations are evident. More than 80 percent of sparehands—41 of 49—had been employed less than a year. Among the low-paid drawers and spinners, almost 60 percent had been employed a year or less, while for the high-paid dressing room hands, only 38 percent had been working for so short a time. At the other end of the experience spectrum, only 1 operative out of 51—less than 2 percent—employed in drawing and spinning had been working 6 or more years at Hamilton; among dressing room hands, this proportion reached 19 percent.

Job transfer provided the mechanism that enabled women workers to improve their earnings over the course of their careers. Harriet Hanson

Robinson and Lucy Larcom, two operatives who have left reminiscences describing their years in the mills, experienced such promotions over the courses of their careers. Harriet Hanson began work in the Lawrence mills at 10 as a bobbin girl, soon moved up to become a spinner and, when she finally left the Boott Corporation to be married in 1848, received an honorable discharge from the dressing room. Similarly, Lucy Larcom moved up the job ladder from bobbin girl to spinner to warper in the dressing room. She found the latter too taxing, however, and transferred to the cloth room, another haven for experienced operatives. [10]

Analysis of the careers of workers who persisted at the Hamilton Company between 1836 and 1850 reinforces the picture of occupational mobility and wage improvement evident in the cross-sectional picture for July 1836. Between July 1836 and August 1850, 46 workers persisted in the Hamilton work force. [11] On the whole, men were overrepresented among persistent workers. About 17 percent of male workers—24 of 148—remained over the fourteen-year period, compared to only 2.5 percent of females—22 of 882. Both men and women, however, advanced to better-paying jobs over the course of their lengthy careers (see tables 11.4 and 11.5).

TABLE 11.4. JOB MOBILITY OF PERSISTENT MEN AT HAMILTON, 1836–1850

Job Category	1836	1850
Operative	10	3
Repair shop	3	4
Second hand	3	5
Overseer	8	12
Overall	24	24

TABLE 11.5. JOB MOBILITY OF PERSISTENT WOMEN AT HAMILTON, 1836–1850

Job Category	1836	1850
Carding	2	1
Spinning	3	1
Weaving	8	4
Dressing	6	14
Other	3	2
Overall	22	22

Career male workers moved into supervisory positions in the mills over these years. In 1836 10 of the 24 men in the group had been operatives; this number had declined to only 3 by 1850. In turn, the number of overseers increased from 8 to 12, while that of second hands went from 3 to 5. In 1836 less than half of the male persistent group had been in supervisory positions; by 1850, the proportion reached 70 percent.[12]

The main avenue of advancement for women was promotion into the dressing department. In 1836 only 6 of the 22 persistent women worked in dressing, but by 1850 that number had reached 14. At every other job level there was a decline in the number of persistent women over the period. In particular, the number in the low-paying carding and spinning departments decreased from 5 to 2, while weavers dropped from 8 to 4. With this movement up the job ladder, the average daily earnings of persistent women increased from 63.5 cents in 1836 to 72.0 cents in 1850. These gains are particularly significant because the mean earnings of all female operatives at Hamilton declined slightly in the same period.

Career female workers were undoubtedly self-supporting. Their earnings for the most part do not appear to have gone to parents. Fully two thirds lived in company boardinghouses and were probably unmarried. Their weekly earnings increased from $3.81 to $4.32, a gain of about 13 percent, while the cost of room and board in company boardinghouses rose 10 percent, from $1.25 to $1.375 per week.[13] Although living expenses were undoubtedly larger than this figure, the women were able to save considerable sums. Almost half of the women—10 of 22—had savings accounts at the Lowell Institution for Savings, and the mean maximum balance of these accounts reached a respectable $153—fully 40 weeks of wages at current rates.[14] In purely economic terms, career women workers did well in the early mills.

The proletarianization of the female work force and the evolution of the family economy led to a significant transformation of the career patterns of women workers in the 1850s. In this decade women had longer careers at Hamilton, but over the course of their lengthened employment they neither changed jobs so often nor improved their earnings so much as persistent women earlier. These changes in career patterns clearly reflect the deteriorating position of women in the Lowell mills between 1836 and 1860.

Operatives working at Hamilton in June 1860 were considerably more experienced than their counterparts in 1836. As table 11.6 indicates, workers in 1860 had been employed at Hamilton about twice as long as in 1836. For men the increase amounted to almost 130 percent; for women, a slightly less dramatic 80 percent.

The differences in means were also reflected in the overall frequency distributions. While more than half of the work force in 1836 had been employed less than a year, by 1860 this proportion had declined to only one third. The proportion working 6 years or more increased correspondingly, from 7.5 to 19 percent.

TABLE 11.6. EXPERIENCE OF HAMILTON OPERATIVES, 1836 AND 1860, BROKEN DOWN BY SEX

	Mean Years at Company	
	1836	1860
Males	2.2 (33)	5.0 (55)
Females	1.8 (233)	3.2 (207)
Overall	1.8 (266)	3.6 (262)
Missing data	5	17

NOTE: Hamilton Mill A sample for July 1836 and Mill AB sample for June 1860. For details see appendixes 1 and 3.

The increasing permanence of the work force was not simply a reflection of the influx of immigrant operatives after 1845. Yankee workers—men and women alike—had longer careers in this period than did immigrant newcomers. In fact the inclusion of immigrants in the 1860 sample masks somewhat the lengthening of the careers of native-born workers. Between 1836 and 1860 the previous work experience of native-born men at Hamilton increased from 2.2 to 6.9 years; for women the parallel increase was from 1.8 to 3.7 years. Evidently a more permanent mill work force emerged quite independently of the coming of the Irish.

Although the influx of immigrants did not contribute to the lengthening of operatives' careers at Hamilton, in one way it did reduce turnover from the high levels of earlier years. The mean length of work stints of operatives rose steadily, with immigrants slightly more likely to work continuously in the mills than the native-born. The mean length of work stints increased from 1.4 years in 1836 to 2.5 years in 1860.[15] The overall figures, however, mask significant variations among subgroups within the work force. The most persistent workers, native-born men, averaged almost six years on each work stint. This group clearly approached the stability of what might be called career operatives. Well below them were immigrant men and women, working an average of 2.5 to 3.0 years on a stint. Finally, the least permanent members of the work force in 1860 were native-born women. The length of their work stints had increased only marginally since 1836, averaging 1.5 years compared to 1.2 earlier, suggesting that many continued to move back and forth between work in the mills and vacation in their rural homes. Given the dramatic changes in the mills in these years, the continuance of this earlier pattern is particularly striking.

Even though Hamilton workers came to remain in the mills for longer periods than earlier, they no longer enjoyed the increases in wages over the course of their careers that had prevailed in the 1830s and 1840s. The large differentials between the earnings of experienced workers and newcomers declined substantially, as is clear in table 11.7 (see also graph 1). The overall wage spread for male operatives declined from 200 percent in 1836 to 105 percent by 1860; for women the differential declined from 40 to 16 percent. The decrease in the mean earnings of experienced operatives led to this narrowing of the wage spread among women workers. In 1836 experienced women operatives—those with six or more years of employment at Hamilton—had earned an average of $0.74 per day; their counterparts in 1860 made only $0.61 daily.

The changing wage prospects of women workers can also be seen in graph 1. In 1836 (the solid line in the graph) women's wages rose steadily

TABLE 11.7. MEAN DAILY PAY OF THE HAMILTON MILL AB SAMPLE, JUNE 1860, BROKEN DOWN BY SEX AND BY PREVIOUS WORK

Previous Work	Mean Daily Pay	
(in years)	Males	Females
0.00–0.99	$0.58 (16)	$0.53 (74)
1.00–2.99	0.86 (8)	0.58 (47)
3.00–5.99	0.93 (11)	0.62 (56)
6.00+	1.29 (20)	0.61 (30)
Total cases	55	207
Missing cases	4	13

GRAPH 1. MEAN DAILY PAY BY EXPERIENCE, 1836 AND 1860, FOR WOMEN
WORKERS AT THE HAMILTON COMPANY

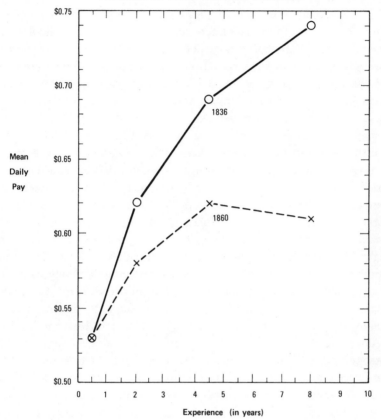

with increasing experience at Hamilton. Beginning with $0.53 per day
for relative newcomers, this figure increased to $0.74 for operatives with
six or more years of experience. In 1860, however (the dotted line), wom-
en's earnings reached their peak after only three years of employment
and even declined for more experienced women workers thereafter.
While newcomers in both 1836 and 1860 averaged $0.53 per day, the gap
in the wage profiles for the two years increased steadily with experience.
The growing distance between the two lines on graph 1 provides clear
evidence of the declining wage prospects for women workers over the
course of their careers at Hamilton. More women were working for ex-

tended periods of time, but the relative rewards of their employment were declining.

This development is further indication of the proletarianization of the female work force in the Hamilton mills. Just as the 1850s saw the narrowing of the differential in wages between native-born and immigrant, the evidence here reveals a reduction in the wage spread between newcomers and experienced operatives. The female wage hierarchy at Hamilton was compressed considerably, and the earnings gap between different groups of workers narrowed over the period. This homogenization of women's wage rates set a new lower limit on the wage gains of women over the course of their careers. One of the consequences of the declining wages of workers in the dressing and weaving departments described earlier was the lowering of the ceiling on female wages so evident here. Weavers and dressers were traditionally the most experienced women workers at Hamilton. Wage reductions for these groups consequently limited the future wage prospects for less experienced workers, who might have expected to move into these occupations as they remained at Hamilton. Opportunity for wage advancement had definitely narrowed as immigrants came to predominate in the mill work force. While this development paralleled the movement of immigrants into the mills, it obviously affected the opportunities available to both Irish and Yankee.

Along with the compression of women's wage scales, we see a growing homogenization of female occupations in the mill. In 1836 female jobs had been organized on a clearly defined job ladder. Newcomers had tended to enter jobs in the carding and spinning departments and to move into weaving and dressing with increased experience. By 1860, however, beginners were more evenly distributed among all women's jobs. Increasingly, female jobs were interchangeable. About one third of women working in spinning and carding—the lowest-paying departments—and the same proportion in weaving—the highest-paying one— were newcomers who had been employed at Hamilton less than a year in June 1860. Only the dressing room, one-sixth newcomer at this date, stood out as substantially different from the other departments. This difference stemmed not from the higher wages or greater skill requirements of dressing, but from the general exclusion of immigrants from the department. Since the vast majority of newcomers in 1860 were Irish, the low proportion of foreign-born in dressing accounted for the relative absence of newcomers as well.

The changing career patterns of women workers revealed in the analysis of the Hamilton work force in 1860 are also apparent in the careers of those who persisted at the company over the decade of the 1850s. Of the 1221 workers employed at Hamilton in August 1850, only 72 persisted in the work force in June 1860.[16] This group was not completely representative of the broader work force, as table 11.8 indicates:

TABLE 11.8. COMPARISON OF 1850–1860 PERSISTENT WORKERS TO 1850 HAMILTON COMPANY WORK FORCE

Characteristic	Persistent Group	1850 Work Force
Percent male	47 (72)	24 (1221)[a]
Percent native-born	61 (72)	61 (1175)
Percent resident in company housing	48 (72)	39 (1168)
Mean male daily wage, 1850	$1.39 (33)	$0.98 (291)
Mean female daily wage, 1850	$0.58 (39)	$0.59 (930)

[a] Total cases vary with missing data on a given variable.

The proportion of men in the persistent group was twice that for the work force as a whole, and these men tended to be the most skilled and highest paid of all male workers. Women who persisted, however, earned wages virtually identical to those of all women at the company, suggesting that they were drawn from throughout the ranks of female operatives at Hamilton. This pattern was itself a departure from earlier traditions, for women who had continued to work at Hamilton over the 1836-1850 period were almost exclusively high-paid weavers and dressers. Female persisters in the 1850s were not entirely the elite of Hamilton's women workers.

Occupational mobility for male workers at Hamilton in the 1850s mirrored earlier patterns. Of the 33 men in the persistent group, the number of operatives declined from 17 to 12 over the decade. Correspondingly, the number of overseers increased from 8 to 13. This pattern of upward occupational mobility is evident in table 11.9, which compares the jobs of persistent male workers in 1850 and 1860.

Male occupational mobility occurred one small step at a time as operatives moved up into the ranks of second hands and second hands became overseers. Although the number of second hands among male

TABLE 11.9. JOB MOBILITY OF PERSISTENT MEN AT HAMILTON, 1850–1860

Job Category	1850	1860
Operative	17	12
Repair shop	4	4
Second hand	4	4
Overseer	8	13
Overall	33	33

persisters remained constant over the course of the decade, the composition of this group changed completely. The 4 second hands in 1850 had all become overseers by 1860, while 4 operatives had moved up to the rank of second hand. In all, 10 of the 33 persistent men at Hamilton moved up the job hierarchy over the decade, a figure comparable to the proportion of occupationally mobile men in the 1836-1850 persistent group once one corrects for the different lengths of the two periods.

Women workers, in contrast, did not fare as well as their male counterparts. Mobility between departments slowed considerably as compared with the earlier period. As table 11.10 demonstrates clearly, few persistent women changed jobs over the course of the 1850s. Overall, only 6 of 39 persistent women—15 percent—moved from one department to another over the course of the decade. This proportion was less than half that for the earlier period.

Between 1836 and 1850 women had tended to move into higher-paying departments, but in the 1850s persistent women remained basically where they were. Over the decade the number of persistent women working in the low-paying carding, spinning, and winding rooms in-

TABLE 11.10. JOB MOBILITY OF PERSISTENT WOMEN AT HAMILTON, 1850–1860

Job Category	1850	1860
Sweeper	7	7
Winding	1	1
Carding	3	4
Spinning	7	7
Weaving	17	13
Dressing	4	7
Overall	39	39

creased from 11 to 12. The continued employment of another 7 women as sweepers—the least skilled group in the mills—was indicative of the narrowing of opportunities for advancement for persistent women.

Just as persistent women did not share in occupational mobility to as great a degree as men, their wage gains over the decade were far less. On average, men employed at Hamilton in 1850 and in 1860 earned an additional $0.49 per day at the latter date, an overall increase of about 35 percent. The average earnings of persistent women remained unchanged.

Native-born and immigrant workers in the persistent group did not share a common fate in this regard, however. As one would expect, the wage gains of native-born men were far more impressive than those of immigrant men; among women, however, the pattern of wage gains was reversed. Over the decade the average earnings of persistent immigrant women increased, while those of their native-born counterparts actually declined. Table 11.11 presents evidence of these contrasting experiences.

TABLE 11.11. DIFFERENCE IN MEAN DAILY PAY OF PERSISTENT OPERATIVES AT HAMILTON, 1850–1860, BROKEN DOWN BY SEX AND ETHNICITY

Ethnicity	Males	Females
Native-born	+$0.63 (24)	−$0.03 (21)
Foreign-born	+ 0.13 (9)	+ 0.03 (18)
Overall	+ 0.49 (33)	+ 0.00 (39)

Native-born men enjoyed wage increases five times as large as those of immigrant men. In contrast, the earnings of foreign-born women rose by 3 cents on average, while the wages of the native-born women declined by the same amount.

Differences in wage increases of native-born and immigrant men resulted from the exclusion of the foreign-born from supervisory positions in the mills. All of the upward occupational mobility of persistent males came through promotion into the ranks of overseers and second hands. With these avenues of mobility closed to them, immigrant men made very limited gains in wages over the decade.

Two factors account for the contrasting wage patterns for native-born and immigrant women: the relative segregation of these two groups of workers and the proletarianization of women's work over the decade.

Persistent Yankee and immigrant women workers were segregated for the most part in different departments at Hamilton. Some 17 of 21 Yankee persisters were employed in the weaving and dressing departments in both 1850 and 1860. Only 3 of 18 persistent immigrant women worked in these high-paying rooms at any time in the decade.

Since these two groups of persistent women workers were concentrated in different departments, they were affected in opposite ways by the relative narrowing of the wage spread among various departments in the mills. Yankee persisters working in dressing and weaving suffered declines in wages along with other women in those jobs. Immigrant persistent women in carding and spinning, however, enjoyed wage gains along with their workmates in those rooms. These developments led to the narrowing of the native-immigrant wage gap for persistent women operatives over the course of the decade.

Persistent women found themselves in fixed job niches in the 1850s. While in the earlier period they had enjoyed occupational mobility, principally into the dressing room, there was little or no such mobility in the 1850s. Four weavers did move into the dressing room, but for each of these women, mean daily earnings actually declined over the decade. Another weaver switched to the carding room, only to see her wages fall by almost 20 percent. Of the 6 women who did experience occupational mobility, only one enjoyed higher wages as a result. The contrast with the gains of persistent women between 1836 and 1850 is striking on both counts. Movement among jobs had diminished over the period, and it no longer was associated with increased earnings. Women's jobs had a dead-end quality in the 1850s that had been absent earlier.

The contrasting wage experiences of native-born and immigrant persistent women reflect the pattern of wages in the overall female work force. The decline in the native-immigrant wage differential described here mirrors that for all women at Hamilton. Table 11.12 presents data on wages for both the persistent group and for the overall female work force in 1850 and 1860.

The evidence here situates female persisters within the larger work force and suggests contrasting patterns of persistence among native-born and immigrant women workers. Native-born persistent women were among the most skilled and highest-paid native women workers at Hamilton. In both 1850 and 1860 their earnings were considerably higher than those of all Yankee women at the company. Persistent im-

TABLE 11.12. MEAN DAILY PAY OF PERSISTENT FEMALES AND ALL WOMEN WORKERS AT HAMILTON, 1850–1860, BROKEN DOWN BY ETHNICITY

	Mean Daily Pay (in cents)			
	1850		1860	
Ethnicity	Persisters	All women	Persisters	All women
Native-born	68.2 (21)	63.2 (539)	65.4 (21)	57.5 (324)
Foreign-born	45.6 (18)	53.6 (370)	48.7 (18)	56.1 (524)
Overall	57.8 (39)	59.3 (909)	57.8 (39)	56.6 (848)

migrant women, in contrast, earned far less than the mean wage for all foreign-born women. They were among the least skilled and lowest-paid immigrant women in the mills. That immigrant women in the lowest ranks persisted over the decade, without significant job mobility, is strong evidence that economic need, rather than prospects for advancement, played the determining role in keeping these women in the mills. The demands of the emerging family economy rather than opportunities for individual advancement and independence seem to have been at work for this group of persistent women workers.

The analysis of the changing career patterns of women workers suggests that between 1836 and 1860 a selection process operated among females employed at the Hamilton Company. For a variety of personal reasons, some women persisted over long periods of time, while others left employment. Between 1836 and 1850 persistent women were drawn almost exclusively from the ranks of the most skilled operatives. By the 1850s, however, they included a fair number of the least skilled. The change in the selection process was only partial by 1860, and more than half of persistent women were still native-born skilled workers. Nevertheless, this partial change is indicative of the transformation that occurred in the textile mills of Lowell over the period. It also presaged the further decline of mill employment relative to other women's occupations which was to take place after 1860. In the 1830s the Lowell mills had attracted an educated group of rural Yankee women who wanted to work for economic and social independence; by the 1850s the mills increasingly employed immigrant women who had to work for their families' subsistence. In this contrast we see evidence of the fundamental transformation of work in the Lowell mills in this period.

CHAPTER TWELVE

The Operatives' Response, 1850-1860

THE PRECEDING CHAPTERS have presented in some detail the nature of the transformation of work and the work force in the Lowell mills between the mid-1840s and 1860. Two major developments stand out in the discussion: the new heterogeneity of the mill work force and the increasing importance of economic necessity as a motivation for women workers in the 1850s. Together these factors help to explain the evident decline in labor protest that accompanied the transformation of mill employment.

In the mid-1830s the homogeneity of the mill work force had been striking. Workers at the Hamilton Company in Lowell, that firm with the best surviving labor records, had been more than 85 percent female and 96 percent native-born in 1836. Almost three fourths of workers resided together in company housing adjacent to the mills. Shared cultural backgrounds and shared experiences in the mills and boarding-houses contributed to the growth of a sense of community among women workers and undoubtedly played a role in the outbreak of collective labor protest before 1850.

This homogeneity, however, began to break down with the influx of Irish immigrants after 1845. The proportion of male operatives rose to almost 30 percent by 1860, while the parallel increase of the foreign-born in the work force—from less than 4 percent in 1836 to amost 62 percent in 1860—was even greater. Furthermore, the concentration of young, single workers in their late teens and early twenties declined significantly. The new heterogeneity in age was evident in the increase in the numbers of boys under 15 and of women over 30. Workers in the mills in 1860 were much more diverse and less unified than earlier.

The diversity of the mill work force was reflected in the residence patterns of workers as well. Newcomers increasingly lived in private boardinghouses and tenements distant from the mills. The proportion of women workers at Hamilton residing in company housing declined from 73 percent to 33 percent over the period. Reflecting and contributing to this change, a growing proportion of women lived at home with their families while working. In 1836 only a ninth of the female work force at Hamilton had resided at home, but in 1860 Lowell fully 35 percent did so.[1] It seems plausible to contend that these women were cut off still further by family emotional ties and economic responsibilities from their fellow operatives. It is likely that both residential dispersal and increasing family bonds contributed to the disjuncture of work and home lives for many female operatives in the 1850s.

Finally, the changed economic circumstances of the immigrant workers in Lowell must have further dampened labor protest. The Yankee women of an earlier era had rural farms to which they might return and thus were not totally dependent on mill earnings for self-support. Even more important, their families in New Hampshire, Maine, and Vermont were not counting on their earnings for basic subsistence. Thus, when they reacted strongly in opposition to wage cuts or increases in the cost of room and board, as they did in February 1834 and October 1836, they were free to act upon their feelings. Turning out imposed no great hardships on the striking women or their families. In each of these respects, the economic situation of the immigrant Irish in the 1850s was strikingly different. Having fled famine-stricken Ireland, immigrant women could not return to their rural homes. Further, as the earlier discussion of the 1860 millhand sample revealed, immigrant families were particularly dependent on the earnings of millhand daughters. In this new context, a turn-out would have led to an immediate loss of income that was crucial for immigrant families. The transformation of the mill work force made it more dependent and undoubtedly undermined the labor movement that had emerged in the earlier period.

All of these factors worked to discourage the growth of collective

protest among women workers in Lowell in the 1850s. Cultural traditions, segregation at the workplace and in housing, and very different
sorts of economic needs and motivations divided Yankee and Irish
women workers. Thus when mill management reduced piece wages or
implemented speedups and stretch-outs, the likelihood of united action
on the part of women workers was slim. Yankee women responded by
leaving the mills, while economic necessity demanded that the Irish continue working. As important, while wages and working conditions for
Yankee women declined, Irish newcomers began moving up the occupational hierarchy within the mills. Limited expectations at first and actually improving conditions gave the Irish little reason to protest. And so
the massive entry of the Irish into the mills signaled the end of the
Yankee labor movement as it had evolved in the 1830s and 1840s. We
see this development not simply because the new workers were Irish,
nor because of their greater economic need, nor because of the new
family labor system, but because of the combined impact of all these
changes. It was this particular constellation of forces working together
that had such a dampening effect on protest.

The changing nature of labor protest in Lowell is most evident in the
history of the Ten Hour Movement. In contrast to the struggle of the
1840s, the movement in the 1850s became primarily a workingmen's
political struggle. As local petition campaigns gave way to ward political
work, women's participation in reform declined drastically. Traditional
electoral activity displaced the public agitation and lobbying of the earlier decade. In 1851 the Democratic and Free Soil parties in Lowell nominated a joint slate of candidates for the state legislature pledged to enact
a strong ten-hour law. In a hotly contested election, with the ten-hour
day as the central issue, the entire coalition slate was elected. Minor
irregularities in returns led local Whig officials to void the returns and
call for a special election. In the second contest, despite extreme pressure
from the corporations on their employees, five of six ten-hour candidates
were returned. Finally, in a vindication of the initial vote, the legislature
voted to seat the entire ten-hour slate originally chosen by Lowell voters.[2] The integration of the labor reform movement into the electoral
process tended to displace women activists and gave workingmen a new
prominence in the movement that they had not enjoyed earlier. Men ran
for office, nominated candidates, participated in ward meetings, and fi-

nally cast their votes in elections. Although women could agitate for passage of the ten-hour law, they were excluded from direct partipation in electoral politics.

Not only were women conspicuously absent from the electoral activity of the Ten Hour Movement, but their role in the more strictly agitational work of the movement declined as well. In 1845 women had comprised fully two thirds of Lowell ten-hour petition signers. As a consequence representative William Schouler had summoned a predominantly female delegation to testify before the committee investigating the mills that winter. In 1846, as the number of petition signers skyrocketed to more than 4,000, women still constituted more than 58 percent of that number. In contrast, less than 40 percent of petition signers in 1851 were females.[3] Clearly the Ten Hour Movement in Lowell in the early 1850s was unable to mobilize women workers as it had earlier.

Reports of ten-hour rallies in Lowell in these years confirm the impression created by extant petitions. A lengthy notice of a ten-hour meeting noted in its final paragraph: "Arrangements will be made for ladies who may attend. . . ." The whole tenor of the notice makes this reference seem like rather an afterthought. In the earlier decade it would have been taken for granted that women would participate and would in fact predominate at ten-hour rallies. The report on this rally a week later noted a large turnout of 1,500 men and 200 or 300 women. These numbers were almost the reverse of the relative proportions of men and women in the mills. At this date women comprised about 75 percent of the mill work force, though they made up less than 20 percent of the participants at the rally. The outcome of the rally was summarized in this newspaper account, and once again women workers were conspicuous by their absence: "The meeting settled the question that the Ten Hour men of Lowell are not going to be satisfied with any Eleven Hour substitute for what they demand and are determined to have. Onward is their word."[4]

Finally, the declining participation of women in the rank and file of the movement was also reflected in the composition of its leadership. The City Committee of the Ten Hour Movement, set up in 1853 to represent Lowell at a statewide Ten Hours Convention, consisted of 20 members, all of them men.[5] The Ten Hour Movement in the 1850s had become primarily a workingmen's reform movement. A scattering of women continued to show their support for the cause, but the mass movement of women operatives of the earlier decade had largely disappeared.

As men became mobilized by the Ten Hour Movement, direct economic action came to play a new part in the struggle. In March 1853 machinists at the Lowell Machine Shop went on strike; their single demand called for establishment of a ten-hour working day.[6] This strike proved unsuccessful, but sparked mounting unrest among overseers in the mills. Overseers had remained entirely aloof from earlier protests within the mills, which had always been dominated by women workers. On this occasion, however, overseers held their own meetings and petitioned mill agents requesting a ten-hour day. Evidently fearful that overseers and operatives might unite to demand reduction of the hours of labor, mill managers took these pleadings seriously. The treasurers of the various Lowell firms met and voted to reduce the daily hours in the mills to eleven.[7] Thus only when the Ten Hour Movement spread from women workers into the ranks of skilled male machinists and overseers did mill management respond to the pressure from below.

The success of these efforts spurred ten-hour supporters. Petitions continued to assail the state legislature and local agitation increased. Frequent rallies in major Massachusetts cities generated support for the election of ten-hour candidates and put pressure on unpledged representatives to come out in favor of legislation. The campaigns peaked in 1855 when the state House of Representatives approved a strong ten-hour bill by a margin of more than two to one. The state senate, however, consistently opposed effective regulation of the hours of labor, and no legislation was enacted until 1874.[8]

The decline in collective action among women workers was also evident in the reduced frequency and scale of strike actions. This decline occurred even though management continued to take actions that earlier had provoked protest. There were at least three cuts in piece wages in the Lowell mills in the decade: in October 1850, January 1855, and late in 1857.[9] In addition, speedups and stretch-outs continued to increase the workload of operatives. Between 1850 and 1860 the average weekly output per worker in Lowell's cotton mills rose from 213 to 248 yards, an overall gain of more than 16 percent.[10] Given the nature of work and the stability of basic technology over these years, this increase could have been achieved only by increasing the speed of machinery or by assigning additional machinery to each worker. Careful examination of company correspondence and of local newspapers reveals, however, that there was no organized opposition among operatives to these practices of management.

There was, in fact, only one turn-out in the Lowell mills during the decade. It was small and apparently very short-lived, though there is little information to illuminate the course of events. In the fall of 1857, in response to the general depression of that year, the Lowell textile companies reduced operations and cut piece-wage rates. By early 1859, however, the mills had resumed production at close to full capacity, and some operatives felt that it was time to increase wage rates to their predepression levels. In February 1859 spinners at the Tremont, Boott, Prescott, and Massachusetts mills turned out, demanding higher wages. The strike brought out from 300 to 500 women operatives, all immigrants according to surviving newspaper accounts.

In several respects the strike was reminiscent of the turn-outs of the 1830s. Strikers repeated tactics employed earlier and "marched in procession along the side-walks of the principal streets, passing the premises of all the mills so as to awaken discontent among those still at work." Like its predecessors, this turn-out sparked labor protests in other New England communities, with strikes in Chicopee, Lawrence, and Manchester following on its heels. [11]

The 1859 strike was, in fact, only a faint echo of the massive protests of the mid-1830s. In 1834 fully a sixth of the work force took part, while even by the smallest estimate the 1836 turn-out involved more than a fourth of all mill operatives. Even taking the highest estimate for the 1859 strike, less than 6 percent of the female mill work force joined in at this later date. [12] Furthermore, newspaper accounts of the strike disappear after the fourth day, suggesting it was very short-lived. Numerous factors worked against striking operatives. The small number of strikers meant they had little impact on production and thus could bring little pressure to bear on management. Their impact was further undermined by the sizable inventories of yarn that mills were able to draw upon during the strike. Finally, firms responded to the strike by recruiting Yankee women in the surrounding countryside. [13] Just as Irish strikebreakers had been brought in during the 1852 strikes in Amesbury and

Salisbury, this time Yankee women were sought to break an Irish strike. The ethnic division of the work force presented a weak point that management could exploit tellingly in times of labor unrest. The solidarity of the earlier turn-outs was conspicuously absent during the 1859 strike. As a result the strike made little impact on mill production, which reached near-record levels for the six-month period including the strike. [14]

The strike is an interesting and important one, despite the fact that it had little impact on the mills. In several respects it differed from the earlier turn-outs. It was the first strike among Lowell textile operatives with what Norman Ware termed an "aggressive" character. Ware distinguished strike activity in the 1840s from that of the 1850s, calling the former "defensive" and the latter "aggressive." With these terms, he sought to stress the fact that the former were essentially attempts by workers to defend themselves against measures taken by employers that threatened either wages or working conditions. In contrast, "aggressive" strikes were autonomous demands for improvements in wages or working conditions. According to Ware, defensive actions were somewhat backward-looking, a reaction to industrial capitalism within a system of values that predated the transformation of work. Aggressive strikes, in contrast, accepted the class divisions that had evolved in this period; rather than challenging the authority of employers, these actions sought limited concessions from that authority. [15]

This framework focuses clearly on a new and important element in the spinners' strike of 1859. In the 1830s women operatives turned out in defense of existing piece wages and room and board rates. Their actions sought to defend the status quo from attack by management. And they justified their actions by a defense of their status as "daughters of freemen." Preindustrial values and beliefs clearly motivated their actions. In 1859, in contrast, women spinners struck to achieve increased wages and not simply to defend existing standards. While strike pronouncements have not survived, it is hard to imagine immigrant spinners invoking images of the "Ould Countrey" to support their demands for wage hikes. In the face of rising prices and the return of prosperity, they simply demanded a larger share of a growing pie.

The turn-out was aggressive in yet another way; it appears to have contributed to the formation of a permanent labor organization among Lowell workers. Although they did not take part in the February strike, male card grinders apparently formed a mutual benefit society. They denied any intention of striking and noted: "We consider that we have as good a right to meet as those who are above us, and shall continue to do so, acting like men and not like boys. Justice to the grinders requires that this statement should be made public." The society hired a hall and announced weekly meetings. Membership was open to any "grinder of good character." In this inconspicuous notice in a Lowell paper, we see the origin of organization in the textile mills that would play an important role in the rebirth of the Ten Hour Movement in the decade after the Civil War. [16]

In addition to its new character, the 1859 strike differed from earlier labor struggles in still another way. It was the first in the history of Lowell to involve extensive participation by the foreign-born. Accounts of earlier strikes and of the Ten Hour Movement indicate that these struggles were carried on almost exclusively by native-born operatives. That this strike was carried out entirely by immigrant women suggests the passing of an era. Native-born operatives were by this date a distinct minority in the mills. At the Hamilton Company in 1860 they comprised less than 40 percent of the work force. By 1859 the attitudes and experiences of immigrants, and particularly of the Irish, determined in large part the extent of protest in the mills.

With the spinners' strike in February 1859 we see the emergence of collective action among Irish mill workers. The strike marks the end of a decade of relative labor peace that had prevailed since the defeat of the Ten Hour Movement in the late 1840s. No longer, however, could the Irish be counted on as a docile, tractable labor force. The spirit that animated the protest in 1859 surfaced frequently thereafter, first in strikes of immigrant mule spinners in the mid-1860s and later in a renewed Ten Hour Movement between 1867 and 1875. [17] In this context it is apparent that the decline of protest among operatives in Lowell in the 1850s was a transitional phenomenon. A new fragmentation replaced the earlier homogeneity in the mill work force. In the face of the massive influx of immigrants, Yankee women workers who might have protested in an earlier era chose to leave the mills for good. Had they chosen to protest, they probably would have found their places taken by immigrant newcomers as happened to striking workers in the Amesbury-Salisbury mills in 1852. [18] Religious and cultural differences and segregation at the workplace and in housing divided native and immigrant workers and effectively undermined collective protest. Finally, the Irish themselves had little reason to protest mill conditions, at least in the early and middle years of the decade. Their hopes and expectations were undoubtedly shaped by the famine experience. They needed jobs and steady income, both of which the mills could offer, and they were unlikely to be overly concerned with specific wage levels or working conditions. Given the growth of a hostile nativism in Lowell, as in much of Massachusetts in the period, the Irish may have made an effort at first to win the respect of their employers. [19] All of these factors contributed to the decline in industrial protest.

By the end of the decade, however, the position of immigrant women in Lowell had changed dramatically. With the continued influx of the Irish, they were no longer a minority in the mills. By 1860 at the Hamilton Company, for instance, immigrants comprised more than 60 percent of the mill work force, the Irish alone accounting for 47 percent. Sheer numbers must have given the Irish a new sense of their power. Furthermore, in these years the expectations of the immigrant newcomers undoubtedly changed. With increased experience in the mills, they must have developed a new sense of what constituted a fair level of earnings and a reasonable pace of work. Their expectations in 1859 were no longer based primarily on the trauma of flight from Ireland but on their industrial experience in Lowell. By this date they were evidently as sensitive to wage cuts and speedups as their native-born counterparts, as the spinners' strike demonstrates. Furthermore, their near majority status in the work force, and their concentration in particular departments within the mills meant that they could turn out with some hope of success.

The changing nature of labor protest in Lowell in the decade of the 1850s reflected a fundamental transformation of work and community in Lowell. In the 1830s and 1840s Yankee women had predominated in the mill work force and had provided leadership to the labor struggles that punctuated the period. In the 1850s with the steady departure of Yankee women from the mills, there was a steady transformation of the labor movement as well. Initially, skilled Yankee workingmen displaced their sisters in the leadership of the political Ten Hour Movement that emerged in the first half of the decade. With the decline of that movement after 1855, we see the emergence of labor protest for the first time among immigant operatives in the 1859 Irish spinners' strike. The displacement of the Yankee woman worker of the earlier era was now complete. By this date immigrant newcomers predominated not only in the mill work force but in the ranks of labor protestors as well. New traditions were in the making; the world of the "daughters of freemen" had passed.

APPENDIX 1

Preparation of the Hamilton Company Payroll, 1836

ANALYSIS of the makeup and earnings of the work force of the Hamilton Manufacturing Company in Lowell in the months of July 1836, August 1850, and June 1860 provides a cornerstone for the interpretation offered in this book. Given the importance of these data, it makes sense to discuss the basis for the selection of this firm and these particular months as well as the methods used in preparing data for analysis.

Payroll records survive for only two major Lowell textile firms, the Hamilton and Lawrence companies. Together these records comprise about 500 large manuscript volumes and provide virtually complete runs of the firms' payrolls between 1834 and 1900.[1] The Hamilton payrolls, beginning in 1826, though with several discontinuities in the first decade, offer a somewhat longer view, but as far as the payroll records themselves are concerned there is little reason to choose one firm over the other. The existence of a separate series of records, register books, for the Hamilton Company was the primary reason for the selection of that firm.[2] Register books recorded each worker's entrance and departure from the mill work force, the room he or she worked in, place of residence in Lowell, and nativity. The possibility of linking together payroll records and registers, and thus knowing more about each worker than simply payroll information, shaped the decision to focus on the Hamilton Company.

Still, the Hamilton payrolls were voluminous and further sampling was required. Given a work force that varied in size between 1,000 and 1,250 over the period 1830-1860, there were on the order of 400,000 individual monthly payroll entries in the volumes covering these years. To examine the changing composition, occupational structure, and wage patterns of the work force, single months of payrolls were chosen for detailed study. In particular, the months of July 1836, August 1850, and June 1860 were chosen in order to optimize linkage with nonmill records. The 1836 date coincided with the preparation of a supplement to the *Lowell Directory* that recorded the names and addresses of women employed in all of the major firms in the city. The choice of the latter months facilitated linkage to the federal manuscript censuses of 1850 and 1860 and coincided with the particular months in which census enumerators passed through the neighborhood surrounding the Hamilton mills. Possible bias resulting from the choice of these months is discussed in appendix 5.

The study of the Hamilton work force in July 1836 began with the coding and keypunching of individual payroll entries. There were three mills at this date and separate payroll volumes provided monthly records of employment and earnings in each mill. Overall, the payrolls included 1,103 separate entries. For each entry name, room, job, days worked, earnings, sex, and literacy were recorded. The determination of literacy was based on the ability of an operative to sign for his or her wages in the appropriate space after the payroll entry. If someone else signed for a given operative—a friend, sister, or parent, for instance—literacy was coded as "missing."

An early difficulty resulted from the frequent occurrence of more than one payroll entry for a given worker. It was necessary to reduce the 1,103 payroll entries to a smaller number of monthly records for individuals. An alphabetical sort of the payroll records revealed numerous double entries. Additional examination of the original payrolls made it possible to distinguish between double entries for the same person and those cases in which two workers had the same names. For literate operatives a comparison of actual signatures settled the issue. For illiterate workers, or those who did not sign for their wages, logical criteria were applied. If the total days worked for the two entries were less than or equal to the number of days in the payroll period, and if wage rates were consistent, the two entries were said to refer to one person. The vast majority of double entries were associated with individuals who had recently entered as sparehands and had switched during the payroll period to a regular position in the same room. They simply had their earnings as sparehands recorded in a separate place in the payrolls from their earnings as regular operatives. Double entries referring to the same person were combined onto a single record giving the total days worked and the total wages earned during the payroll period. The job in which the operative worked longer during the month was coded on the combined record. This consolidation reduced 1,103 payroll entries to 1,030 operatives' payroll records.

With the payroll entries reduced to individual records, the next step was to trace workers in company register books.[3] Three pieces of data found in the registers were used in the linkage process: name, room, and entry and departure dates. Ideally for a given individual in the payroll it would have been possible to find a register entry with name spelled exactly as in the payroll, with the correct room given, and with dates of entry and departure indicating that the worker had been employed in July. Needless to say there were numerous discrepancies between payroll and register entries, even in cases clearly referring to the same individual. Names were often spelled correctly in one source and phonetically in the other. Surnames were often misspelled in logical ways. Catherine McKenney, for instance, turned up in the register book as Catherine M. Kenney. With experience it became possible to anticipate the more common discrepancies and to look for a given individual in a number of places in the register book. To ensure against false links—that is, incorrectly concluding that a payroll and register entry referred to the same person, when in fact they did not—agreement on two of the three linkage variables—name, room, and entry and departure date—was required. If any two of the three pairs of variables differed, the register entry was not linked to the payroll individual. In other words, if the name in the register were misspelled, then room and entry information had to match. If the rooms in the payroll and register did not agree, then name and entry information had to match in the two records. Using these criteria, 83 percent of the individuals listed in the payrolls were linked in register books.[4]

The company register books gave additional data on linked individuals. They provided the nativity and local residence of operatives and recorded whether operatives were "old" or "new" workers at the company and whether they brought with them a certificate of school attendance.

At this stage of the preparation, 13 variables had been coded for Hamilton operatives successfully traced in company register books:

Variable	Nature of Coding
Name	Alphabetic
Job	Numeric
Status	Overseer/Second hand/Operative
Days worked	Numeric
Earnings	Numeric (in dollars and cents)
Sex	Male/Female
Literacy	Literate/Illiterate/Missing
Nativity	Numeric code
Residence	Numeric code
Experience	Old/New
School certificate	Yes/No
Entry date on work stint	Numeric code for year and month
Departure from work stint	Numeric code for year and month

There remained two potential difficulties at this point in the linkage process. First, there was the possibility of systematic bias. There may have been a consistent—as opposed to a random—reason why it was impossible to link all payroll individuals in the registers. Perhaps the clerk had failed to record Irish as carefully as native workers, or nonresidents of company housing as fully as residents. Since the purpose of the analysis was to gain an accurate picture of the ethnic makeup and residence of the work force it seemed important to minimize missing data and thereby reduce the magnitude of possible bias. The second problem stemmed from the nature of the company register book. The clerk recorded the residence of each operative when he first began the book or when the operative entered the mill. A year or two could separate an operative's entrance and the payroll date. An operative might have moved in the intervening months, raising the possibility that the summation of all such individual moves might change the aggregate findings in one direction.

Neither of these proved an insuperable problem, and the payroll date was chosen to meet the potential difficulties. Beginning in 1832 printers in Lowell published annually the *Lowell Directory,* an alphabetical listing of workingmen in the city. This source gave business and residence addresses of a good proportion of the skilled, male work force in Lowell. It had limitations though; it systematically underreported unskilled Irish laborers and dependent, employed sons living at home and did not list women at all. In 1836, for the first and only time, the editors of the directory prepared a supplement that gave the name, residence, and employer of women working in the mills.[5] The date of July 1836 was chosen specifically to facilitate the linkage of payroll individuals in this additional source.

In the next step in the linkage process, men on the payroll were traced in the 1836 *Directory* and women in the *Female Supplement* for that year. A comparison of listings in the supplement and in the register book indicated that the former had been compiled in mid-August. If the register book indicated that an individual remained at Hamilton continuously between July 23, the payroll date, and mid-August, the city directory residence was accepted as correct. If the individual had not been linked in the register book, the city directory or supplement address was accepted provided that it gave Hamilton as the employer. With the additional information gained from these two sources, it was possible to reduce missing data on the residence of operatives considerably. Linkage on this variable reached 91.5 percent, indicating that about 40 percent of those initially unlinked in the register books were found in the directories. Not only were additional linkages made but numerous initial linkages were corrected with the more current addresses listed in the directories.

Interestingly, use of the *Directory* and the *Supplement,* although reducing the amount of missing data, had little effect on the residence patterns reported in chapter 3. Table A.1 presents the findings, before and after the additional linkage.

Missing data declined by more than a third, but the proportion of operatives living in company housing increased by only 2 percent. The basic conclusions concerning the existence of a close-knit community of female operatives were not dependent on this additional linkage work. The limited impact of the directory and supplement linkage, however, could not have been predicted, and it seemed important to minimize

TABLE A.1. COMPARISON OF RESIDENCE PATTERNS OF HAMILTON
WORK FORCE, JULY 1836, BEFORE AND AFTER DIRECTORY LINKAGE

| | Proportions Residing in Company Housing | |
	Register book linkage alone	Register and directory linkage
Males	66.1% (111)	69.9% (122)
Females	72.8 (785)	74.2 (823)
Overall	71.7 (896)	73.7 (945)

potential bias arising out of missing data. The reduction in missing data has, in fact, increased the reliability of the findings.

At this point in the preparation of the 1836 payroll, I felt it important to expand the focus beyond the single month of July. I decided to prepare a 6-month payroll and also to record for workers the date of their first entrance in the Hamilton work force. To reduce the record linkage and keypunching to manageable proportions, sampling seemed appropriate.

Since both the 6-month payroll and the first entrance linkage required tracing the payroll entries of individuals over time, it proved most useful to sample entirely from one of the company's three mills. Given the focus on a single mill, it remained to consider which mill seemed most representative of the company as a whole. Summary accounts indicated that fluctuations in the dollar payroll of Mill A during 1836 most closely approximated those of the overall company payroll.[6] Mill A differed significantly from the other company mills only in the fact that it had a winding room in addition to the other main departments. To assure that the sample group was representative of the firm as a whole, winding room operatives were excluded from the sample.[7]

This sample, comprised of 271 operatives employed in the four major departments of Mill A in July 1836, was traced in company payrolls for 6 months between April and October of that year. Payrolls for the four departments were keypunched, sorted alphabetically, and checked to determine whether similar or identical names actually referred to the same individual.[8] Examination of register books permitted tracing of operatives who had switched to or from another mill during the period, and a few additional entries in payroll volumes for mills B and C were added. These steps resulted in a data file organized by individuals with a single record for each month of employment and additional register book data drawn from the earlier linkage. From this file, those individuals who had entered employment for the first time in May, June, and July 1836 were selected for analysis of newcomers' work experiences.

The sample also provided the basis for the analysis of operatives' careers presented in chapter 11. Detailed linkage in payroll and register volumes determined the date of first employment of Mill A sample members. This linkage was complicated by gaps in extant register volumes. Earlier registers survive for the periods between December 1834 and July 1836 and between June 1830 and July 1832.[9] For these periods the tracing process was relatively straightforward. For each operative I recorded entry and departure, working backwards from July 1836. Name and nativity provided suitable linkage variables. Agreement on both variables for successive register entries was required before they were said to refer to the same individual. In other words, if the entries for two Mary Grants indicated that "both" operatives came from Derby, New Hampshire, they were called linked. Discrepancies on either name or nativity led to the rejection of potential links.[10]

Completion of linkage in the register books still left a large number of operatives with no precise date of first employment. Many of these had clearly entered between July 1832 and December 1834, the period lacking extant registers. For this group, company payrolls were examined. Names and signatures of operatives were checked to determine the first entry of the remaining sample members. These procedures reduced the number of operatives with unknown dates of first employment to only 6 out of 271.

Preliminary analysis began at this point, but it soon became apparent that I was also interested in determining the proportion of women living with their families. Analysis of the housing and families of female mill-hands in 1860 (in chapter 10) particularly underscored the importance of this additional variable.

For residents of Hamilton Company housing, it was a relatively simple matter to check company rental records to determine whether an individual lived in a company tenement or boardinghouse and whether or not she lived with her family. Company records noted the rent for each dwelling, from which one could conclude whether a given numbered household was a tenement or boardinghouse. The records also gave the name of the principal tenant—the household heads for tenements and the keepers of boardinghouses. [11] If an operative's surname agreed with that of the tenant, she was said to be living with her family.

For residents of private housing, the task was more involved. First, an operative's exact address as given in the company register book was recorded. For about a third of these individuals, the register book noted that they were living "at home" or with "parents," so one could determine family membership directly. The remainder lived in either private boardinghouses or tenements. The register book often gave the names of the household heads in these private dwellings, and recourse to the *Lowell Directory* and the *Female Supplement* generally enabled one to determine whether the household was a boardinghouse or tenement.

In a number of cases, family membership and household type had to be inferred from available evidence. About 5 percent of the female operatives resided in Appleton Company housing adjacent to the Hamilton mills. Lacking rental records of the Appleton Company, I inferred that these operatives were all boarders in boardinghouses. This decision seemed reasonable since 95 percent of female operatives living in Hamilton Company housing resided in boardinghouses, and 98 percent were boarders rather than family members. For the remaining cases family membership was inferred by a comparison of the surnames of millhands and household heads. If the surnames of millhand and household head were the same, an individual was coded as a family member; if the names differed, the worker was said to be a boarder. This procedure sought to balance possible linkage errors. A number of boarders with common surnames were probably miscoded as family members, but cousins and nephews and nieces incorrectly recorded as boarders may well have balanced them.

For about 14 percent of female operatives successfully linked in company register books or in the directory supplement, it was not possible to determine directly whether or not they lived in tenements or boardinghouses. This group consisted entirely of women living in private households. To help in making inferences, I prepared household cards giving the name of the operative, her residence as given in the register or directory supplement, and the name of the head of her household. These cards were sorted by the names of household heads to determine how many Hamilton operatives lived in each household. With this additional information I made the following inferences:

1. If a single Hamilton operative or two operatives with the same surname live in the household, then the household coded a tenement.

2. If the individual's surname differs from that of the household head, and if two unrelated or three or more related operatives live in the household, then household coded a boardinghouse.

The final results from these procedures—the relative proportions of known and inferred family members and tenement and boardinghouse residents—are given in tables A.2 and A.3.

One final task remained to complete the preparation of data for the Hamilton 1836 work force. The reliability of data on the length of work stints of operatives was limited by the incompleteness of entry and departure dates in Hamilton registers. Several volumes were either missing or illegible, and as a result more than 40 percent of Hamilton operatives

TABLE A.2. FAMILY RESIDENCE OF FEMALE OPERATIVES IN THE
HAMILTON COMPANY, JULY 1836

Category	Proportion (%)
Family member, known	11.5
Boarder, known	83.7
Boarder, inferred	4.8
Total cases	818
Missing cases	63

TABLE A.3. HOUSING OF FEMALE OPERATIVES IN THE
HAMILTON COMPANY, JULY 1836

Category	Proportion (%)
Tenement, known	13.5
Tenement, inferred	5.9
Boardinghouse, known	72.3
Boardinghouse, inferred	8.3
Total cases	815
Missing cases	66

had missing data on the length of their work stints. Time-consuming hand linkage in payroll volumes was required to fill in these gaps, and as in the earlier first-entry analysis, it was decided to sample in order to reduce the clerical work involved.

Initially it had been hoped that the Mill A Sample could be traced, but two difficulties arose. One volume of Mill A payrolls—that for May 1835-April 1836—was missing from the Hamilton Company records. In addition Mill A closed down for 6 months in 1837, so operatives in this mill could not have worked beyond May 1837. These facts meant that one could not trace entrances into the mill between May 1835 and April 1836 and also that operatives in Mill A had their work stints cut off prematurely by the closing of that mill in 1837.

To avoid these problems I focused on reducing missing data on work-stint entry and departure dates for operatives in Mill C. Those with missing data on either stint entry or stint departure were traced directly in payrolls for every third month before and after July 1836. If an individual was found to be missing in a given month, he or she was traced in payrolls for the adjoining months to determine the exact month of entry or departure. Individuals were traced for 5 years prior to and after the payroll period, giving a maximum stint length of 10 years. The same procedure was employed in tracing operatives in 1850 and 1860 to ensure comparability.

In each of the additional linkage steps—first entry, family membership, and stint length—the number of individuals with missing data on residence and nativity was further reduced. The new data found in successive passes through the register books were added to the appropriate records. The fact that each "updated" data file differed slightly from the previous ones made it important to recalculate the proportions of native-born operatives and of company residents after each step. The recalculation of these proportions several times made it possible to estimate bias in the findings due to the incompleteness of payroll-register linkage. If each successive update changed the findings on a particular variable consistently in the same direction, this fact would be evidence that the population of unlinked individuals differed significantly from the linked population with respect to this variable. Appendix 5 analyzes the nature of any bias arising from this source.

Appendix 2

The Social Origins Study

THE REGISTER BOOKS of the Hamilton Company in Lowell provided the starting point for the social origins study. To identify rural communities that sent large numbers into the mills, the native towns of all workers entering employment between January and June 1836, some 700 in all, were recorded. An alphabetical sort of these records provided a list of towns that sent large numbers to work at Hamilton. Excluding Lowell itself twelve of the fourteen leading towns were found in New Hampshire, five in central Merrimack County.[1] A county-level study seemed a possibility, but with twenty-seven towns and a population of more than 34,000 in 1830, Merrimack County seemed rather formidable.[2] In order to reduce the dimensions of record linkage and to maximize the likelihood of success, it was necessary to find the intersection of those towns sending the most workers to Hamilton with those having the best published genealogical records. This process led to the final decision to focus on workers from three Merrimack County towns, Boscawen, Canterbury, and Sutton.

With the selection of specific towns, the process of transcribing data and record linkage began. As a first step all entrances, departures, or room changes recorded in the Hamilton register books that indicated these communities in the nativity column were keypunched. Each initial record noted the name of the operative, native town, room working in, residence in Lowell, entry and departure dates where given, and any miscellaneous information recorded by the company clerk. All such entries were recorded for volumes extending from 1830 to 1850.[3] The vast majority of cases fell in the 1830s, and the drastic decline in the 1840s led to the decision to set 1850 as the final cutoff year.

These records were next alphabetized, and entries and departures pertaining to the same individual were grouped together and recorded onto index cards. Further attempts were made later to trace individuals in company payrolls, and in a number of cases entry or departure dates were modified to reflect these additional linkages. On occasion the register books noted that an individual brought a discharge paper from another textile firm, and these cases were recorded as well.[4] Surviving register volumes for the Nashua Manufacturing Company for the period 1837-1839 were searched for additional entries for operatives from the three towns, as were fragmentary records of the Amoskeag Company in Manchester, New Hampshire. From these two sources only one additional link to a Hamilton operative was found, and it was added to the appropriate record.[5]

At this point operatives were separated according to native town, and linkage in local genealogical and vital records began. Published genealogies were employed first, the towns having been chosen in part to assure this valuable source.[6] For each individual successfully linked, birthdate, parents' names, and birthdates and names of siblings were recorded. Marriage date and place, spouse's name and residence, dates and places of children's births, and date and place of death (where given) were added as well. Any evidence that parents, siblings, or children worked, married, bore children, or died in Lowell or other mill towns was noted. If the genealogist indicated that the operative did not marry, or if the death date revealed as much, this too was recorded. Care was taken to record any siblings or other relatives (on the father's side only) who also worked at the Hamilton Company.

Genealogical records were the first step in the vital record linkage process, but only the first. Genealogists have their limitations and biases; in particular, they gathered data in the last third of the nineteenth century with a special interest in those families that continued to reside in their community at that date. Families that had moved out of the three towns in intervening years were undoubtedly underrepresented among those linked in genealogies.[7] Since the study had a primary interest in the residence of operatives after their years in Lowell, it seemed crucial to exhaust all possible sources before completing the linkage process.

To expand the framework, church, town, and state vital records were searched as well. These sources included cemetery inscriptions, records of town meetings (often with vital records interspersed), and records of births, deaths, and marriages kept by local churches and ministers. Town vital records proved valuable, particularly an alphabetical file of Boscawen records prepared over many years from the original manuscript volumes. [8]

Once local sources were exhausted, the vital record registration system for the state of New Hampshire provided additional linkages. In this massive, but uneven, collection of records, various strategies were employed to increase links. At first those unlinked in any source were traced in birth records. Because of the commonality of names, positive identification of the individual record with the appropriate home town was required. Marriage and death records were searched in the same manner. Links increased most often, however, for those individuals already linked in some source. Birth linkage, and thus generally the parents' names, greatly facilitated further marriage links. Marriage links provided women's married surnames and aided in determining additional death links. Using the registration system proved tedious, but steadily rewarding, as one link invariably led to another, and further tracing often cleared up earlier ambiguities.

Following extensive work in local and New Hampshire vital records, examination of Lowell and Massachusetts records completed vital record linkage. Published volumes of births, marriages, and deaths in Lowell before 1849, local manuscript records in the city clerk's office, and the records of the state registration system in Boston were all employed. [9] A fair number of operatives married, bore children, or died in Lowell, and these additional links were added to individual records.

The federal manuscript census enumerations for the three New Hampshire towns provided another valuable source for record linkage. [10] This searching worked in successive stages, and as additional linkages were made in other sources, census listings were reexamined. The 1850 and 1860 censuses were traced, and all operatives, parents, and spouses were noted. Census links often provided age data on the operative or her spouse not readily available elsewhere. On several occasions the census provided clear evidence of marriages not found in vital records. Most importantly the census noted occupational and property data for fathers and husbands that played an important role in placing operatives' families within the social and economic structure of their home towns.

To facilitate study of the property ownership and occupations of fathers and spouses, the census enumerations of all household heads in the three towns were keypunched for 1830, 1840, 1850, and 1860. For the first two decennial censuses, only the names of household heads were recorded. For 1850 and 1860 data on the sex, age, property ownership, and occupation of each household head were noted. The nominal lists were invaluable in the subsequent analysis of tax records; the census data for 1850 and 1860 facilitated placing fathers and spouses in the larger setting of their home towns.

Further tracing procedures supplemented the earlier marriage linkage. Each husband was traced in Lowell city directories, beginning 2 years before his marriage and continuing until he had disappeared from two successive directories, or for at least 2 years after the marriage date. Husbands were traced in the Hamilton register books and operatives under their married names in the years after their marriages. Following these various linkage efforts, summary data were noted on each operative's record: spouse's residence before marriage, place of marriage, couple's place of residence after marriage, birthplace of first child, and operative's place of death.

Individual records were repeatedly updated throughout the linkage process. Names spelled phonetically or simply misspelled in company register books were corrected. Sometimes records for two "individuals" were combined when, for instance, it became apparent that an operative continued to work after her marriage. The linkage, though described here as sequential, had more of a circular character. After corrections were made following one linkage step, or after new linkages were made, old sources were reexamined to see whether new links could be found which would take into consideration the new information. City directory and census linkage, for instance, were repeated numerous times, as the number of marriage links increased.

Once the vital record linkage was complete, parents and husbands were traced in local tax inventories. The entire tax inventory for each town in 1830, 1840, and 1850 was coded and keypunched. The actual data recorded vary from one year to the next, but each town acted under state-enabling legislation that assures comparability among towns in a given year.[11] Data recorded included (where given) the number of polls, value of livestock, value of improved and unimproved lands, value of personal estate, and total tax. Where it was not given, in 1830 for instance, it was possible to compute the total value of taxed property. Nonresidents were excluded from the analysis, as were units of property designated in the name of heirs of an individual's estate. All three towns occasionally taxed individuals who occupied land or kept livestock for someone else, usually a nonresident, and these holdings were also excluded. Where two individuals held property in the form of a partnership, efforts were made to determine the identity of partners and to assign shares of the property to the appropriate individuals.[12]

To complete the analysis of property ownership in these communities it seemed important to identify more fully those taxed. Tax inventories were thus linked to an alphabetical list of household heads as enumerated in the federal manuscript census for each year. The sex and household status of each property owner were recorded. Household status was recorded simply as head of household or nonhead. Finally the parents and spouses of Hamilton operatives were noted to allow comparison of these individuals with all taxpayers.

To facilitate analysis of the ages at first marriage of millhands and their husbands, further genealogical linkage was required. All husbands were traced separately in local genealogies to determine the dates of their births. These additional links supplemented data derived earlier from manuscript censuses and local vital records. Even with this linkage, data for the operatives themselves were more complete than for their spouses. The age at first marriage could be determined for 80 women workers but for only 36 of their husbands.

Finally several of the calculations in the analysis required that individual families of women workers be analyzed separately. To this end individual records were sorted and a single record created for each family. In all, 111 individuals had been traced in some way back to their families of birth; 75 separate families were represented in this population. This additional step made it possible to vary the level at which the analysis was performed.[13]

APPENDIX 3

The Hamilton Company Work Force, August 1850 and June 1860

THE PAYROLLS of the Hamilton Company in August 1850 and July 1860 were chosen for detailed analysis to maximize the possibility of linking payroll individuals in the federal manuscript censuses of those years. Examination of the censuses revealed that enumerators passed through the neighborhood surrounding the Hamilton mills in these months.[1] The preparation of these payrolls followed the sequence of steps outlined for the 1836 payroll in appendix 1, and the focus here will be on significant departures from the procedures outlined there.

These two latter payrolls differed from those in 1836 in that they included volumes for the Hamilton Print Works in addition to those for the company's mills. Examination of the register books indicated that print works' employees were not systematically recorded in these volumes. This fact, and the desire to insure that the 1850 and 1860 work forces were comparable to that of 1836, led to the exclusion of print works' employees.[2]

As in 1836 payroll entries for 1850 were keypunched and alphabetically sorted to facilitate the combining of double entries for the same individual. The same criteria were used as before—if signatures matched, entries were combined; if both entries referred to illiterate workers, logical criteria were applied. If the number of days on these

entries added up to 30 or less—the number of days in the payroll period—and the daily wage rates were comparable, the entries were said to
refer to the same individual. Overall, this process reduced the 1,232
entries to 1,221 individual payroll records—a much smaller reduction
than in 1836.

Linkage of payroll records to the Hamilton register books and to the
federal manuscript census for Lowell came next. As before objective
criteria had to be satisfied before register and payroll entries were considered linked. Two of the three linkage variables—name, room, and
entry and departure dates—had to agree for a positive linkage. Individuals were traced in successive register volumes, and their nativity, place
of residence, and school attendance recorded. Entry and departure dates
on the work stint including August 1850 were also noted. Individuals not
found in the register volume for this date were traced in the subsequent
volume that began in November 1850 and then in previous registers. In
using earlier or later volumes of the register, both name and room had to
agree because most entries referred to time periods that did not include
August 1850.[3]

For the entire 1850 work force an effort was made to find the date of
first employment for each operative. For this linkage I began with the
register for 1850 and worked backward through successive volumes.
Each earlier register provided less new data on first entrances of operatives, until with the fourth volume first entry data changed for only 8
percent of the work force. I might have continued tracing in still earlier
volumes, but concluded that the earlier entry dates on perhaps 2 percent
of the work force would not merit the additional investment of time.[4]
To supplement register linkage, however, I did examine the linked pairs
of workers found in Hamilton payrolls for both July 1836 and August
1850 and added earlier entrance dates on individuals traced in the previous linkage.

To aid in determination of stint entry and departure dates and to
provide data on the yearly earnings of workers, I keypunched the payroll
of the four main departments in Mill A—carding, spinning, weaving,
and dressing—for the entire year of 1850. These payrolls were merged
and alphabetically sorted to provide records of the yearly employment of
workers in Mill A in August 1850. The yearly payroll, coupled with
register book linkage and tracing in payrolls before and after 1850, pro-

vided stint entry and departure dates for all but 12 of the 230 operatives employed in Mill A in August 1850. To make the findings comparable to 1836 data, those who worked continuously between 1845 and 1855 were recorded as working a stint of 10 years, regardless of the actual length of continuous service.

The fact that in 1850 the Federal Manuscript Census recorded for the first time the names of all individuals enumerated provided an additional resource for record linkage. The census was particularly valuable because no city directory was published in 1850. Linkage proceeded in two distinct steps. First the census entries for residents of Hamilton tenements and boardinghouses were keypunched in their entirety. This list of about 700 residents was then merged with the payroll data deck and combined into a single alphabetical list. Linkage variables for this procedure included name, nativity, and residence. There was considerable discrepant data, especially in the spelling of names. The Hamilton register and payroll volumes were prepared by the same individual, and while there were some discrepancies on names, the payroll and register volumes were usually consistent. The census listings, however, were prepared by enumerators and were probably based on oral communication with boardinghouse keepers and household heads while most household residents were at work. It is understandable that quite a few names became transformed in the process. Thus, to complete linkage between payroll individuals and residents of company housing, I had to relax previous linkage standards somewhat. If name, interpreted quite broadly to allow phonetic and handwriting discrepancies, and either residence or nativity agreed, a payroll individual and a census listing were considered linked. If the census and register listings disagreed on place of residence, the census was accepted since the register book usually gave operatives' addresses as of the date they had entered the mill, often a year or more before the payroll period.

Only about 40 percent of payroll individuals lived in company housing, however, and it was also necessary to link workers residing in private housing. I prepared an alphabetical listing of those not linked to company housing and began a visual search through the microfilm listing of the census. If the payroll listing and a census entry agreed on name and nativity, they were said to be linked. When more than one census listing seemed acceptable for a given payroll individual, the street address recorded in the register book and the occupation of the operative were checked. If linkage still remained ambiguous, the entries were said not to be linked. Ambiguous cases were particularly frequent among Irish with common names. Still, it seemed important to limit linkage at this time to clearly "correct" links, even at the expense of having a higher level of missing data.

At the end of payroll-register and payroll-census linkage only 4 percent of payroll individuals remained unlinked in either the register books or census. Over 90 percent had been linked in the register books, and 45 percent in the census. Only 1.4 percent, however, were found in the census but not in company registers.

The failure to link a greater proportion of the work force in the census was a real disappointment. I had hoped to analyze the age composition of the work force and the relationship between age and earnings. The data on the careers of operatives would have been more valuable with age at entry and departure also known. The extent of missing data on age precluded any such studies. The unrepresentativeness of the sample linked to the census clearly limited any analysis based on these data.[5]

There were few differences between the preparation of the 1860 payroll and that for earlier years. The 1860 register volume included information not systematically recorded in previous years. First the clerk recorded entrants as "new" or "old" much more regularly than had been the case in 1850. Second he recorded whether or not an individual had worked at another mill in Lowell or in some other New England mill town. These additional data were recorded for 1860 payroll individuals. Except for these minor differences, register linkage for 1860 was identical to that for earlier years.[6]

Census linkage proceeded somewhat differently for 1860, based on the difficulties encountered with the 1850 linkage. Payroll individuals were linked only to the census listings of residents of Hamilton Company housing. The census was used to check the accuracy of register book entries and to reduce missing data on residence and nativity. No attempt was made to trace 1860 operatives throughout the manuscript census. Because of this approach the age of linked operatives was not added to the records. Any distribution of ages based on these operatives would have been highly misleading because of the unrepresentativeness of the group living in company housing.[7]

The payroll-census linkage for the 1860 work force did prove useful in reducing missing data and in correcting register entries on residence. It was necessary, however, to deal with discrepant data in a consistent fashion, as census and register did not always agree on the residence of a given individual. In all there were 407 individuals in the June 1860 payroll of Hamilton listed by either the register book or the census, or both, as living in Hamilton Company housing. Two thirds were recorded as residents of company housing in both sources. For another 77 workers listed in only one source there was no problem accepting that linkage. At this point there remained 54 cases in which census and register data could not be reconciled. In 20 cases for which there were two identical register entries—one before the payroll period and one in November 1860—the register book residence was accepted over that given in the census. In the remaining cases, where there was only one register book entry, the census listing was accepted as correct.

At the end of this process there remained only 75 cases unlinked in either the register book or the census—about 6 percent of the mill work force. Since only company housing census entries had been linked to the payroll, it seemed likely that the remaining unlinked individuals lived almost entirely in noncompany housing. I had been able to find 48 of 50 company dwellings in the census, so this premise seemed reasonable. I calculated residence in two ways, first considering residences of unlinked individuals as missing, and second recording them as noncompany. By these two methods I found that either 34 or 32 percent of the Hamilton work force in June 1860 resided in company housing. The mean of these figures, 33 percent, has been reported in chapter 8.

To make the 1860 data comparable to those for earlier years, I still had to determine the date of first employment for a sample of operatives. Since the 1860 payroll volumes combined the payrolls of four mills into two volumes, it was not practicable to sample entirely from one mill. I drew a random sample of 279 operatives from the four main rooms in mills A and B and traced these individuals through earlier register books to determine their dates of first employment. I utilized the 1850-1860 linked pairs' data (discussed in chapter 11) to supplement register book records.

I used the same Mill AB sample for the study of stint entry and departure dates. A yearly payroll for mills A and B, the company register book, and earlier and later payrolls were employed to determine dates when workers entered or left on the work stint that included June 1860. [8] The methods were comparable to those for 1850 except that tracing after 1860 continued only until July 1862. After that date Hamilton reduced operations and closed, company officials preferring to sell raw cotton during the war shortage than to produce finished cloth. Given this fact it is particularly striking that stint lengths of operatives in 1860 were still considerably longer than earlier. This pattern held even though stints could only be traced for two years after the payroll date.

APPENDIX 4

The 1860 Millhand Sample

A BRIEF EXAMINATION of the 1860 census for Lowell indicated that about 10,000 millhands were enumerated in the city's six wards.[1] It was evident from this rough estimate that it would be necessary to sample in order to study operatives in any detail. I chose to take a 1-in-10 selective sample, making the expected sample size about 1,000, a figure I had found reasonable in my earlier studies of Hamilton payrolls. This figure seemed a reasonable compromise between the desire to keep clerical work under control and the need to have enough cases for meaningful comparison among subgroups.

"Millhand" was, however, only one, though the most common, of the census designations of individuals employed in the Lowell mills in 1860, and care was required in sampling. The practices of enumerators differed somewhat from ward to ward, a second factor that had to be taken into account. In some wards overseers were designated as such, but in others they were simply called "millhands." In order to select comparable groups from each ward I decided to include as acceptable occupations for sample members individuals designated overseer, second hand, millhand, mill operative, weaver, carder, spinner, or any other term that indicated a worker in a textile mill. I specifically excluded individuals likely to have been employed in related, nonmill occupations such as machinists, millwrights, and harness and bobbin makers. The ambiguity of occupation tended to affect males more often than females. It is possible that the sample includes some males who were overseers in non-textile establishments and excludes some machinists who worked for textile companies, but overall it mirrors mill payrolls as closely as possible.

One additional source of bias should be considered separately. Curious as to how the census enumerators had treated employees of textile print works, I linked together the 1860 millhand sample with payrolls of the Hamilton Print Works. Several individuals listed in the census as millhands were in fact employed in the print works—as bleachers and dyers. Thus the 1860 millhand sample includes a certain, unfortunately indeterminate, number of individuals who worked in textiles, but not directly in the mills. In this sense, the millhand sample is not completely comparable to the 1860 Hamilton work force.

I began the study of the sample by coding and keypunching a certain amount of data for each sample member. For both males and females I recorded the following variables:

Variable	*Nature of Coding*
name	alphabetic
ward number	numeric
age	numeric
sex	male/female
occupation	categorical
real property	yes/no
personal property	yes/no
birthplace	categorical
married within year	yes/no
attended school	yes/no
literacy	yes/no

The initial data were easily coded and keypunched from the manuscript census and required no inferences from the historical record.

In the course of preliminary study, it became evident that I would need additional information on the households and families of sample members. Since the sample included 1,090 individuals residing in over 550 households the prospect of recording these additional data proved quite formidable. The average number of residents in a household appeared to be about 20, so that if I were to prepare individual records for each person living in a sample member's household, over 10,000 census listings would have been required. Clearly I needed to find a way to reduce the clerical work and yet produce a meaningful study.

I decided to examine the census listings for all households of sample members and to code data pertaining to the family and household of each millhand without generating separate records for each resident. To further reduce preparation time, I decided to code household and family data for female sample members only. Given the limitation of 1836 family data to women workers at Hamilton, the similar focus for 1860 made sense.

For each of the 761 females in the millhand sample I recorded the variables listed below:

Variable	*Nature of Coding*
number in household	numeric
number in family	numeric
marital status	categorical
relation to household head	categorical
sex of household head	male/female
nativity of hh. head	categorical
occupation of hh. head	categorical
number in hh. employed	numeric
number in hh. employed in mills	numeric
number in fam. employed	numeric
number in fam. employed in mills	numeric
ownership of dwelling	company/private
kind of household	boardinghouse/tenement
fam. membership	boarder/family member
(If boarder)	
number of relatives in hh.	numeric
(If family member)	
no. of children in family	numeric
no. of children employed	numeric
no. of children in mills	numeric
no. of children at school	numeric
age of oldest child in fam.	numeric
occupation of oldest child	categorical
age of youngest child working in mills	numeric
school attendance of above	yes/no
age of oldest child in school, but	
not working	numeric

Most of the new variables were self-coding. Some simply required counting, as in the number living in the same household; others required establishing mutually exclusive categories, such as those used to code occupations or birthplaces of household heads. A number of variables, however, required inferences based on an examination of all the residents of a sample member's household.[2]

The number of individuals in a sample member's family was not always self-evident. Initially I decided to include only household members with the same surname. As I examined the census listings, however, I found two kinds of exceptions where family membership could be inferred although surnames did not agree. First, married daughters living at home with their parents had different surnames. From the ages of children in a household and the order of the listings one could generally infer whether or not a given resident was a married daughter of the household head. When I concluded that a woman was a married daughter, I counted her and her husband and any children as family members. The reader should realize that unless the couple had been married within the year, or unless the occupation of the female was given as "wife," it was only by inference that I concluded the couple was married.

Second, I found a small number of elderly men and women of the appropriate age to be parents of a female head of a household or of the wife of a male household head. I inferred that these individuals were parents of a family member and included them in the family count. Failure to have modified the definition of family membership in this way would have systematically understated the proportion of extended families among the families of sample members.

Marital status also had to be inferred from census listings. Occasionally women were listed as "wife" or recorded as having "married within the year," but these cases comprised a relatively small proportion of those who appeared to be married. In recording a female millhand as "married" I chose to set rather minimal criteria in order to set an upper limit on the proportion of female millhands who were married. In a boardinghouse, if a male and female listed in succession had the same surname and were roughly the same age, I called them married. Within family settings, since most brothers and sisters would have met these criteria, I required more evidence. Young children of the appropriate age, or the listing of a couple out of the normal age order among children in a household, provided positive evidence on this score. Ambiguous cases were coded both ways and minimum and maximum proportions of married female sample members computed. In addition numerous women were listed in the census as heading households that included children with the same surname, but with no husband in the listing. There were also a few females living in boardinghouses with young children. I coded these females as "widowed," understanding that this category also included women separated from their husbands, women whose husbands may have been temporarily absent from Lowell, and women who may never have married.

The head of a household was defined as the first person listed in a given household by the census enumerator. In coding the occupation and nativity of the household head, it was a simple matter to set up mutually exclusive categories that included all the possibilities found for the sample.

The relationship of a sample member to the household head had to be inferred from census listings. Age, sex, and placement in the household listing were used to assign the category that seemed most appropriate. I did not use hard criteria (i.e., a child had to be at least fifteen years younger than a parent, or a spouse had to be within fifteen years of the age of the household head), as I had no objective grounds on which to base such standards. Rather I evaluated each sample member, household by household, and tried to make intelligent coding decisions.[3] Placement in the census listing proved particularly helpful, as individuals related to the household head were invariably listed first in each household, with single children generally appearing in order of descending age. Individuals with surnames differing from that of the household head, who could not be inferred to be family members on the grounds described above, were designated boarders. Possible categories for family members included household head, spouse, parent, sibling, or child. No female sample members were in-laws or granddaughters of the household head.

The numbers of employed individuals in the household and in the family were computed by counting those within each unit who were given occupations other than "wife" or "student." Housekeeping, a frequent occupation of married women, or women heading their own households, was considered a form of employment although housekeepers probably worked within their own homes. The number of household and family members working in the mills was determined by counting those whose occupations placed them within the textile mills. I used the same criteria here as in the initial selection of sample members.

The numbers of children in the family, employed, employed in the mills, and attending school were simple to determine once one had inferred the relationship of all family members to the household head. In the few families that had three generations, only children in the third, and youngest, generation were included in this count. Thus, although a married 38-year old woman might be a child of the household head, if her children lived in the same household, neither she, nor her unmarried siblings, were included in the count of children in the family.

In the analysis of family structure, only the families of sample members were coded in detail. If a millhand boarded away from home, data on the family of the household head were not recorded. Only when the sample member resided with her own family—family by blood or by marriage—did I record family data.

The remaining family variables were self-coding. Given my interest in child labor in the mills, I recorded the ages of the oldest child employed, of the youngest child working in the mills, and of the oldest child not working in the mills but attending school. I also recorded the occupation of the oldest child and whether or not the youngest child working in the mills also attended school. While I did not record all possible data on children in the families of female millhands, these data gave a fair picture of the age spread and employment of children.

Two remaining variables that were crucial to the study of the residence of millhand sample members had to be inferred from the historical record: the ownership of dwelling—company or private—and the kind of household—boardinghouse or tenement. Neither of these was recorded directly in the census, but both could be determined with additional record linkage.

The ownership of the dwelling was particularly difficult to determine. To code this variable I first recorded the census household number and the name of the household head. I alphabetized these records by surname and traced household heads in the 1859 *Lowell Directory*. On each household card I then keypunched the address of the household according to the directory, or, where the address was ambiguous, the alternative possibilities. I then sorted the household cards and returned them to the original order within the census. A listing of the addresses in the order of enumeration provided a reasonably accurate map of the addresses of households listed in the 1860 census.[4]

I accepted as correct all addresses that fit logically into the pattern of addresses surrounding them. If I found ten consecutive households listed as "12 Boott Company," "16 Boott Company," etc., I coded these households as company dwellings. If I had six straight households listed on "Cady St.," I considered these private dwellings. However, a Lawrence Company listing among a series of Cady St. households was considered uncertain. The fact that the census enumerators recorded households a year after the compiling of the city directory meant that a fair number of household heads may have moved in the interval. By using the city directory I was able to determine directly the ownership of 55 percent of the dwellings of sample members.

For the remaining 45 percent of sample dwellings not linked unambiguously in the city directory, I had to infer ownership from the pattern of ownership of adjacent dwellings listed in the manuscript census. If an unlinked household was situated among numerous other company dwellings, it was inferred to be company-owned. A parallel inference was made for households located among private dwellings. For households on the borderline between company and private neighborhoods, I traced additional adjacent census households in the directory to locate more precisely the dividing line between company and private housing. In this manner I inferred the ownership of the remaining dwellings of females in the sample.

I also had to infer whether a given household was a boardinghouse or a tenement. Often the head of a household was listed with an occupation of "boarding house" by the census enumerator, and these households were easily coded. Otherwise, if a household had ten or more residents, more than half of whom were nonfamily members, or less than ten residents, at least two thirds of whom were nonfamily members, the household was considered a boardinghouse. The criteria were arbitrary, but it seemed important to have consistent standards to distinguish between households consisting primarily of members of a single family and others primarily housing boarders.

Boarders, by the definition used here, did not live in the household of their own families, but I did record the number of relatives boarding in the same household. I defined a relative as any co-resident with the same surname and with the same birthplace (state or country) as the sample member. Where I had coded the relative as a child or husband, I did not require that birthplace agree. Relatives included brothers, sisters, cousins, spouses, children, and parents. In the sample all categories were represented with the exception of parents.

Although the initial coding scheme for the 1860 Millhand Sample provided considerable data on the housing and families of women operatives, a number of limitations became apparent as the analysis proceeded. First, the nature of the initial family data recorded limited the sorts of questions I could answer using the sample. For instance, I knew the ages of the youngest and oldest employed children in the families, but not their sexes. At numerous points in the initial analysis, I wanted to go beyond the summary family data I had coded. Second, the initial sample of 1,090 was quite small for purposes of analyzing differences among millhands living at home. There were only 204 millhand daughters in the sample, limiting possibilities of breaking the sample down along lines of ethnicity or of sex or occupation of household head. To increase the size of the sample and to broaden the analysis, I decided to code individual census records for all household members of sample members living at home. This decision created a new data set of 1,449 individuals in the 253 families of female millhands. [5]

Data recorded for each household member included the same variables coded for the millhand sample as a whole: name, age, sex, occupation, value of real and personal property, birthplace, marriage within the year, school attendance, and literacy. I also added to each individual's record the family and household summary data recorded for each female millhand. For each individual I also inferred family status and relationship to the head of the household, along the lines of my earlier coding for female sample members. On the records of household heads, I recorded the number of generations of co-residing family members and the age of the youngest child. These variables were essentially self-coding once I had made decisions about the family status and relationship to the head of the household of each resident.

The additional data recorded in this extension of the original millhand sample enabled me to broaden the analysis in chapter 10 considerably. Tables 10.5 through 10.8 are based on these findings. Only with the inclusion of a significant number of boys in mill families, is it possible to place the experience of millhand daughters within a broad perspective. The new data also permit consideration of the changing proportions of boys and girls among children in mill families. Finally, the new data provide a more accurate measure of the age spread among children living at home and thus a better estimate of children's contribution to the family economy.

Although the tiered data structure utilized in the study of mill families in Lowell in 1860 developed by trial and error in the course of this research, in several respects it is particularly well suited to the task at hand. Given limitations of time and resources in individual research of this kind, this structure enables one to tailor data coded and keypunched to the specific analytical situation. Thus for comparison with Hamilton Company data, I coded individual-level data for both males and females in the original millhand sample. Then in order to generate data comparable to the findings for housing patterns of female operatives at Hamilton in 1836, I coded household and family data on female millhands only. Finally in order to expand the analysis of the family economy in 1860, I coded individual data on all household members of female millhands living at home. In the best of research worlds, one might like to have such data on all residents of Lowell; in the real world a tiered data structure proves a useful compromise.

APPENDIX 5

Sources of Bias and Considerations of Representativeness

THROUGHOUT THIS book I have self-consciously examined relatively narrow samples in order to draw broader conclusions concerning the work and lives of women operatives in the Lowell textile mills in the antebellum period. In chapter 1 I discussed the representativeness of the Lowell mills and of the Hamilton Company in particular. At this point it makes sense to consider a number of narrower questions concerning possible sources of bias in the findings.

Even granting that the Hamilton payrolls are representative, a potential difficulty remains. The vast size of Hamilton records required sampling of extant payroll volumes. Three months of payrolls—July 1836, August 1850, and June 1860—provided the bulk of data on the experience of Hamilton workers in this period. The existence of additional, noncompany records—the city directory supplement and manuscript censuses—was the primary consideration in the choice of months.

The first question to pose is how the choice of these particular months may have affected the findings. For instance, were these periods of expansion or depression for the northern New England textile industry? The answer is that each of these years is best described as a "mixed" year for the industry. According to data compiled by Davis and Stettler, production in Waltham-Lowell type firms increased and then declined over the course of each year. Table A.4 presents data on quarterly output of fifteen Waltham-Lowell firms in 1836, 1850, and 1860.[1]

For each year we can see that production in the Waltham-Lowell mills peaked and then declined. Each time, the quarter of maximum output included the payroll month selected for detailed study. This fact is important because it offers some assurance that the payroll months are reasonably comparable.

TABLE A.4. QUARTERLY OUTPUT OF SELECTED WALTHAM-LOWELL FIRMS, 1836, 1850, 1860 (THOUSANDS OF YARDS)

Year	1st quarter	2d quarter	3d quarter	4th quarter
1836	11,534	12,238	12,642	12,186
1850	27,782	27,604	29,129	28,022
1860	43,084	43,229	40,881	40,447

In terms of wages the payroll periods are also comparable. None followed immediately after a wage cut. In fact for each month the most recent wage reduction had been about 2 years earlier.[2] Wages generally moved cyclically, reaching low points immediately after the periodic cuts in piece rates and then increasing steadily as productivity increased, until once again piece rates were cut. Given this cycle, each of the payroll months was at a point of relatively high daily earnings.

The earnings of women workers during these months are probably somewhat above average for a second reason. Women were generally paid a piece wage, and the longer they worked the more they could produce and thus the higher their earnings. Since the mills ran somewhat longer in the summer than in winter, the mean daily pay of operatives was greater then. In 1840, for instance, the mills ran 12 hours 45 minutes daily between May and September, although for the year as a whole they averaged only 12 hours 13 minutes daily. In the 1850s variation in the length of the working day declined, but operatives still averaged an extra 15 minutes daily during the summer months.[3]

Although the earnings reported here may be somewhat above the true average over the entire year, comparisons among the payroll periods are not affected. Throughout the antebellum period, the mills maintained longer hours between May and August. In other words the choice of these specific months does not introduce any relative biases into the findings. Each month was one of longer than average working hours. This fact gives added support to the contention that the findings are representative of the basic trends for wages in the antebellum period. They have not been unduly biased by the choice of payroll months.

Another source of possible bias stems from the impossibility of linking all workers in company registers, city directories, or the manuscript census. The incompleteness of record linkage left a certain amount of missing data on the nativity and residence of operatives. To the extent that unlinked workers were markedly different than linked ones, the findings reported may be misleading. To examine this question I shall estimate bias in the findings for the Hamilton work force in 1836, the year for which linkage was least complete.

One possible source of bias stems from the fact that men more often than women could not be traced in company register books. The longer work stints of male workers meant that they were signed into and out of the register volumes less frequently than women. Also, when clerks began filling out new register volumes, recording workers employed at that date, they tended to leave many entry columns, including nativity, blank. Because male workers worked more continuously than women, their entries were more likely to be affected by this practice. Due to these factors missing data on nativity occurred for 34 percent of Hamilton men, but only 14 percent of women. Assuming that immigrants comprised as large a proportion of unlinked men and women as of their linked counterparts, one can estimate the ethnic composition of the mill work force as a whole. Correcting in this way for missing data, the proportion of foreign-born at Hamilton increases from 3.7 to 3.8 percent.

However one might argue that the major source of bias results from the fact that individuals unlinked in the register books were more likely to be foreign-born than those linked. The clerk, for instance, may have been more likely to misspell Irish or English names, and thus the criteria used in determining links may have unduly discriminated against the foreign-born.

The fact that successive computer runs were made on the data each time they were updated means that it is possible to estimate bias due to missing data. Successive linkages reduced missing data on nativity from 205 to 167 cases, a decline of 18.5 percent. In this process, the proportion of immigrants increased slightly from 3.6 to 3.7 percent. As hypothesized immigrants were somewhat overrepresented among those initially un-linked in the company register volumes. Two of the additional 38 opera-tives linked were foreign-born. In other words, 5.3 percent of those with missing data compared to only 3.6 percent of those initially linked were foreign-born. If the remaining 167 cases with missing data also have this higher proportion of foreign-born, the proportion of immigrants among the overall work force would increase to 4.0 percent. Even if 10 percent of the remaining unlinked operatives were foreign-born, an unlikely figure, the proportion of immigrants at Hamilton would increase only to 4.8 percent. These two figures—4.0 and 4.8 percent—set reasonable up-per bounds on the proportion of immigrants at Hamilton in July 1836. Any error due to missing data—either 0.3 or 1.1 out of 3.7 percent—is of a relatively small magnitude. The impact of this error is insignificant when compared to the overall findings, that the proportion of foreign-born at Hamilton increased from 3.7 to 61.8 percent between 1836 and 1860.

Similar calculations may be made to estimate any error in the pattern of residence for operatives. Repeated linkage efforts reduced missing data on residence by 30 between the first and last computer analyses of the 1836 work force. Of the 30 operatives thus linked in either the company register volumes or city directories, 29—or 97 percent—resided in company housing. It is likely then that the figure of 73.7 percent living in company housing may set a lower limit for Hamilton operatives in 1836.

It is difficult however to estimate the correction of the residence find-ings due to missing data because of the nature of the sources. Most of the decline in missing data resulted from linkage in the *Lowell Directory* and its *Female Supplement*, particularly the latter. A brief analysis of the supplement indicated that this source had its own bias. According to the Hamilton register book, corrected and supplemented by the city direc-tory sources, 25.8 percent of female operatives lived in private housing. However a 1-in-10 selective sample of the supplement revealed that only 8 percent of Hamilton female operatives in the sample—5 of 66—resided in noncompany housing. In other words the supplement appeared to be systematically biased, overrepresenting operatives living in company boardinghouses. Supplement enumerators probably went to company boardinghouses and to the larger private ones in the course of compiling lists of operatives. They may well have missed some operatives who lived at home with their parents or who boarded with families in private tenements. Given this fact I would hesitate to use the changing proportion of company residents which resulted from further linkage in the city directory supplement to "correct" the overall findings reported in chapter 3.

This last example illustrates particularly well the pitfalls which await the overzealous quantifier who focuses too intensely on sophisticated linkage techniques and statistical tests. The data presented in this study are no better than the sources from which they are drawn. To the extent that company clerks and directory and census enumerators introduced systematic bias into their work, the historian's accuracy is limited. Sometimes, with care, one can estimate the error due to bias. At other times, while trying to reduce bias, one can introduce still further sources of error. Such appears to have been the case, to an unknown extent, in the payroll-city directory supplement linkage carried out for the 1836 Hamilton work force. This result indicates that there are, after all, limits to the accuracy with which we can determine the ethnic makeup and residence of Hamilton Company operatives in the 1830s. No matter how carefully we work to "reduce" missing data, the final result can be no better than the sources on which it is based.

On some occasions sources of bias may work in opposite directions, making the final results quite representative of the true population parameters in spite of incompleteness of record linkage. Such appears to have been the case in the analysis of the age distribution of operatives in 1850 presented in chapter 8. Overall only 45 percent of the mill work force were linked in the census. Because of conflicting biases, however, that fact had a minimal impact on the findings reported in table 8.3.

The 1850 census-linked group was a highly biased cross section of the Hamilton work force. It included relatively more men, more native-born, and more residents of company housing than the work force as a whole, as table A.5 reveals.

The differences between the census-linked group and the overall work force are clear and systematic. Linkage was more complete for those residing in company housing, and this group included larger numbers of native-born operatives than immigrants. Similarly linkage was more complete for those who headed households, a factor tending to favor the

TABLE A.5. COMPARISON OF THE 1850 CENSUS-LINKED GROUP AND THE
HAMILTON 1850 WORK FORCE

Characteristic	Census-Linked	Work Force
Percent male	30%	22%
Percent native-born	80	61
Percent in company housing	61	39
Total cases	531	1221

inclusion of men in the linked group. Finally linkage was more complete for individuals with uncommon names, another factor tending to exclude immigrants. The census-linked group was higher-paid than the work force as a whole, a fact that reflected the overrepresentation of males and of native-born in the group.

Aware from the outset of the incompleteness of the payroll-census linkage, I hesitated to use the data on age that the linkage had produced. Thus no effort was made to analyze the relationship of age and daily pay or to determine the mean age of 1850 operatives when they began and ended their careers at Hamilton. I did decide to estimate the age distribution of the Hamilton work force from these data, doing so only after I had been convinced that the findings were reasonably accurate.

The earlier analysis of the makeup of the Hamilton work force in 1836 guided my testing of the accuracy of the age distribution for 1850. In 1836 only 27 percent of the work force lived in private housing, but more than 50 percent of children working in the mills—23 of 44—did so. It seemed important to correct for the fact that the census-linked group underrepresented those living in private housing, and thus may have underestimated the proportion of children in the mill work force.

I also knew from the payroll-register linkage for 1850 that the proportion of children among males working in the mill was much higher than for females. Register book linkage demonstrated that 7.6 percent of males brought with them certificates of school attendance; for females the comparable figure was only 1.2 percent. This difference suggested that the census-linked group, because it overrepresented males, might overstate the proportion of children in the mill work force.

I attempted to correct for these possible sources of error by dividing the linked group into four subgroups: males living in company housing; males living in private housing; females living in company housing; and females living in private housing. I then determined the age distribution for each of these subgroups. Up to this point I had considered only the census-linked group.

In the estimating procedure I calculated the age distributions of the four subgroups—males and females in company and private housing—based on the linked population of 531 individuals. Then I weighted these four distributions by the actual proportions each subgroup comprised of the overall work force. In this procedure I extrapolated my findings to the remaining 690 individuals who had not been linked in the census. After this extrapolation I combined my findings to produce an age distribution for the overall work force, one that corrected for bias due to the incompleteness of payroll-census linkage. The results of these calculations are given in table A.6:

TABLE A.6. CORRECTED AGE DISTRIBUTION OF THE HAMILTON
1850 WORK FORCE

Age Group	Males	Females	Overall
Under 15	18.0%	2.9%	6.5%
15–19	12.1	32.0	27.2
20–29	46.0	43.6	44.2
30–39	14.2	13.4	13.6
40 and over	9.7	8.0	8.4

As had been predicted the new estimate indicates that the census-linked group understated the proportion of both males and females under 15 years of age. For the census-linked population 15.4 and 2.7 percent of males and females respectively were under 15, compared to 18.0 and 2.9 percent estimated here. Given the incompleteness of payroll-census linkage, these figures are remarkably close to the overall estimates. Interestingly the overall figure reported in table 8.3 is actually closer to the latest estimate than the separate male or female figures. In table 8.3 the overall proportion under 15 was 6.6 percent compared to 6.5 percent here. The greater accuracy of the overall figure is due to the fact that table 8.3 is based on data weighted by the inclusion of males in the census-linked group in a proportion far above their actual numbers in the overall work force. That bias has been corrected in the figures given here.

The striking fact in comparing the two tables is that they really do not differ greatly from one another. Three of the five figures in the "overall" columns differ from each other by less than one half of a percent. There are systematic errors introduced into the findings of table 8.3, but they work in opposite directions, tending to cancel each other out. This comparison suggests that the figures in chapter 8 are reasonable estimates for the overall age distribution of Hamilton workers in 1850, and no further corrections seem called for.

Up to this point the discussion of representativeness has considered the findings for the Hamilton work force in isolation. The selection of a separate sample of millhands from the 1860 census of Lowell provides another source for consideration of these questions. The 1860 census presents the first opportunity of drawing a sample of Lowell operatives comparable to the Hamilton Company work force. Previously the census recorded the occupations of males only, so that it was not possible to generate a representative sample earlier. The substantive findings regarding this sample were reported in chapter 10; the discussion here will be limited to points of comparison between the Hamilton work force and the census sample.

There are a number of differences between the two populations. The Hamilton Company produced only cotton goods in 1860, while the Lowell textile industry included a large-scale carpet factory and a woolen mill as well as eight major cotton textile firms. In addition, examination of the census revealed that operatives in print works and the Lowell Bleachery were considered "millhands" by enumerators. The sample was drawn from a population of textile and textile-related operatives, rather than from cotton textile workers in the large-scale corporations.

Comparative data on the two populations of textile operatives are given in table A.7.

TABLE A.7. COMPARISON OF THE 1860 HAMILTON WORK FORCE AND THE 1860 MILLHAND SAMPLE

Characteristic	Hamilton	Millhand Sample
Percent male	29.6%	30.1%
Percent native-born	38.1	51.1
Percent under fifteen	6.5	3.6
Percent residing in company housing	33.0	51.2
Total cases	1258	1090

The two groups evidently had similar proportions of males and females, but the remaining characteristics indicate considerable variation. The Hamilton work force included more foreign-born operatives, more children, and more noncompany residents than the census sample. These three differences however may in fact reduce to only one. Earlier discussions indicated that the residence and age distributions of operatives were highly correlated with ethnicity. Native-born operatives tended to live in company housing; immigrants, in private tenements and boardinghouses. Similarly, children in the mill work force were more likely to be immigrants than native-born in this period. Thus all three differences may be consequences of the fact that Hamilton apparently had a higher proportion of immigrants in its work force than the Lowell mill work force as a whole.

There are two possible explanations for this difference. Hamilton may have employed a greater proportion of immigrants than did other firms in Lowell. It is also possible however that there were systematic differences in the manner in which census enumerators and the clerk of the Hamilton Company recorded nativity.

A closer analysis of the 1860 millhand sample offers a possible basis for the apparent nativity difference. In the examination of the families of millhands, it was shown that 61 percent of female millhands living at home were foreign-born. However 80 percent of their parent-household heads were foreign-born.[4] In other words 19 percent of millhand daughters living at home were native-born children of immigrants. It is very possible that the census enumerator correctly recorded the birthplace of these operatives, but that the Hamilton clerk recorded what we would call the ethnicity of operatives. It is likely that the clerk recorded all Margaret Callahans and Peggy Flynns as "Irish" whether or not they were born in Ireland.

If this was in fact the case, the data presented in chapter 8 may overstate the proportion of the Irish in the work force.[5] Yet in a sense the clerk was correct in recording these native-born operatives as "Irish." As the children of immigrants, they were more closely tied to the immigrant than to the Yankee community. In other words the "ethnicity" of the company clerk may be more useful than the census enumerators' "birthplace" for studying the community of female operatives.

The only way to verify this explanation is to trace a group of Hamilton Company workers in both company register volumes and in the Federal

Manuscript Census and compare the results. Steven Dubnoff, a sociologist, carried out just this sort of linkage work in the course of his research.[6] His findings confirm the reasoning offered here. Dubnoff took all workers in the four main departments of mills A and B at Hamilton in June 1860 and successfully linked about two thirds in the manuscript census. In contrast to the 1850 census-linked group discussed above, Dubnoff's linked sample does not appear to overrepresent the native-born or residents of company housing. The ethnic makeup and residence patterns of those traced are similar to the work force as a whole.

For individuals successfully linked in both Hamilton registers and the census, we see clear evidence of a systematic difference in the recording of nativity in the two sources. According to the register books, 37.1 percent of this group are native-born; according to the census, 42.7 percent are native-born. Table A.8 presents data on the census and register nativity of the 348 Hamilton operatives linked in both sources.

TABLE A.8. SUMMARY OF CENSUS AND REGISTER NATIVITY OF HAMILTON
OPERATIVES IN MILLS A AND B, JUNE 1860

Nativity	Census	Register
United States	42.7%	37.1%
Canada	4.6	5.7
Great Britain	6.0	7.8
Ireland	46.6	49.1
Other Foreign	0.0	0.3
Total cases	348	348

For this sample the census enumerator recorded an additional 5.6 percent as native-born in comparison to the notations of the Hamilton Company clerk. A more detailed breakdown of listings reveals that 40 operatives were called "native" in the census but "immigrant" in register volumes. A smaller number, 21 overall, were recorded as immigrants in the census and native-born in the register. The net effect of these opposing trends is that census enumerators recorded 19 more operatives native-born than did the company clerk.

A certain, but indeterminate, proportion of the discrepancies in the two sources is due to linkage error. It is reasonable to assume, especially given the commonness of both Yankee and Irish names, that some of the links made between the payrolls and the census and register book listings were incorrect. Because the payrolls and register books were kept by one company and allowed the use of name, room, and entry and departure dates as linkage variables, the chances are that there are fewer errors in the payroll-register than in the payroll-census linkage.

Even if the entire 5.6 percent ethnicity difference is due to the nature of the initial data collection by census enumerators and the Hamilton clerk, there remains a substantial difference in the ethnic makeup of the Hamilton work force and the 1860 millhand sample. According to the data presented in chapters 8 and 10, 38 percent of the Hamilton work force and 53 percent of the 1860 millhand sample were native-born. The source of error just described can account for only about one third of this difference. It is reasonable to conclude that at any one point in time Hamilton was not entirely representative of the entire textile industry in Lowell. It may well have had in 1860 a larger proportion of immigrants in its work force than was true of the industry as a whole. However, I would contend that the basic trends evident in the work force of the Hamilton Company between 1836 and 1860 were duplicated in the other Lowell mills. Hamilton may have led in the employment of immigrants, but over time the other companies would certainly have followed its practice. In other words, although we may not be able to conclude that the mill work force in Lowell in 1860 was 62 percent immigrant, there is no doubt that a dramatic increase in the proportion of immigrants in the mill work force did occur between 1845 and 1860 and that a family-oriented labor system developed in this period. It is the trends reported in this study, and not the specific statistics at any single date, that are crucial to the interpretation made here.

Abbreviations

Locations of manuscripts frequently cited

BL   Baker Library, Harvard Graduate School of Business Administration, Boston, Massachusetts

HPL   Haverhill, Massachusetts, Public Library

LHSC   Lowell Historical Society Collection, University of Lowell

MHA   Manchester (N.H.) Historic Association

MVTM   Merrimack Valley Textile Museum, North Andover, Massachusetts

NHHS   New Hampshire Historical Society, Concord, New Hampshire

Private   Private Collections

SL   Arthur and Elizabeth Schlesinger Library on the History of Women in America, Radcliffe College, Cambridge, Massachusetts

UL   University of Lowell, Special Collections

VHS   Vermont Historical Society, Montpelier, Vermont

Notes

1. WOMEN WORKERS AND EARLY INDUSTRIALIZATION

1. Richard B. Morris, *Studies in the History of American Law: With Special Reference to the Seventeenth and Eighteenth Centuries* (New York: Columbia University Press, 1930), ch. 3; Julia Cherry Spruill, *Women's Life and Work in the Southern Colonies* (New York: Norton, 1972; originally published in 1938), ch. 16.

2. Karl Marx, *A Contribution to the Critique of Political Economy* (Chicago: Kerr, 1911), p. 11.

3. For a recent expression of the importance of human agency within a Marxist framework, see E. P. Thompson, *The Making of the English Working Class*, p. 9.

4. U.S. Bureau of the Census, *Historical Statistics of the United States*, p. 72.

5. Paul W. Gates, *The Farmer's Age: Agriculture, 1815-1860* (New York: Harper & Row, 1960), ch. 2.

6. George Rogers Taylor, *The Transportation Revolution*, p. 6. For more on these cities see David T. Gilchrist, ed., *The Growth of Seaport Cities, 1790-1825* (Charlottesville: University Press of Virginia, 1967).

7. Taylor, *Transportation Revolution*, pp. 210-11. See also Rolla Tryon, *Household Manufactures in the United States, 1640-1860*.

8. Nancy Cott, *The Bonds of Womanhood*, ch. 1; Tryon, *Household Manufactures*; Blanche Brown Bryant and Gertrude Elaine Baker, eds., *The Diaries of Sally and Pamela Brown*; "Diary Kept by Elizabeth Fuller," in Francis Blake, *History of the Town of Princeton . . . Massachusetts*, pp. 302-23.

9. U.S. Bureau of the Census, *Historical Statistics*, p. 72; Taylor, *Transportation Revolution*, p. 249.

10. Caroline Ware, *The Early New England Cotton Manufacture*. See also chapter 2 of this book.

11. Percy Bidwell, "The Agricultural Revolution in New England," pp. 235, 240.

12. U.S. Bureau of the Census, *Manufactures of the United States in 1860*, pp. xxi, xxxv.

13. John R. Commons et al., *History of Labour in the United States*, set the trend for much subsequent work. Even an outright revisionist such as Alan Dawley, *Class and Community*, while integrating women in his conceptual framework slights them in the basic quantitative work of his study. A notable exception to this general trend is Milton Cantor and Bruce Laurie, eds., *Class, Sex, and the Woman Worker*, with a fine introduction by Caroline Ware.

14. Paul Gustaf Faler, "Workingmen, Mechanics, and Social Change: Lynn, Massachusetts, 1800-1860" (Ph.D. diss., University of Wisconsin, 1971); Faler, "Cultural Aspects of the Industrial Revolution: Lynn, Massachusetts, Shoemakers and Industrial Morality, 1826-1860," *Labor History* (1974), 15:367-94; Faler and Dawley, "Working-Class Culture and Politics in the Industrial Revolution"; Bruce Laurie, "'Nothing on Compulsion': Life Styles of Philadelphia Artisans, 1820-1850," *Labor History* (1974), 15:339-66.

15. Shorter, "Female Emancipation, Birth Control, and Fertility in European History"; Shorter, "Illegitimacy, Sexual Revolution, and Social Change in Modern Europe," *Journal of Interdisciplinary History* (1971), 2:237-72.

16. Scott and Tilly, "Women's Work and the Family in Nineteenth-Century Europe"; Tilly, Scott, and Cohen, "Women's Work and European Fertility Patterns."

17. Recent interpretations of American women in the antebellum period place considerable emphasis on the growth of a new prescriptive literature expressing a new feminine ideal. See Barbara Welter, "The Cult of True Womanhood," for the fullest elaboration of this ideal. Both Gerda Lerner, "The Lady and the Mill Girl," and Cott, *Bonds of Womanhood*, place this image within the material context of women's actual work roles.

18. George S. Gibb, *The Saco-Lowell Shops*; John Ewing and Nancy Norton, *A History of the Bigelow-Sanford Carpet Company: Broadlooms and Businessmen* (Cambridge: Harvard University Press, 1955); Robert G. Layer, "Wages, Earnings, and Output of Four Cotton Textile Companies in New England, 1825-1860"; Layer, *Earnings of Cotton Mill Operatives, 1825-1914*; Paul F. McGouldrick, *New England Textiles in the Nineteenth Century*; Robert Brooke Zevin, "The Growth of Cotton Textile Production After 1815."

19. A number of more focused community studies are also useful. See Vera Shlakman, *Economic History of a Factory Town*; Constance M. Green, *Holyoke*.

20. Lowell was representative at the beginning of this period of only the northern sector of the New England cotton textile industry; the Rhode Island and Philadelphia regions had distinctive experiences. Over time, however, the differences between southern and northern New England declined considerably until by 1860 the features of shared technology and organization of production clearly outweighed earlier differences. For evidence on this convergence from the southern New England perspective see Jonathan Prude, "The Coming of Industrial Order." For a view of mill villages in the Philadelphia region, see Anthony F. C. Wallace, *Rockdale: The Growth of an American Village in the Early Industrial Revolution* (New York: Knopf, 1978).

21. Among other Lowell firms, only the Lawrence Company has a good run of surviving payrolls. The Lawrence, however, lacks register volumes that provide crucial evidence on workers' nativity and residence in Lowell. The studies of the social origins of workers in chapter 3 and of discrimination against the Irish in chapter 9 could be carried out only for Hamilton workers. The existence, however, of considerable aggregate data for the Lawrence and other Waltham-Lowell

firms has provided important evidence for checking the representativeness of Hamilton findings.

22. Lawrence Manufacturing Company Records, Correspondence, vol. MAB-1, broadside, Jan. 30, 1834; vol. MA-1, March 13, 1840. Company records hereafter cited as [Name] Co. Merrimack Co., Directors' Records, vol. 1, July 13, 1842; Tremont-Suffolk Mills Records, vol. FB-1, March 17, 1840 (hereafter cited as T-S Mills). All BL. *Timetable of the Lowell Mills to Take Effect September 21, 1853*, BL; Green, *Holyoke*, p. 48.

23. Lance Davis, "Capital Mobility and American Growth," p. 294; Shlakman, *Economic History*, table 1, pp. 39-42; Ware, *Early New England Cotton Manufacture*, pp. 148-50, 320-21; McGouldrick, *New England Textiles*, pp. 20-21. The conclusion regarding multiple treasurerships is based on correspondence in company records.

24. Nashua Co., Correspondence, Nov. 27, 1829, BL; Dover Co., Letter book, July 2, 1827, NHHS; Appleton Co., Agent's letter book, July 28, 1853, July 18, 1855, August [30], 1857, MVTM; Massachusetts Mills, Directors' Records, July 15, 1842, Jan. 30, 1843, Feb. 13, 1843, Oct. 18, 1851, Sept. 10, 1853, in Pepperell Co., vol. I-A-1, BL; Shlakman, *Economic History*, p. 42; Caroline Sloat, "The Dover Manufacturing Company," p. 54, note 6.

25. Nashua Co., Correspondence, Dec. 12, 1832, BL; Poignand and Plant Papers, June 25, 1829, as quoted in Ware, *Early New England Cotton Manufacture*, pp. 269-70. See also T-S Mills, vol. FB-1, Henry Hall to Robert Means, Jan. 21, Feb. 18, 1834, BL; Shlakman, *Economic History*, p. 62; Green, *Holyoke*, p. 48.

26. Layer, *Earnings*, p. 11; Layer, "Wages, Earnings, and Output," pp. 158, 167.

27. Stanley Lebergott, *Manpower in Economic Growth*, table A-12, p. 520.

2. THE EARLY TEXTILE INDUSTRY AND THE RISE OF LOWELL

1. Taylor, *Transportation Revolution*, pp. 210-11.

2. "Diary Kept by Elizabeth Fuller," in Blake, *History of Princeton*, pp. 306, 309-10, 315.

3. E. H. Cameron, *Samuel Slater*, pp. 37-56; Paul Rivard, "Textile Experiments in Rhode Island," significantly revises earlier accounts of Slater's contribution and demonstrates convincingly that Slater built upon the earlier work of Rhode Island mechanics.

4. Cameron, *Samuel Slater*, pp. 58-76; Peter J. Coleman, *The Transformation of Rhode Island, 1790-1860*, ch. 3; James B. Hedges, *The Browns of Providence Plantations*, ch. 8.

5. Ware, *Early New England Cotton Manufacture*, pp. 23, 32.

6. William R. Bagnall, *Samuel Slater and the Cotton Manufacture*, p. 46; Smith Wilkinson as quoted in George S. White, *Memoir of Samuel Slater*, p. 106.

7. Ware, *Early New England Cotton Manufacture*, ch. 3.

8. Victor S. Clark, *History of Manufactures in the United States*, p. 539. See also Coleman, *Transformation of Rhode Island*, pp. 80-81.

9. Clark, *History of Manufactures*, p. 539.

10. James Montgomery, *A Practical Detail of the Cotton Manufacture of the United States*, p. 13. For a broader view of the differences see Ware, *Early New England Cotton Manufacture*, pp. 29-30, 199.

11. Gary Kulik, "Pawtucket Village and the Strike of 1824," p. 13; Prude, "Coming of Industrial Order," p. 116.

12. Coleman, *Transformation of Rhode Island*, p. 91.

13. Nathan Appleton, *Introduction of the Power Loom*, pp. 7-9.

14. Coleman, *Transformation of Rhode Island*, p. 93, reports that the typical Rhode Island mill in 1832 was capitalized at less than $40,000.

15. Howard M. Gitelman, "The Waltham System and the Coming of the Irish," p. 231.

16. Appleton, *Introduction of the Power Loom*, pp. 15-16, attributed the boarding-house system and corporate paternalism to the far-sightedness of the mill's founders, but technological difficulties and economic necessity more adequately explain these developments. See also chapter 5 in this book.

17. Ware, *Early New England Cotton Manufacture*, pp. 212-14; Prude, "Coming of Industrial Order," pp. 115, 191-200.

18. Ware, *Early New England Cotton Manufacture*, p. 153; George S. Gibb, *The Saco-Lowell Shops*, p. 27. On this score I stand in sharp disagreement with the recent revisionist work of Robert Dalzell, who argues that the Boston Associates were more interested in the security of their investments than in the actual level of returns. See his "The Rise of the Waltham-Lowell System."

19. White, *Memoir of Samuel Slater*, p. 215. See also Appleton, *Introduction of the Power Loom*, p. 13.

20. Appleton, *Introduction of the Power Loom*, p. 19.

21. Charles Cowley, *Illustrated History of Lowell* (Boston: Lee and Shepard, 1868), pp. 25-28, 33; Appleton, *Introduction of the Power Loom*, p. 19. For more on the Middlesex Canal, see Mary Stetson Clark, *The Old Middlesex Canal* (Melrose, Mass.: Hilltop Press, 1974) and Christopher Roberts, *The Middlesex Canal, 1793-1860* (Cambridge: Harvard University Press, 1938).

22. For contemporary accounts of the growth of Lowell see Henry Miles, *Lowell As It Was*, and Appleton, *Introduction of the Power Loom*.

23. Merrimack Co., vol. 1, Directors' Records, 1822-1843, BL; Appleton, *Introduction of the Power Loom*, p. 24; Gibb, *Saco-Lowell Shops*, pp. 55-58.

24. Appleton, *Introduction of the Power Loom*, p. 17. The Merrimack Company was probably not the first textile firm to introduce calico printing, but it was certainly the most successful. See Sloat, "The Dover Manufacturing Company."

25. Gibb, *Saco-Lowell Shops*, ch. 3; Frances Gregory, *Nathan Appleton: Merchant and Entrepreneur, 1779-1861*, p. 203.

26. *The Lowell Directory*, 1836, pp. 7-9.

27. Arthur L. Eno Jr., ed., *Cotton Was King*, p. 255.

28. David J. Bruck, "The Schools of Lowell, 1824-1861," ch. 3, presents a fine discussion of the arrogance with which Kirk Boott attempted to "run" Lowell as well as the corporation under his control. Similar attitudes are evident in other

mill towns as well. Consider the line in a letter from the agent of the Nashua Manufacturing Company to his treasurer following the local election in March 1827: "I should think no man can have an office here without our consent." Nashua Co., vol. GB-1, March 14, 1827, BL.

29. Lance Davis, "Capital Mobility and American Growth," p. 294; Ware, *Early New England Cotton Manufacture*, Appendix K.

30. McGouldrick, *New England Textiles*, p. 21.

31. Women's letters occasionally describe the process of finding a job in some detail and refer to the role of the overseer in this process. See Mary Paul to Bela Paul, Nov. 5, 1848, Mary Paul Letters, VHS; Julia A. Dutton to Lucretia Dutton, Sept. 26, 1847, Dutton Family Letters, Private. Courtesy of Mrs. Aileen Eurich, Waitsfield, Vermont.

3. THE LOWELL WORKFORCE, 1836, AND THE SOCIAL ORIGINS OF WOMEN WORKERS

1. Miles, *Lowell As It Was*, pp. 162-94; Mass. House Document No. 50 (1845), in Commons et al., eds., *A Documentary History of American Industrial Society*, 8:133-51. For subsequent historians' accounts see Ware, *Early New England Cotton Manufacture*, ch. 8; Josephson, *Golden Threads*, ch. 4; Layer, *Earnings of Cotton Mill Operatives*, pp. 70-71; Layer, "Wages, Earnings, and Output," table 27, p. 226 ff.

2. Mary Hall Diary, *passim*, NHHS; New Hampshire Bureau of Vital Statistics, marriage of Mary Hall to Albert G. Capen, June 5, 1838; Lowell *City Directory*, 1834-1855.

3. Lawrence Co., vols. GA-1, GA-2, GA-3, BL. Hall worked in the Lower Weaving Room and her wages are recorded with that room in the monthly payroll series.

4. Harriet Hanson Robinson, *Loom and Spindle*, chs. 2-4, 8.

5. The actual choice of which Lowell firm to study is limited by the fact that payrolls are extant for only the Hamilton and Lawrence companies. The earlier starting point for the Hamilton payroll series, 1826 compared to 1833, coupled with the existence of separate register volumes providing the nativity and residence of workers, led to the selection of the Hamilton Company. For a fuller discussion of this choice and of the methods used in analyzing Hamilton records, see appendix 1.

6. The work force consisted of employees in the company's three mills at this time, in the repair shop, in the millyard, and on the firm's night watch force.

7. Layer, *Earnings of Cotton Mill Operatives*, pp. 70-71, presents almost identical figures for the ethnic makeup of the Hamilton work force at this date although utilizing somewhat different techniques to analyze company registers. He computes the ethnic composition of the work force by drawing samples of entrants as recorded in registers between 1830 and 1876. His figures thus indicate the makeup of those entering the mills in a given period, not of those actually working at a single point in time.

8. For a discussion of potential bias in the findings reported here see appen-

dix 5. There an attempt is made to estimate bias due to the incompleteness of linkage between payrolls and register volumes. That this problem is worth consideration should be evident from the fact that table 3.1 indicates that 167 of 1030 workers—more than 16 percent—could not be traced in register volumes. For men, this proportion reached fully a third.

9. Age analysis based on examination of the enumerations for Hamilton Company boardinghouses in the manuscript censuses for Lowell in 1830 and 1840. Linkage of Hamilton rental records and the census located 49 of 50 Hamilton tenants in 1830 and 48 of 50 in 1840. In the computation children under 10 and all males in the households were excluded from consideration. The overall female age distribution, summarized in chapter 3, is given in table N.1.

TABLE N.1. ESTIMATE OF AGE DISTRIBUTION OF FEMALE OPERATIVES AT THE HAMILTON COMPANY, 1830 AND 1840

Age (in years)	1830	1840
10–14	2.8%	3.9%
15–19	32.9	28.2
20–29	51.7	51.7
30–39	6.0	10.6
40–49	5.1	4.7
50+	1.4	1.0
Total cases	431	407

On the reasonableness of the assumption that girls under ten were not working in the mills see Robinson, *Loom and Spindle*, p. 30; Lucy Larcom, *A New England Girlhood*, p. 153. For a discussion of census schedules and instructions to enumerators see Carroll D. Wright, *The History and Growth of the United States Census*, pp. 28-52, 138-55. For corroborating findings see William Scoresby, *American Factories and Their Female Operatives*, p. 53; Mass. House Document No. 50 (1845), in Commons et al., *Documentary History*, 8:146; Edith Abbott, *Women in Industry*, p. 124.

10. Children's jobs included doffers in spinning and lap boys in carding. Register books recorded children who brought with them certificates of school attendance and noted only 24, about 2 percent of the work force. Lowell School Committee, *26th Annual Report* (Lowell, 1852), noted that 2,000 school certificates had been issued in the previous fourteen years, making an average of about 150 per year, consistent with the findings for Hamilton alone. On school attendance legislation see Charles Persons, "The Early History of Factory Legislation in Massachusetts," pp. 19, 21.

11. Hamilton Co., vols. 506-508, BL, lists all tenants of company houses and from the rental figures one can determine whether a given unit was a boardinghouse or a tenement.

12. The Boott Manufacturing Company agent in 1841 analyzed his company's register book and found that only 9 percent of operatives had permanent homes in Lowell, a finding comparable to the Hamilton data. Mass. House Document, No. 50 (1845), Appendix A, p. 19, as quoted in Ware, *Early New England Cotton Manufacture*, p. 219.

13. This study will be at once an examination of rural-urban migration and of the place of mill employment in the female life cycle. Earlier works that have influenced the approach taken here include Michael Anderson, *Family Structure in Nineteenth-Century Lancashire*, chs. 4, 5, 7; Peter R. Uhlenberg, "A Study of Cohort Life Cycles"; Laurence Glasco, "The Life Cycles and Household Structure of American Ethnic Groups"; Tamara Hareven, "The Family as Process: The Historical Study of the Family Cycle," *Journal of Social History* (1974), 7:322-29; Hareven, "The Dynamics of Kin in an Industrial Community."

14. Appendix 2 provides a fuller consideration of sampling procedures and methods employed in record linkage. Published sources included Charles Coffin, *The History of Boscawen and Webster; One Hundred and Fiftieth Anniversary of the Settlement of Boscawen and Webster*; James Otis Lyford, *History of the Town of Canterbury, New Hampshire, 1727-1912*; Augusta Harvey Worthen, *The History of Sutton, New Hampshire*; Willis Burton, *History: Boscawen-Webster, Fifty Years, 1883-1933*.

15. D. Hamilton Hurd, ed., *History of Merrimack and Belknap Counties*, pp. 181, 229, 627; Alonzo J. Fogg, *The Statistics and Gazetteer of New Hampshire*, pp. 69-73, 83-86, 345-46; Bryn E. Evans, "Sutton, New Hampshire and the Kearsarge Valley."

16. For overviews of the general difficulties confronting the majority of towns in New Hampshire in the period see Harold Fisher Wilson, *The Hill Country of Northern New England*, chs. 1-4; Norman W. Smith, "A Mature Frontier—The New Hampshire Economy, 1790-1850," *Historical New Hampshire* (1969), 24:3-19; Stewart Holbrook, *The Yankee Exodus*; Lois Kimball Mathews, *The Expansion of New England*; Lewis Stilwell, *Migration from Vermont*.

17. U.S. Department of State, *Compendium of the Enumeration . . . From the Returns of the Sixth Census*, pp. 106-17; 1840 Manuscript Census of Merrimack County, M704, Roll 240; Worthen, *History of Sutton*, pp. 285-91; Lyford, *History of Canterbury*, ch. 8; U.S. Department of Treasury, *Documents Relative to the Manufactures of the Unites States*, Document 5, Nos. 2, 6, 9, 20, 21; C. Benton and S. F. Barry, *A Statistical View of the Number of Sheep . . . in 1836* (Cambridge: Folsom, Willson and Thurston, 1837), pp. 13, 122. In terms of industry, Canterbury stood out somewhat from the other two towns as it included a thriving Shaker community with strong traditions of craft production. There is no evidence however that any Shakers were included in the Lowell migration, and in the analysis of tax inventories and census occupations Shakers have been excluded from consideration.

18. Fogg, *Statistics and Gazetteer*, pp. 69, 83, 345; Evans, "Sutton, New Hampshire," p. 8. The 1850 Agricultural Census for Merrimack County (manuscript volume in State Library, Concord, N.H.) provides the first breakdown at the town level of principal agricultural commodities for these three communities.

Boscawen and Canterbury per capita yields of oats and Indian corn were substantially above those of Sutton, while the latter had relatively larger herds of sheep than the other two.

19. Based on analysis of 1830 tax inventories for Boscawen, Canterbury, and Sutton. Means are for resident taxpayers only, and exclude property held in the names of heirs of estates. See also appendix 2.

20. Figures based on counting the number of individuals who entered or departed the company with nativity recorded in the appropriate register volume as Boscawen, Canterbury, or Sutton. Undoubtedly, a certain proportion of those for whom nativity was left blank came from these towns. Furthermore, one volume had faded so thoroughly that names and nativity could not be determined. Finally, register volumes are not extant for a period in the first half of the 1830s. Taken together, the difficulties suggest that the figure of 175 understates the actual number of women from these towns who worked at Hamilton.

21. *Boston Quarterly Review* (1840), 3:369-70. Whether the 15 percent figure for never married is high or low is difficult to judge without comparable studies for this time period. Robert V. Wells, "Quaker Marriage Patterns in a Colonial Perspective," *William and Mary Quarterly*, (1972), 3d ser., 29:415-42, found 15.9 percent of females in two Quaker meetings living to 50 without marrying. Uhlenberg, "A Study in Cohort Life Cycles," p. 411, found 12.9 percent of an 1830 cohort never marrying. Yasukichi Yasuba, *Birth Rates of the White Population in the United States, 1800-1860*, p. 109, found less than 10 percent of women born in cohorts after 1835 single between the ages of 45 and 54. The figures here suggest that millhands did not differ significantly from other rural women.

22. An earlier linkage would have been preferred, but the 1850 census provides the first enumeration of occupations. Unfortunately death and migration limited the number of fathers who could be traced at that date. The combination of census occupations and tax inventories gives some assurance, however, that fathers of millhands were primarily farmers.

23. Since the fathers of millhands were all household heads it seemed important to find a similar group for purposes of comparison. Therefore the tax inventories were linked with the enumeration of household heads in the manuscript census for the same year. All taxpayers were then recorded either as household heads or nonheads and the comparison made accordingly. For a fuller discussion of methods see appendix 2.

The findings here undoubtedly are subject to a certain amount of bias from the nature of the linkage process. Only parents of millhands linked in genealogies or local vital records could be traced in tax inventories. This process necessarily excludes millhands who lived in the three towns but were born and married elsewhere. The tendency would be to exclude millhands who were rather transient and to include those who persisted for relatively long periods of time. Given what we know from studies of geographical mobility, it is likely that the linkage process overstates somewhat the property holdings of the families of millhands. Unfortunately it is impossible to estimate the magnitude of any error resulting from this bias.

24. In order to insure that aggregate patterns did not mask significant variations among the three towns, I analyzed the data initially at the town level. The individual town results did vary, but in a manner that seemed to reinforce rather than contradict the main argument. In Boscawen and Sutton the median property holdings of fathers of millhands were below those for all male household heads. In Canterbury, the reverse was true. In all three towns, property holdings of millhand fathers were distributed in the middle tiers of assessed valuations. On the comparability of assessment practices over the 1830-1860 period see *Laws of the State of New Hampshire . . . Published by Authority* (Hopkinton: Isaac Long, Jr., 1830), pp. 551-59; *General Statutes of the State of New Hampshire* (Concord: B. W. Sanborn, 1867), pp. 115-23.

25. Persistent fathers obviously aged over this period and an attempt was made to compare them each census year with an appropriate control group. In 1850, 97 percent of linked fathers were 50 or over, and their property holdings were compared with those of male household heads of that age. Similarly, for 1860, millhand fathers were compared with household heads 60 and over.

26. This pattern contrasts with evidence on European working women presented in Joan Scott and Louise Tilly, "Women's Work and the Family in Nineteenth-Century Europe"; Tilly, Scott, and Cohen, "Women's Work and European Fertility Patterns." Unfortunately Scott and Tilly's recent book, *Women, Work, and Family* (New York: Holt, Rinehart and Winston, 1978), was not available at the time of this writing.

27. Mary Paul to Bela Paul, Sept. 13, 1845, Nov. 27, 1853, Dec. 18, 1853, VHS. Mary Paul, 21, and her father, 60, were recorded living in dwelling 533 in Claremont, New Hampshire. Manuscript Census (1850), M432, Roll 441.

28. Nell Kull, ed., "'I Can Never Be Happy There In Among So Many Mountains'—The Letters of Sally Rice," pp. 49-57; quote, p. 52.

29. Kull, "The Letters of Sally Rice," pp. 54, 57.

30. Loriman Brigham, ed., "An Independent Voice: A Mill Girl from Vermont Speaks Her Mind," pp. 142-46; quote, p. 144.

31. Elizabeth H. Hodgdon to Sarah D. Hodgdon, March 29, 1840, Rochester, N.H., Hodgdon Letters, NHHS.

32. Eben Jennison to Elizabeth Jennison, Charleston, Maine, Sept. 2, 1849; Eben Jennison to Elizabeth and Amelia Jennison, July 13, 1858. Jennison Letters, Private, in possession of Mary A. Dinmore, of Lowell, Mass. My thanks to Harry and Mary Dinmore for sharing these letters and permitting their use here.

33. *Lowell Offering*, 1:161-71, 263-66; 2:145-55, 246-250. Here I differ also with Cott, *Bonds of Womanhood*, p. 55, who argues that women operatives "usually engaged in wage earning in order to help sustain their families." This is certainly the conventional wisdom, but the evidence marshalled here calls this view into question.

34. Scott and Tilly, "Women's Work and the Family," pp. 42, 50-55.

35. Bryant and Baker, eds., *Diaries of Sally and Pamela Brown*, Feb. 11, 1832, May 31, Oct. 30, Nov. 7, Dec. 2, 7, 1833, Nov. 3, Dec. 5, 1837.

36. Scott and Tilly, "Women's Work and the Family," pp. 61-62.

37. In determining the proportion of first-, second-born (and so on) children working at Hamilton, I excluded five operatives who were only daughters in their families.

38. Tamara Hareven, "Dynamics of Kin," describes a similar phenomenon among French Canadians in the Manchester (N.H.) mills at the turn of the twentieth century. For the classic sociological statement of this pattern of chain migration see John S. MacDonald and Leatrice MacDonald, "Chain Migration, Ethnic Neighborhood Formation, and Social Networks," *Milbank Memorial Fund Quarterly* (1964), 42:82-97; see also Anderson, *Family Structure*, pp. 62, 152-60.

39. The description of the White family experience and other examples for operatives from Boscawen, Canterbury, and Sutton are based on the record linkage carried out in the social origins study. For each woman worker I prepared a separate index card and with each successive linkage I added new data to the card. Finally, I coded the data and prepared it in machine-readable form for statistical analysis. The index cards provide a rich source for the biographical information presented here.

40. For literary evidence on boardinghouse families in early Lowell, see Robinson, *Loom and Spindle*, chs. 2, 4, 5; Larcom, *New England Girlhood*, ch. 7.

41. Julia A. Dutton to Lucretia Dutton, Sept. 26, 1847, Clintonville, Massachusetts, Dutton Family Letters, Private. Martha Coffren may have been a sister. Earlier, another sister, Jane Dutton Witherby, had written to sister Martha encouraging her to come work in the mills. Jane Witherby to Martha Dutton, Feb. 28, 1847, Grafton, Massachusetts.

42. Eben Jennison to Elizabeth Jennison, Sept. 2, 1849, Jennison Letters, Private.

43. Wealthy Page to "Respected friends," June 6, 1830; Sarah Hodgdon to "Sister and mother," June ——; Wealthy Page to "Dear friends," n.d., Hodgdon Letters, NHHS.

44. Mary Paul to Bela Paul, Sept. 13, Nov. 20, 1845, April 12, 1846, Mary Paul Letters, VHS.

45. Louisa A. Sawyer to Sabrina Bennett, Dec. 30, ——, Bennett Family Letters, HPL.

46. Mary Hall Diary, *passim*, NHHS.

47. Sarah Hodgdon to Mary Hodgdon, June ——, Hodgdon Letters, NHHS. See also *Lowell Offering*, 1:245.

48. Visiting, care of sick neighbors, and the exchange of work were common elements in women's rural lives and provided bases for close same-sex relations among rural women. See Bryant and Brown, eds., *Diaries of Sally and Pamela Brown*, May 31, 1833, May 19, July 27, 1836, and Feb. 10, 1837. For an urban, middle-class variant, see Carroll Smith-Rosenberg, "The Female World of Love

and Ritual." In this pioneering piece, Smith-Rosenberg argues for the centrality of intimate same-sex relationships in the lives of women in the nineteenth century. Although she bases her argument on letters and diaries of upper- and middle-class women, the evidence presented in this chapter suggests that support networks of female friends and kin may have played as important a role in the lives of working-class women.

49. For similar findings among mill operatives in other communities see Anderson, *Family Structure*, pp. 118-20; Hareven, "Dynamics of Kin," pp. 17-21. Both these cases, however, examine kin networks in which parents played a significant role. In early Lowell, parents were conspicuously absent from the mills.

50. The difference in means reported here was paralleled by the actual distributions of the lengths of careers. More than 45 percent of those without relatives worked less than a year for the company, while only 24 percent were so transient among those with relatives. At the other end of the spectrum, 19.4 percent of those with relatives stayed six years or longer at Hamilton, compared to only 8.6 percent among those who came alone.

51. Occupational data on husbands came from disparate sources: marriage records, Lowell city directories, and the 1850 and 1860 federal manuscript censuses. For numerous individuals, more than one occupation was found. Since some of the men worked in Lowell briefly before settling in Boscawen, Sutton, and Canterbury, the latest occupational linkage (in point of time) was taken as the husband's occupation. Thus a Lowell machinist who returned to a Sutton farm was coded a farmer. This procedure attempted to make husbands of millhands as comparable to fathers as sources would permit.

52. Of the 24 husbands found in the 1850 census heading their own households, 75 percent were between the ages of 30 and 49, providing the basis for choosing this control group. The gap between husbands and their age peers continued through 1860, when 50.0 percent of husbands—9 of 18—were listed as farmers, compared to 63.1 percent of all male household heads between 40 and 59.

53. Thomas Monahan, *The Pattern of Age at First Marriage in the United States*, pp. 161, 174-76, 316-18; Nancy Osterud and J. Fulton, "Family Limitation and Age at Marriage"; Marc Harris, "A Demographic Study of Concord, Massachusetts, 1750-1850," p. 42; Daniel Scott Smith, "Parental Power and Marriage Patterns: An Analysis of Historical Trends in Hingham, Massachusetts," *Journal of Marriage and the Family* (1973), 35:419-28.

I have to acknowledge at this point that the strongest test of age at marriage data for millhands in the sample would be to compare millhands with non-millhands from the same three towns, or perhaps even with non-millhand sisters in the same families. This comparison, however, would require additional nominal record linkage far beyond the scope of this study. The uniformity of all the other studies of age at first marriage, and their contrast to the findings for women operatives, provide assurance of the distinctiveness of the patterns described here.

54. David Levine, *Family Formation in an Age of Nascent Capitalism*, pp. 51, 61-62.

55. Marriage records, genealogies, and city directories were utilized to determine spouse's place of residence before marriage. These sources plus the federal manuscript censuses of Boscawen, Canterbury, and Sutton were used to trace couples' residences after their marriage. Families were followed until the birth of their first child but attrition in the sample introduced considerable bias at this point. Table N.2 presents data on the overall marriage residence patterns of women workers.

TABLE N.2. MARRIAGE RESIDENCE PATTERNS OF NEW HAMPSHIRE
WOMEN WORKERS

Place	Husband's Residence Before Marriage[a]	Couple's Residence After Marriage[b]
Millhand's home town	35.5%	45.0%
Lowell	35.5	33.3
Other rural	22.8	13.3
Other urban	10.1	8.3
Total cases	79	60

[a] Proportions in this column add to more than 100.0% because a few men resided before marriage in both the millhand's home town and Lowell.
[b] Taken to be the first residence found after the marriage date through linkage in city directories, manuscript censuses, and local genealogies.

56. Worthen, *History of Sutton*, p. 192.

57. Zadock Thompson, *The History of Vermont*, p. 39, as quoted in Nicholas Ward, "Pianos, Parasols, and Poppa," p. 44.

58. "Farming Life in New England," *Atlantic Monthly* (August 1858), 2:341; also quoted in Joseph Kett, *Rites of Passage: Adolescence in America, 1790 to the Present* (New York: Basic Books, 1977), p. 96, and Wilson, *Hill Country*, p. 72.

59. Lura Currier to Harriet Hanson, Dec. 14, 1845; Maria Currier to Harriet Hanson, April 5, 1846, in Harriet Hanson Robinson Collection, SL. For published, but occasionally inaccurate, typescripts of these letters, see Allis Rosenberg Wolfe, "Letters of a Lowell Mill Girl and Friends, 1845-1846," pp. 96-102; for corrections and a successful attempt to place these letters in context see Lise Vogel, "Humorous Incidents and Sound Common Sense." My thanks to Lise Vogel for sharing her work in manuscript.

60. Mary Paul to Bela Paul, June 11, 1855, Mary Paul Letters, VHS.

4. THE SOCIAL RELATIONS OF PRODUCTION IN THE EARLY MILLS

1. Patrick Tracy Jackson, an early investor in Lowell, expressed this vision well when he first visited the undeveloped East Chelmsford site in 1821 and

predicted that within his lifetime the population of this new town would reach 20,000. Nathan Appleton, *Introduction of the Power Loom*, p. 19.

2. David Jeremy, "Innovation in American Textile Technology During the Nineteenth Century," pp. 54, 55; Samuel Batchelder, *Introduction and Early Progress of the Cotton Manufacture in the United States*, p. 68; Appleton, *Introduction of the Power Loom*, p. 9.

3. "Regulations agreed upon by Ag[en]ts of the Merr[imack] Mg. Co., Hamilton Mg. Co., A[ppleton] Co.," 1829, Unbound papers, Appleton Co., MVTM. The first blacklist references I have found in Hamilton register volumes in the 1830s appear in 1835 and 1836, suggesting that the company probably did not actually exchange lists with other companies until the turn-outs in Feb. 1834 and Oct. 1836. See Hamilton Co., vol. 283, entries for Lucinda Clough, Eliza Cross, Angeline Graves, Lucinda Giles, Belinda Gilson, Nancy Nutt, Lucinda Rollins, and Rosina Thompson, BL.

4. A straightforward tracing of a sample of women with surnames beginning with the letter "A" in Hamilton registers revealed numerous cases of workers who departed early or without regular notice and yet were rehired at a subsequent date. Hamilton Co., vols. 481-485, entries for Rosina Armon, Sarah Atkinson, Mary Jane Aiken, and Eliza Adams, BL. For a fuller discussion of discipline at Hamilton see Carl Gersuny, "'A Devil in Petticoats' and Just Cause." Gersuny's discussion, however, tends to remain a bit removed from actual conditions and fails to consider adequately limitations on corporate power.

5. John Coolidge, *Mill and Mansion*, figures 2, 3, pp. 251 ff.

6. Miles, *Lowell As It Was*, p. 64.

7. Richard D. Trevellick, in *Fincher's Trades Review*, (n.d.), reprinted in George E. McNeill, *The Labor Movement: The Problem of Today* as quoted in Herbert Gutman, "Work, Culture, and Society in Industrializing America, 1815-1919," pp. 556-57.

8. The tyranny of the bells in early Lowell was a repeated theme in operatives' complaints about industrial time-discipline. See *Lowell Offering*, 1:111. On this broader issue see E. P. Thompson, "Time, Work-Discipline, and Industrial Capitalism."

9. Alternative arrangements of floors were possible. The location of weaving and dressing might be reversed. Since warp yarn went to the dressing room and filling to weaving, either setup was equally efficient. Locks and Canals Collection, Shelf 112, Nos. 2245, 2259; Shelf 105, Nos. 581, 582, UL; Miles, *Lowell As It Was*, pp. 76-84; Montgomery, *Practical Detail*, p. 16; Theodore Sande, "The Architecture of the Cotton Textile Mills of Lowell, Massachusetts, 1822-1860."

10. Picking involved serious fire hazards. High operating speeds caused bearings to overheat, which, coupled with the flammability of both cotton and lubricating oil, proved dangerous. Fire destroyed one of the first mills of the Merrimack Company in 1829 and led to the separation of picking operations from the mills.

11. I am deeply indebted to Theodore Penn, Researcher in Technology at Old Sturbridge Village, and to Professor John Goodwin of the University of Lowell and the Lowell Historical Society for their careful readings and criticism of drafts of this section.

12. The conclusion that double carding predominated is based on inventories of several firms: Merrimack Co., Directors' Records, Inventory, May 19, 1830, BL; Tremont-Suffolk Mills, Unbound Letters, vol. FN-1, Oct. 3, 1833 (hereafter cited as T-S Mills), BL; Hamilton Co., Directors' Records, Inventory, April 1830, BL; Appleton Co., Unbound papers, Benjamin French to William Amory, Dec. 31, 1834, and Hamilton Mill B inventory (c. 1834), MVTM; William Burke, "Statistics Relating to the Cost of Manufacturing Drillings and Standard Sheetings in 1838 and 1876," pp. 6-7; Gibb, *Saco-Lowell Shops*, p. 632.

13. Montgomery, *Practical Detail*, p. 55; Walter English, *The Textile Industry*, pp. 67-68.

14. If drawing combined four ends and if the process were repeated three times in series, the final sliver would be the product of 4 × 4 × 4 or 64 doublings of the original card ends. The sliver would have been doubled this many times and have been stretched so that the final diameter remained unchanged. More importantly, it would be more even and uniform than the original slivers, a factor crucial to the quality of yarn in later steps.

15. English, *Textile Industry*, p. 169; Montgomery, *Practical Detail*, pp. 60-69. For wage data on speeders see table 4.1.

16. Larcom, *New England Girlhood*, p. 226. See also Jeremy, "Innovation in American Textile Technology," p. 55; Montgomery, *Practical Detail*, p. 97.

17. Montgomery, *Practical Detail*, pp. 101-4; Burke, "Statistics," pp. 6-8; John L. Hayes, *American Textile Machinery*, p. 91; Jeremy, "Innovation in American Textile Technology," pp. 60-61.

18. Gitelman, "Waltham System," pp. 231-32.

19. Although women earned varying piece wages, the fact that payrolls also recorded days worked and total earnings made it possible to compute mean daily earnings. Several men earned more than $100 in the payroll period. It is unclear whether they were extremely skilled operatives or sub-contractors who also had to pay assistants out of gross earnings, and they have been excluded from this analysis.

20. Each of these machines was equipped with a large clock, geared to revolve with the take-up beam, that measured the machine's output. Montgomery, *Practical Detail*, p. 68.

21. George Draper, *Facts and Figures for Textile Manufacturers*, p. 172.

22. Larcom, *New England Girlhood*, p. 226.

23. Robinson, *Loom and Spindle*, p. 38.

24. Eliza Adams, Lowell, to John Karr, Londonderry, N.H., Feb. 27, 1842, Private. Courtesy of Joanne Preston, Cambridge, Mass.

25. Robinson, *Loom and Spindle*, p. 30.

26. For a striking contrast in the social nature of work, see the treatment of

textile employment in the twentieth century in Robert Blauner, *Alienation and Freedom: The Factory Worker and His Industry*, (Chicago: University of Chicago Press, 1964).

27. Lucy Davis to Sabrina Bennett, Nashua (N.H.), Sept. 25, 1846, Bennett Family Letters, HPL.

28. *Lowell Offering*, 1:169.

29. *Ibid.*, 4:145-48, 169-72, 237-40, 257-59.

30. *Ibid.*, 4:170.

31. Findings for sparehands based on analysis of first four months' employment of newcomers in Mill A of Hamilton who began work between April and July 1836. Of 37 newcomers, only one was male. Of 36 females, two began work as regular operatives, while 34 began as sparehands and comprise the group described here.

32. Robinson, *Loom and Spindle*, p. 91; *Voice of Industry*, May 15, 1846; Lucy Larcom, *An Idyl of Work*, p. 81.

33. Wealthy Page to "Respected Friends," June 6, 1830, Hodgdon Letters, NHHS.

34. A Factory Girl, *Lights and Shadows of Factory Life*, p. 18.

5. THE BOARDINGHOUSE

1. Robinson, *Loom and Spindle*, p. 89.

2. Ware, *Early New England Cotton Manufacture*, pp. 198-202.

3. Gitelman, "Waltham System," p. 21.

4. Ware, *Early New England Cotton Manufacture*, p. 21.

5. Coburn, *History of Lowell*, p. 162.

6. Valuations of the Town of Lowell, 1826, 1830, 1860.

7. Appleton, *Introduction of the Power Loom*, pp. 15-16.

8. *Ibid.*, p. 16.

9. Miles, *Lowell As It Was*, p. 128.

10. For a view of corporate paternalism similar to that expressed here, see Gitelman, "Waltham System," p. 232. I take issue with the entirely moralistic view of John Kasson, *Civilizing the Machine: Technology and Republican Values in America, 1776-1900* (New York: Grossman Viking, 1976), ch. 2.

11. "Regulations to be Observed by all Persons Employed by the Suffolk Manufacturing Company," n.d.; "Regulations of Boarding Houses," n.d., Lawrence Co., LHSC; See also Lawrence Co., "Regulations to be Observed by all Persons Employed by the Lawrence Manufacturing Company," n.d.; "Regulations of Boarding Houses," 1833, BL.

12. "Regulations to be Observed by all Persons Employed in the Factories of the Middlesex Company," 1846; "Regulations for the Boarding Houses of the Middlesex Company," n.d., LHSC. See also *Handbook for the Visiter* [sic] *to Lowell*, pp. 42-46.

13. "Regulations of Boarding Houses," Lawrence Co., n.d., LHSC; "Regulations for the Boarding Houses of the Middlesex Company," n.d., LHSC. For

broader discussion see Ware, *Early New England Cotton Manufacture*, pp. 266-67; Gersuny, "'A Devil in Petticoats' and Just Cause."

14. Appleton Co., Unbound papers, MVTM.

15. Mary Paul to Bela Paul, April 12, 1846, Mary Paul Letters, VHS.

16. Montgomery, *Practical Detail*, pp. 173-74.

17. Based on analysis of the enumeration of Hamilton boardinghouses in manuscript censuses of Lowell for 1830 and 1840 and examination of later photographs of buildings, Locks and Canals Collection, UL. See also Coolidge, *Mill and Mansion*, Figures 4, 5, 8, 9, 19, 21, following p. 251.

18. *Operatives' Magazine*, 2:100, in Abbott, *Women in Industry*, p. 129; H. E. Back to Harriet Hanson, Sept. 7, 1846, Harriet Hanson Robinson Collection, SL; *Voice of Industry*, March 26, 1847.

19. *Lowell Offering*, 1:169.

20. *Ibid.*, 2:65-79, 5:218.

21. Robinson, *Loom and Spindle*, pp. 65-66.

22. *Lowell Offering*, 1:5, 4:148.

23. Robinson, *Loom and Spindle*, p. 89; Larcom, *New England Girlhood*, p. 200; *Voice of Industry*, Jan. 9, 1846, Dec. 26, 1845.

24. Cott, *Bonds of Womanhood*, pp. 176-77; see also Smith-Rosenberg, "Female World of Love and Ritual," p. 19.

25. Miles, *Lowell As It Was*, pp. 144-45.

26. B. H. Piper to Luther M. Trussell, Sept. 4, 1860; R. M. Piper to LMT, Sept. 20, 1860; LMT to Delia Page, Sept. 7, 11, Nov. 16, 25, 1860, Delia Page Letters, Private. Courtesy of Mildred Tunis, New London, N.H.

27. *Lowell Offering*, 4:14-23.

6. THE EARLY STRIKES: THE 1830s

1. Proclamation of striking women workers, Lowell, February 1834, *Boston Evening Transcript*, Feb. 18, 1834.

2. For a fine analysis of exactly this process in a shoemaking town see Dawley, *Class and Community*.

3. Commons et al., *History of Labour in the United States*, vol. 1, parts 2 and 3; Philip S. Foner, *History of the Labor Movement in the United States*, vol. 1, chs. 7-12.

4. Commons, *History of Labour*, vol. 1, part 3.

5. *Ibid.*, pp. 195-284, 458-66; Foner, *History of the Labor Movement*, ch. 8; Edward Pessen, *Most Uncommon Jacksonians: The Radical Leaders of the Early Labor Movement* (Albany: State University of New York Press, 1967); Walter Hugins, *Jacksonian Democracy and the Working Class: A Study of the New York Workingmen's Movement, 1829-1837* (Stanford: Stanford University Press, 1960).

6. Commons, *History of Labour*, 1:389-92.

7. *Ibid.*, pp. 454-58.

8. Ware, *Early New England Cotton Manufacture*, p. 291. See also Gutman, "Work, Culture, and Society," p. 551; Gitelman, "Waltham System," p. 237.

9. On the efforts of the New England Association of Farmers, Mechanics, and

Other Working Men to attract factory operatives, see Commons, *History of Labour*, 1:304-6.

10. Lawrence Co., vol. MAB-1, broadside, Jan. 30, 1834, BL.

11. Tremont-Suffolk Mills, Correspondence, vol. FN-1, Henry Hall to Robert Means, Jan. 21, 1834, BL. Hereafter cited as T-S Mills.

12. Lawrence Co., vol. MAB-1, William Austin to Henry Hall, Feb. 12, 1834, BL; see also T-S Mills, vol. FN-1, John Aiken to Henry Hall, Feb. 12, 1834, BL. The single best source for the lively agent-treasurer correspondence on the turn-out is Layer, "Wages, Earnings, and Output," pp. 496-503.

13. T-S Mills, vol. FN-1, John Aiken to Henry Hall, Feb. 12, 1834, BL.

14. Appleton Co., Unbound Papers, MVTM.

15. Lawrence Co., vol. MAB-1, William Austin to Henry Hall, Feb. 15, 1834, BL.

16. Boston *Evening Transcript*, Feb. 17, 1834.

17. *Ibid.*, Feb. 18, 1834.

18. Lawrence Co., vol. MAB-1, William Austin to Henry Hall, Feb. 17, 20, 24, 28, March 4, 9, 1834, BL.

19. *Ibid.*, Feb. 15, 1834.

20. *Ibid.*, Feb. 14, 1834. Would that we had comparable first-person accounts from the perspective of the women workers themselves. All that survives is the briefest mention of the turn-out in the diary of a worker who it seems did not take part. Mary Hall's diary for this period reads: "Feb. 14: To day some excitement amongst the girls in the Factories respecting the wages and many of the girls have left their work. Feb. 15: The excitement increases & many more have left." Mary Hall Diary, NHHS.

21. Boston *Evening Transcript*, Feb. 18, 1834. Women in the great shoemakers' strike in Lynn in February 1860 carried a banner that mirrored the rhetoric of Lowell workers: "American Ladies Will Not Be Slaves: Give Us a Fair Compensation And We Labour Cheerfully." Dawley, *Class and Community*, p. 82.

22. *The Man*, Feb. 22, 1834, quoted in Ware, *Early New England Cotton Manufacture*, p. 274.

23. Seth Luther, *An Address to the Working-Men of New-England*, p. 26; Dawley, *Class and Community*, pp. 71, 80.

24. One stanza of a song expressed this pride well:

> The overseers they need not think,
> Because they higher stand;
> That they are better than the girls
> That work at their command.

"The Lowell Factory Girl," broadside, LHSC, also quoted in Philip Foner, *The Factory Girls*, p. 8. See also Robinson, *Loom and Spindle*, p. 72; *Lowell Offering*, Feb. 1841, p. 45.

25. See chapters 3 and 11 for a fuller discussion of the economic independence of operatives in the period.

26. In yet another way the wage cuts might have been seen as threatening to

"enslave," in that they would have required women on piece wages to speed up their work simply to maintain their customary level of earnings.

27. Appleton Co., Unbound papers, MVTM.

28. Boston *Evening Transcript*, Feb. 17, 1834; Lawrence Co., vol. MAB-1, William Austin to Henry Hall, Feb. 17, 1834, BL.

29. Lawrence Co., vol. MAB-1, Feb. 15, 1834, BL.

30. Boston *Evening Transcript*, Feb. 17, 1834. The protests were far from "spontaneous outbreaks of blind protest," as described in Gitelman, "Waltham System," p. 237.

31. Lawrence Co., vol. MAB-1, William Austin to Henry Hall, March 1, 1834, BL; *Lowell Directory* (1834), pp. 6-8.

32. Lawrence Co., vol. MAB-1, William Austin to Henry Hall, Feb. 14, 1834, BL; see also Feb. 15, March 4, 1834.

33. Lawrence Co., vol. MAB-1, Henry Hall to William Austin, Feb. 15, 1834, BL.

34. Mary Paul Letters, *passim*, VHS, provide numerous indications of the quoting of wages in terms of that portion above the price of room and board. Robinson, *Loom and Spindle*, p. 83, errs when she recalls that a cut in wages prompted the turn-out. Her mistake, however, confirms the point I am making here, that women workers viewed the increase in board rates as a reduction in wages.

35. Robinson, *Loom and Spindle*, p. 84.

36. T-S Mills, vol. FB-1, Henry Hall to Robert Means, Sept. 27, 1836, BL.

37. Robinson, *Loom and Spindle*, pp. 84-85.

38. Lawrence Co., vol. MAB-1, William Austin to Henry Hall, Aug. 13, 1836, BL.

39. Robinson, *Loom and Spindle*, p. 83; Boston *Evening Transcript*, Oct. 4, 6, 1836; *Zion's Herald*, Oct. 5, 1836; Boston *Daily Times*, Oct. 6, 1836; *Lowell Directory* (1836), pp. 6-9.

40. T-S Mills, vol. FN-1, John Aiken to Henry Hall, Oct. 14, 17, 1836, BL. For a fuller discussion of methods in determining strike participation at the Hamilton Company, see appendix 1. On the closing of Mill A, see Hamilton Co., vol. 285, BL.

41. Lawrence Co., vol. MAB-1, John Aiken to Henry Hall, Oct. 3 and 4, 1836, Bl; *Lowell Directory* (1836), p. 9.

42. *National Labourer*, Oct. 29, 1836, as quoted in John B. Andrews and W. D. P. Bliss, *History of Women in Trade Unions*, p. 30; Boston *Daily Times*, Oct. 6, 1836.

43. T-S Mills, vol. FN-1, John Aiken to Henry Hall, Oct. 10, 1836, BL.

44. Herbert J. Lahne, *The Cotton Mill Worker*, ch. 13; David Montgomery, *Beyond Equality*, chs. 6 and 7.

45. "Records of Some of the Principal Events in the Life of Aaron Lummus," p. 287. MS autobiographical memoir of an itinerant Methodist minister, written 1850-1857, Old Sturbridge Village.

46. *Zion's Herald*, Oct. 19, 1836. Proportion of Hamilton workers paid on a daily basis computed from table 4.1; Lawrence Co., vol. MAB-1, John Aiken to Henry Hall, Oct. 17, 1836, BL.

47. Appleton Co., Unbound papers, MVTM; *Lowell Directory* (1834), pp. 6-8; The typical room distribution for women workers is taken from that obtaining at the Hamilton Company in July 1836.

48. *Zion's Herald*, Oct. 19, 1836. The October figure cannot be accounted for by normal seasonal fluctuations. See Layer, "Wages, Earnings, and Output," table 27. Variations in turnover in September, October, and November were typically 25 percent or less between 1831 and 1840, far lower than the 100 percent differences evident here.

49. Gutman, "Work, Culture, and Society," p. 543, makes this same general point as he establishes a conceptual framework for examining the experience of the American working class in the years 1815-1919. In his treatment of women workers in early Lowell, however, he is incorrect in suggesting that there is "little evidence before 1840 of organized protest."

50. *Manufacturers and Farmers' Journal*, May 31, 1824, as quoted in Kulik, "Pawtucket Village," pp. 22-23.

51. Kulik, "Pawtucket Village," pp. 20-26.

52. Andrews and Bliss, *History of Women in Trade Unions*, pp. 23-24. For an account of another brief, and apparently unsuccessful turn-out, see Almond H. Davis, *The Female Preacher, or Memoir of Salome Lincoln* (New York: Arno Press, 1972; originally published in 1843.), pp. 51-52.

53. T-S Mills, vol. FB-1, Henry Hall to Robert Means, Jan. 21, Feb. 18, 1834, BL.

54. *The Man*, as cited in Ware, *Early New England Cotton Manufacture*, p. 274; T-S Mills, vol. FN-1, C. L. Tilden to Henry Hall, March 4, 1834, BL.

55. *The Man*, March 8, 1834, as quoted in Shlakman, *Economic History*, pp. 60-61; Andrews and Bliss, *History of Women in Trade Unions*, p. 26.

56. T-S Mills, vol. FB-1, Henry Hall to Robert Means, Sept. 24, 1836, BL; Shlakman, *Economic History*, p. 62.

7. THE TEN HOUR MOVEMENT: THE 1840s

1. *Voice of Industry*, Jan. 9, 1846 (hereafter cited as *Voice*).

2. Tremont-Suffolk Mills, vol. FB-1, Henry Hall to Robert Means, May 11, 13, 1837, vol. FB-2, Henry Hall to Robert Means, March 17, 1840 (hereafter cited as T-S Mills); Hamilton Co., Directors' Records, p. 225, also vol. 670, Thomas Cary to John Avery, March 14, 1840; Merrimack Co., Directors' Records, March 21, 1840; Lawrence Co., Letters, Agent to Treasurer, March 13, 20, May 6, 1840. All BL.

3. The fullest secondary account of the labor struggles in the 1840s is found in Norman Ware, *The Industrial Worker, 1840-1860*; Persons, "Early History of Factory Legislation," ch. 1.

4. The specific terms "speedup" and "stretch-out" were not used in contemporary Lowell, but have come into common usage since that time, particularly with reference to the textile industry.

5. Scoresby, *American Factories*, pp. 30-31.

6. *Voice*, Sept. 11, 1846.

7. *Voice*, March 13, 1846.

8. Hamilton Co., vols. 288-290, 330-332; *Statistics of Lowell Manufactures*, 1840, 1854, BL. In these calculations, doffers and male overseers and their assistants have been excluded.

9. *Voice*, May 15, 1846. For a similar protest a decade earlier in Amesbury (Mass.), see Andrews and Bliss, *History of Women in Trade Unions*, pp. 35-36.

10. Appleton Co., Unbound papers, "Memo Relating to Prem[ium]s," MVTM.

11. *Voice*, Jan. 8, 1847.

12. *Voice*, Jan. 30, 1846; see also Sept. 11, 1846, Feb. 11, 1847.

13. Thompson, "Time, Work-Discipline, and Industrial Capitalism," p. 85.

14. Commons et al., *History of Labor*, pp. 185-92, 302-12, 384-95; Commons et al., *Documentary History*, 6:39-49, 76-99, 253.

15. Persons, "Early History," pp. 24-28, 42-46.

16. Petitions 1587/8 and 1587/9 (1845), Mass. State Archives.

17. *Voice*, Sept. 18, 1846.

18. Mass. House Document, No. 50 (1845) in Commons et al., *Documentary History*, 8:134-38. One of those giving testimony, Sarah Bagley, later claimed that the committee report distorted the women's accounts. See *Voice*, Jan. 9, 1846.

19. Commons et al., *Documentary History*, 8:148-51.

20. *Voice*, Jan. 9, 1846, Nov. 28, 1845.

21. Petition 11983 (1846), Mass. State Archives; *Voice*, April 24, 1846.

22. *The Operative*, Dec. 28, 1844. The Lowell FLRA was not the first female labor reform organization formed in the period. Women in Fall River organized a Ten Hour Association as early as May 1844. See Fall River *Mechanic*, May 4, 11, June 1, 1844. My thanks to Sue Benson for sharing selections from this early labor paper.

23. *Voice*, April 3, 1846.

24. N. Ware, *Industrial Worker*, pp. 206-7; Andrews and Bliss, *History of Women in Trade Unions*, p. 54; quote, *Voice*, June 5, 1845.

25. *Voice*, July 10, Sept. 18, Nov. 7, 1845, Jan. 23, Oct. 2, 1846; Andrews and Bliss, *History of Women in Trade Unions*, pp. 53-55. Accounts of the meetings of the NEWA and the reports of the LFLRA are in Commons et al., *Documentary History*, 8:86-132.

26. Andrews and Bliss, *History of Women in Trade Unions*, p. 70; *Voice*, Jan. 23, Feb. 13, 20, 1846; Huldah J. Stone to Thomas W. Dorr, April 12, 1846, Hay Library, Brown University.

27. William Henry Channing was a Boston minister and supporter of Associationism in the 1840s and an active participant in labor reform activity. John Allen was an active labor and land reformer, editor for a time of the *Voice of Industry*, and a candidate for Massachusetts Lieutenant-Governor on a land reform ticket in 1846.

28. *Voice*, May 22, 1846; Andrews and Bliss, *History of Women in Trade Unions*, p. 76; quote, Huldah J. Stone to Thomas W. Dorr, April 12, 1846.

29. *The Operative*, Feb. 15, 1845; *Vox Populi*, March 13, 1846.

30. *Voice*, July 31, Nov. 7, 1845, March 6, 1846, June 4, 25, July 2, 30, 1847.

31. *Ibid.*, Jan. 9, 23, Feb. 13, May 15, 22, 1846; see also Jan. 9, 1845.

32. *Ibid.*, Jan. 9, 1845.

33. *Ibid.*, Dec. 19, 1845, July 25, 1846.

34. *Ibid.*, Dec. 26, 1845, June 19, July 24, 1846, April 9, 1847.

35. *Ibid.*, May 22, 1846, March 11, April 8, 22, 1847.

36. *Ibid.*, Oct. 16, 30, Nov. 13, 1846; quote, Sept. 11, 1846.

37. Essex Co., Samuel Lawrence to Charles Storrow, March 6, 1847, MS 306, MVTM.

38. *Voice*, Jan. 8, 1847. N. Ware, *Industrial Worker*, p. 219, argues that Lowell women were instrumental in the adoption by the NEWA of its new constitution and its new name, and indicates that they had modified their own constitution somewhat earlier. It was only in January 1847, however, after the emergence of the New England Labor Reform League, that the LFLRA drastically modified its constitution to add mutual insurance features.

39. *Voice*, Sept. 18, 1846; Lowell *American*, Dec. 1, 1849. On Associationism, see N. Ware, *Industrial Worker*, ch. 11; Commons et al., *Documentary History*, 7:185-284. On cooperatives see N. Ware, *Industrial Worker*, ch. 13; Commons et al., *Documentary History*, 8:263-79; Edwin Rozwenc, *Cooperatives Come to America: The History of Protective Union Store Movement, 1845-1867* (Mount Vernon, Iowa: Hawkeye-Record Press, 1941), pp. 62-63, 88, 125-35.

40. Petition 11983 (1846), Mass. State Archives. The estimate of 2,500 is based on analysis of the 4,281 signers of the petition. Women comprised 58 percent of those whose names could be clearly distinguished, while in 355 cases names were either illegible or the use of initials made it impossible to determine sex. Assuming that women made up the same proportion of these remaining cases, I estimate a total of 2,495 female petition signers. For the number of women in the mill work force see *Statistics of Lowell Manufactures* (1846), BL.

41. Faler and Dawley, "Working-Class Culture and Politics in the Industrial Revolution," pp. 468-69.

42. *Lowell Offering*, 2:24, 5:263.

43. *Ibid.*, 3:48, 5:263. For evidence on corporation support of the *Offering*, see Josephson, *Golden Threads*, pp. 196-203; N. Ware, *Industrial Worker*, p. 90.

44. *Voice*, Nov. 13, 1846, also quoted in N. Ware, *Industrial Worker*, p. 144; Commons et al., *Documentary History*, 8:139; *Lowell Offering*, 5:96.

45. Commons et al., *Documentary History*, 8:148-51.

46. *Voice*, March 13, 1846.

47. Barbara Welter, "The Cult of True Womanhood"; Gerda Lerner, "The Lady and the Mill Girl."

48. *Voice*, Dec. 26, 1845, Jan. 9, 1846.

49. *Ibid.*, Jan. 9, Mar. 6, 1846.

50. *Ibid.*, March 13, 1846, April 16, 1847.

51. Gerda Lerner, *The Grimke Sisters of South Carolina: Rebels Against Slavery* (Boston: Houghton Mifflin, 1967), chs. 11, 12; Carroll Smith-Rosenberg, "Beauty,

the Beast, and the Militant Woman"; Susan Porter Benson, "Women, Networks, and Reform: The Providence Employment Society, 1837-1858," paper presented at the Berkshire Conference on the History of Women, June 1976.

52. Smith-Rosenberg, "Beauty, the Beast, and the Militant Woman," pp. 577-78; Cott, *Bonds of Womanhood*, ch. 5.

53. Welter, "True Womanhood," pp. 158-63. For more on the relationship of the new ideal to the changing economic position of women, see Lerner, "The Lady and the Mill Girl."

54. The "cult" ideal of dependence stood in sharp contrast to the value of independence stressed repeatedly in women's writings and in popular culture in mill towns. Consider the popular "Song of the Spinners" (*Lowell Offering*, 1:32):

> Despite of toil we all agree,
> or out of the Mills, or in,
> Dependent on others we ne'er will be
> So long as we're able to spin.

See also *Lowell Offering*, 5:140. The theme of independence was of such widespread appeal among mill operatives that it bridged the gulf between rebels and traditionalists.

55. *Voice*, March 13, 1846, April 16, 1846.

56. *Lowell Offering*, 1:130-31. For a contrasting view see *ibid.*, 1:191-92.

57. *Voice*, May 8, 1846.

58. *Ibid.*, Jan. 23, 1846.

8. THE TRANSFORMATION OF LOWELL, 1836-1850, AND THE NEW MILL WORKFORCE

1. Robert Brook Zevin, "The Growth of Cotton Textile Production After 1815"; Victor S. Clark, *History of Manufactures in the United States*, ch. 20.

2. *Statistics of Lowell Manufactures*, 1840, 1850, BL; *Compendium of the Enumeration . . . of the Sixth Census*, pp. 106-29; J. D. B. Debow, *Statistical View of the United States . . . Being a Compendium of the Seventh Census*, p. 180.,

3. Donald B. Cole, *Immigrant City: Lawrence, Massachusetts, 1845-1921* (Chapel Hill: University of North Carolina Press, 1963); Green, *Holyoke*.

4. *Statistics of Lowell Manufactures*, 1835, 1845, 1847, 1848, BL.

5. John Coolidge, *Mill and Mansion*, pp. 69-70; *Statistics of Lowell Manufactures*, 1845, 1846, BL; McGouldrick, *New England Textiles*, p. 20.

6. Expansion after the Civil War carried this process still further as the mills added one and sometimes two additional stories to their original structures, removing the attractive pitched clerestory roofs and topping the buildings off with a flat roof that provided more work space in the uppermost story.

7. Patrick Malone and Larry Lankton, "Water Power in Lowell, Massachusetts" (1974), pp. 13-20. Manuscript.

8. Coolidge, *Mill and Mansion*, p. 69.

9. *Ibid.*, p. 76.

10. Josiah Curtis, "Brief Remarks on Hygiene of Massachusetts," p. 36; also quoted in Coolidge, *Mill and Mansion*, p. 188, note 53.

11. Clark, *History of Manufactures*, pp. 386-87; Ware, *Early New England Cotton Manufacture*, p. 111; McGouldrick, *New England Textiles*, p. 32.

12. Ware, *Early New England Cotton Manufacture*, p. 111; McGouldrick, *New England Textiles*, p. 33, describes the failure of an 1842 effort on the part of Lowell companies to restrict their output and thereby stabilize the price of their products.

13. Ware, *Early New England Cotton Manufacture*, p. 113. Several historians since Ware have contested her analysis. See Shlakman, *Economic History*, pp. 109-17; McGouldrick, *New England Textiles*, ch. 4.

14. *Statistics of Lowell Manufactures*, 1840, 1854, BL; Hamilton Co., vols. 288-290, 330-332, BL. The analysis is based on a comparison of the actual numbers of operatives in the spinning and weaving departments with the numbers of spindles and looms in production. Male overseers and their assistants have been excluded for both departments; for spinning, bobbin hands have also been excluded. All studies acknowledge that a speedup occurred in this period, but scholars differ over whether women had to work harder because of it; some argue that improved machinery accounted for the increase in productivity. See McGouldrick, *New England Textiles*, p. 41; Layer, "Wages, Earnings, and Output," p. 234.

15. *Statistics of Lowell Manufactures*, 1840, 1854, BL.

16. Layer, *Earnings of Cotton Mill Operatives*, pp. 24-27; Ware, *Early New England Cotton Manufacture*, pp. 112-13.

17. Hamilton Co., vols. 315, 316, BL. Mule spinning could not totally displace throstle spinning, as the yarn produced on mules was generally not strong enough to be used as warp. It produced a fine, soft yarn particularly well suited for use as filling.

18. Based on a comparison of Hamilton payrolls and a July 1852 inventory of machinery. There were 25 job hands employed in mulespinning and 52 mule-spinning frames with 18,240 spindles overall. Hamilton Co., vol. 19, "Inventories—Costs—Valuations, Machinery and Property, 1833-1907"; payrolls, vols. 330, 332, BL.

19. Hamilton findings are confirmed by an independent analysis in Layer, "Wages, Earnings, and Output," p. 186. This development also reflected the broader changes throughout the cotton textile industry of New England in this period. See Shlakman, *Economic History*, p. 139; Green, *Holyoke*, p. 30n; Gitelman, "Waltham System," p. 242. Even smaller factory villages such as Webster, Massachusetts, site of several of Samuel Slater's mills, were not immune from this general trend. Prude, "Coming of Industrial Order," p. 330, shows that the proportion of immigrants among textile workers enumerated in the federal manuscript censuses rose from 40.2 to 74.1 percent in the period 1850-1860.

20. These figures are drawn from an analysis of the monthly payrolls at Ham-

ilton for July 1836, August 1850, and June 1860. While the number of Yankee females at Hamilton declined steadily over the period, the number of identifiable immigrant women skyrocketed from 26 in 1836 to 370 in 1850 to 524 in 1860.

21. John Clark to Jesse Huse, July 27, 1847, LHSC. For an operative's view, see *Voice of Industry*, Jan. 2, 1846.

22. *Fifth Census: Or Enumeration of the Inhabitants of the United States*, pp. 10–11; *Compendium of the . . . Sixth Census*, p. 26. Unfortunately the published 1850 census does not provide breakdowns for the age distribution of individual towns for comparison with earlier data. It does, however, give detailed population figures for Merrimack County as a whole, and by estimating the number of females between the ages of 15 and 29 in Concord, one can by subtraction estimate the number of females in rural Merrimack County. This method suggests a decline of 5 percent among females 15 to 29—from 4,267 to 4,046—over the twenty-year period, figures consistent with the data for Boscawen, Canterbury, and Sutton given in chapter 3. For 1850 data, see Debow, *Statistical View . . . of the Seventh Census*, p. 18.

23. Richard M. Bernard and Maris Vinovskis, "The Female School Teacher in Ante-bellum Massachusetts," *Journal of Social History* (1977), 10:332–45, graphs 1, 5; Lebergott, *Manpower in Economic Growth*, p. 500. See also Gitelman, "Waltham System," p. 238.

24. For a similar development see Gitelman, "Waltham System," pp. 244–45. In this respect, the smaller mills of the southern New England variety appear to have been moving in just the opposite direction. At Slater's mills, for instance, the proportion of the work force less than 16 years old declined from more than 50 percent before 1830 to only 9 percent in 1860. See Prude, "Coming of Industrial Order," pp. 118, 324.

25. For a discussion of the methods used in the preparation of the Hamilton 1850 work force and in record linkage with the 1850 federal manuscript census, see appendix 3. The representativeness of the census-linked group and possible bias in the findings on age are discussed in appendix 5.

26. An age distribution for residents of Hamilton Company boardinghouses in 1830 and 1840 is given in chapter 3, note 9.

27. *Statistics of Lowell Manufactures*, 1836, 1850, 1860, BL. Proportions based on all employees in the major cotton textile firms in Lowell. For similar data on the increasing proportion of males in other New England textile firms see Abbott, *Women in Industry*, p. 103; Shlakman, *Economic History*, p. 139; Gitelman, "Waltham System," p. 247n; Prude, "Coming of Industrial Order," p. 323.

28. The hiring of men as mule spinners resulted from the initial dependence on immigrants to operate these machines. For a description of English traditions, see Harold Catling, *The Spinning Mule* (Newton Abbott, Eng.: David & Charles, 1970). Mule spinning in England was an entirely male occupation and quickly became so in the United States as well. For a brief period at the outset, however, some women did tend mules. See Abbott, *Women in Industry*, p. 92.

29. The 1860 figures exclude two weavers for whom nativity could not be determined.

30. The requirement of regular church attendance, though not formally discontinued, seems to have been observed only in the breach. Harriet Farley complained of the hypocrisy of the corporations on this score and argued that the regulation should either be enforced or dropped. See *Lowell Offering*, 3:239-40.

31. Lahne, *Cotton Mill Worker*.

32. Once again, the convergence of the Lowell pattern with that of the mills of southern New England is striking. As the proportion of family members among operatives at Hamilton increased, the like proportion at Samuel Slater's Green Mill declined. In 1820, 87 percent of the workers at the Green Mill lived with their families in nearby East Village; by 1850 this proportion had declined to less than 56 percent. See Prude, "Coming of Industrial Order," pp. 116, 322. The processes of transformation in the northern and southern New England mills were working in opposite directions, until by 1860 the makeup of the work forces in the two regions came to approximate one another.

9. IMMIGRANTS IN THE MILLS, 1850-1860

1. Old Residents' Historical Association (ORHA), *Contributions*, 2:165-79, 3:42, 233-34; *Proceedings in the City of Lowell at the Semi-Centennial Celebration of the Incorporation of the Town of Lowell*, pp. 38, 112.

2. ORHA, *Contributions*, 3:234; see also George F. O'Dwyer, *The Irish Catholic Genesis of Lowell*, pp. 7-8. The employment of itinerant Irish laborers in heavy construction in early Lowell was part of the larger pattern evident throughout much of the Northeast in these years. Oscar Handlin, *Boston's Immigrants*, pp. 71-73.

3. These proportions were computed directly from the Manuscript Census of Lowell (1830), M19, Roll 167. Nativity for household heads was not given, but enumerators recorded the total numbers of residents and of aliens in each household. Households more than 50 percent foreign-born were coded as alien households; the remainder were considered native.

4. From the Portsmouth (N.H.) *Journal*, as quoted in O'Dwyer, *Irish Catholic Genesis*, p. 8; see also Coolidge, *Mill and Mansion*, p. 39.

5. *Semi-Centennial*, p. 38; ORHA, *Contributions*, 2:168, 171.

6. Manuscript Census of Lowell (1830); *Lowell Directory*, 1832; Proprietors of Locks and Canals, payroll volumes, BL. Conclusions based on nominal record linkage of the 1830 census enumerations with payroll records and the 1832 directory.

7. See note 4 above.

8. O'Dwyer, *Irish Catholic Genesis*, pp. 8-19, provides the best account of early religious life among Lowell's Irish. O'Dwyer, pp. 14, 30-39, describes the founding of the first Irish schools and their eventual acceptance by the Yankee majority.

9. Robinson, *Loom and Spindle*, p. 12.

10. On this point, consider the comments of Eliza Adams, a New Hampshire-born operative, after attending a Catholic Mass in Lowell: "I saw so many manoeuvres, rising up and sitting down, bowing, kneeling and making the holy cross, it made my eyes ache a week afterwards." Eliza Adams to John Karr, Feb. 27, 1842, Private.

11. Handlin, *Boston's Immigrants*, p. 52, notes 35,000 Irish in Boston in 1850.

12. The difficulties of recruiting in the prosperous 1840s were noted in chapter 8 and are evident in a number of contemporary sources. See John Clark to Jesse Huse, July 27, 1847, LHSC; *Voice of Industry*, Jan. 2, 1846.

13. Layer, "Wages, Earnings, and Ouput," pp. 184-89. See also table 8.2.

14. The same pattern held at the Boston Manufacturing Company. See Gitelman, "Waltham System," p. 243.

15. Mass. State Board of Education, *Fifth Annual Report*, (1841), pp. 91, 98.

16. McGouldrick, *New England Textiles*, pp. 38, 147; Lance Davis and H. Louis Stettler, "The New England Textile Industry, 1825-1860," pp. 213-28.

17. Harriet Farley, *Operatives' Reply to Hon. Jere. Clemens*, p. 13; also quoted in Harold Luft, "New England Textile Labor in the 1840s," p. 28. My thanks to Professor Luft, currently at Stanford University, School of Medicine, for sharing this paper with me.

18. Based on analysis of residents enumerated in Hamilton Company housing in 1850 Federal Manuscript Census, M432, Roll 326; see also Hamilton Co., vols. 506-508, BL.

19. McGouldrick, *New England Textiles*, pp. 41, 275, quotes the treasurer of the Merrimack Company who justified the provision of company housing in broad economic terms. He wrote: "the amount of direct income from houses and tenements, it is true, is less than the interest on the investment. But the advantage of providing good and comfortable tenements for employees having families and boarding houses for others is important, as it secures an excellent class of work people which tells materially in the prosperity of the company." See also John Coolidge, "Low-cost Housing: The New England Tradition," *New England Quarterly* (1941), 14:6-24.

20. One might argue that the growth of the family labor system meant that there were few immigrant workers interested in living in company boarding-houses. However, the analysis of the housing of operatives in 1860, in chapter 10, indicates that more than half of immigrant women operatives in Lowell were boardinghouse residents. Exclusion from company housing forced them to pay the higher room and board rates of private boardinghouses.

21. Treasurer's Report of the Salmon Falls Manufacturing Company, 1854, in A. A. Lawrence Papers, Massachusetts Historical Society. My thanks to Richard Candee and Gary Kulik for bringing this document to my attention. Despite the emphasis on the uniqueness of Salmon Falls as a rather small mill village, I do not believe the problems described here were absent from large cities such as

Lowell. All of the mills had the difficulty of immigrants supplanting native-born workers, and all had to develop strategies accordingly.

22. Luft, "New England Textile Labor," pp. 34-36.

23. Appleton Co., Letter book, George Motley to Thomas G. Cary, Sept. 24, 1850, MVTM.

24. *Ibid.*, Sept. 30, 1850.

25. The differential between the earnings of native-born and immigrant men actually increased over the decade. In 1850 native males earned on average 38.5 percent more than immigrants; by 1860 they earned 51.3 percent more. It is hard to tell, however, whether the differential for adult males followed this trend, as increasing numbers of boys entered the mills in this period. Boys were immigrant for the most part, so that the increasing male differential may reflect the changing age makeup of the two groups. Since the proportion under 15 in the female work force remained constant—at less than 3 per cent—no such compositional effect influences the trends discussed in this chapter.

26. A similar analysis, restricted to regular operatives, confirms the pattern of declining wage differentials.

27. I have reported actual rather than real wages here because I hesitate to use the existing cost-of-living indexes as measures of the living expenses of women operatives. In 1836 almost three fourths of the women working at Hamilton resided in company housing and their cost of room and board came to only $1.25 weekly. By 1860, however, only a third of women at Hamilton continued to reside in company housing, another third lived in private boardinghouses (with higher room and board charges), and the remainder lived at home with their families. This last group used their earnings to help support families, another distinguishing element in the 1850s. Had women lived in essentially similar settings throughout the period the cost-of-living index might help in comparing earnings over time.

28. Gitelman, "Waltham System," p. 243, presents data on the ethnic makeup of rooms at the Boston Manufacturing Company between 1850 and 1865 and the average monthly earnings of women in these rooms. While there were some differences between the two companies, the basic trends remained the same. Dressing had consistently the smallest proportion of Irish; spinning and carding, the largest. In turn, weaving and dressing generally paid the highest wages. In Waltham there were some large deviations in the pay and makeup of rooms over five-year intervals that suggest either major policy changes at the company or difficulties in Gitelman's record linkage. The findings are based on nominal record linkage between payrolls and census and are more liable to error than the payroll-register book linkage for Hamilton.

10. HOUSING AND FAMILIES OF WOMEN OPERATIVES

1. For discussion of the antebellum censuses and copies of census schedules, see Wright, *History and Growth of the United States Census*. The decision *not* to link

Hamilton operatives in the 1860 census followed the difficulties in linking the 1850 work force. Only 45 percent of Hamilton workers were successfully traced, providing an unrepresentative segment of the overall work force. For fuller consideration of sampling for the 1860 census and methods used in preparing data, see appendix 4.

2. While comparisons will be made throughout this discussion with patterns evident for the 1836 Hamilton work force and for the sample of New Hampshire operatives analyzed in chapter 3, it should be noted here that the 1860 census sample is not strictly comparable to the Hamilton work force. I discuss differences between the two populations in appendix 5.

3. Since the completion of the initial research for the 1860 census sample, Steven Dubnoff, a sociologist, has linked a sample of Hamilton operatives in the 1860 census. In a remarkable piece of work, Dubnoff successfully traced 64 percent of Hamilton workers to their entries in the census. Periodically I shall draw on his work for comparative purposes. The existence of these two independent studies of mill families in 1860 Lowell greatly enhances the value of either study. See Dubnoff, "The Family and Absence from Work," tables 1, 3, pp. 44, 46. Dubnoff finds that 47.1 percent of Irish females at Hamilton lived with their parents, compared to my finding of 34.6 percent among immigrants in the census sample.

4. Although one might conclude from these data that married immigrant women were more likely to work in the mills than the native-born, such a conclusion would not be justified. To argue in this manner would require analysis of a random sample drawn from the census, rather than a sample consisting entirely of millhands.

5. Katz, *The People of Hamilton, Canada West*, pp. 256-60; Katz and Davey, "Youth and Industrialization in a Canadian City," pp. 14-15.

6. Robinson, *Loom and Spindle*; Larcom, *New England Girlhood*; Walkowitz, "Working-Class Women in the Gilded Age," table 7.

7. Handlin, *Boston's Immigrants*, p. 71.

8. Dubnoff, "Family and Absence from Work," ch. 5, esp. pp. 68-70.

9. Walkowitz, "Working-Class Women in the Gilded Age," p. 479; Carol Groneman Pernicone, "The 'Bloody Ould Sixth,'" p. 74; A. Gibbs Mitchell, "Irish Family Patterns in Nineteenth-Century Ireland and Lowell, Massachusetts," p. 323.

10. Since only 9 of the 204 families kept boardinghouses, these families were excluded so that their large numbers of boarders would not distort the findings for the tenement households that predominated in the sample.

11. On the standard of living of mill families across the family cycle, see Dubnoff, "Family and Absence from Work," pp. 54-58, esp. graph 1; Anderson, *Family Structure* pp. 29-32.

12. Gitelman, "Waltham System," p. 250, argues that both Yankee women in the early period and Irish in the 1850s were secondary workers and that their

places in the labor system were essentially similar. This view, however, neglects the changing family patterns of women operatives. Yankee women earlier had been separated from their families for the most part, while an increasing proportion of Irish operatives in the 1850s resided at home with their parents. Yankee women supported themselves alone out of their earnings, while the Irish must have made substantial contributions to their families. To gloss over this difference and to argue that both were secondary workers is to overlook the basic transformation of family relations for operatives over these years.

13. Clarence D. Long, *Wages and Earnings in the United States, 1860-1890* (Princeton: Princeton University Press, 1960), p. 99; Lebergott, *Manpower in American Economic Growth*, p. 541.

14. Mass. Bureau of Statistics of Labor, *Fourth Annual Report* (1873), p. 94; cited in Stephan Thernstrom, *Poverty and Progress*, pp. 20, 244.

15. Other scholars' estimates for Irish laborers in 1860 have been somewhat higher than that given here. See Dubnoff, "Family and Absence from Work," pp. 50, 51; Thernstrom, *Poverty and Progress*, p. 22. Dubnoff deflates 1875 Mass. Bureau of Statistics of Labor data to take into account changing wage levels for laborers between 1860 and 1875. His figure of $269 is reasonably close to the estimate used here. Thernstrom uses an average daily wage figure of $1.33 to estimate annual earnings of Irish laborers in 1860 at $320; his mean wage, however, is considerably higher than the estimates of Long and Lebergott cited in note 13 above.

16. Estimation of the earnings of children began with an analysis of the age distribution of working children in the families of female millhands. Overall, about 12 percent of employed children were under 15 and were assumed to be employed in children's jobs in the mills earning on average $2.00 per week. The remaining 88 percent were said to be earning $3.40 per week, regular adult wages in the mills. Annual earnings of children under 15 were set at $75, assuming nine months of employment; for those 15 and over earnings were set at $170, based on fifty weeks' work each year. Given an average of 2.96 children employed in these families, total children's earnings come to $470. In families headed by unskilled laborers, likely to have earned $250 annually, these earnings would constitute 65.3 percent of overall family income. I decided not to estimate income from boarders; only 9 of 204 families maintained boarding-houses, and for the remaining families, the mean number of boarders was only 0.6. Fully two thirds of the families had no boarders at all. Interestingly, families with native-born household heads had twice as many boarders on average as immigrant families. For similar findings for a commercial city, see Katz and Davey, "Youth and Early Industrialization," p. 13.

17. I expected to find children's contributions to family income peaking at some point and then declining as children married and left the home. I broke down the group of families with oldest child 23 years old and above into a 23-27 year-old group and a 28+ group, and was surprised to discover that the 28+

group had the greatest number of children still living at home and the highest proportion employed of any group of mill families—4.54 children and 89.9 percent employed.

18. Calculations reported here utilize the same assumptions described in note 16 above. Table N.3 provides data used in the calculation. Once again, I assume each family is headed by an unskilled male laborer.

TABLE N.3. CONTRIBUTIONS OF EMPLOYED CHILDREN, BROKEN
BY AGE OF OLDEST CHILD

	Age of Oldest Child Living at Home		
Variable	14–17	18–22	23+
Children employed	1.78	2.81	3.66
% under 15	26.7%	17.6%	5.2%
Children's earnings	$260	$431	$606
Father's earnings	250	250	250
Children's earnings as % of family income	50.8%	63.3%	70.8%

19. It seems reasonable to assume that female household heads earned on average about half that of male laborers, especially since fully 80 percent of those employed were recorded as housekeepers. Given this assumption, children's earnings would have comprised between 67.5 and 82.9 percent of family income, depending on the age of the oldest child living at home. Even these figures probably understate children's contributions as it is not clear that housekeepers actually earned wages. The category housekeeper appears to have been used almost exclusively with female heads of households. A much smaller number of women were specifically recorded as boardinghouse keepers or domestics, two groups likely to have been contributing to family earnings.

20. Jemima Sanborn to Richard and Sabrina Bennett, Nashville [N.H.], May 14, 1843. Bennett Family Letters, HPL.

21. Gardner Plimpton to Werden Babcock, Whitinsville [Mass.], Jan. 10, 1847, VHS.

22. Joseph Hollingworth to William Rawcliff, South Leicester [Mass.], Nov. 7, 1829, in Thomas Leavitt, ed., *The Hollingworth Letters: Technical Change in the Textile Industry, 1826-1837*, pp. 53-55.

23. Of the 761 women in the sample, only 18 were married and living with their husbands. They had on average only 1.8 children; six of the families had none. The mean age of the oldest child was only 9.2 years, reinforcing the argument that married women who worked did so because they needed the income and had no or few children old enough to seek employment.

24. Earlier writers have generally used the term "life cycle." I follow the usage of sociologist Glen Elder, who has argued for adoption of the concept of the life

course to refer to career patterns over individuals' lifetimes. See Elder, "Family History and the Life Course," *Journal of Family History* (1977), 2:279-304.

25. Glasco, "Life Cycles and Household Structure," pp. 339-64, has discussed the limitations of inferring family cycle patterns from cross-sectional data.

26. With the next tables the sample on which the findings are based switches. Thus far I have been presenting data concerning the 265 female millhands residing at home with their families. Tables 10.6, 10.7, and 10.8 are derived from analysis of all children residing in the families of female millhands, about 900 in all. By examining the work and school patterns of this larger group, it is possible to present a much more detailed analysis. The increase in sample size allows one to break down the findings along lines of sex, ethnicity, and age in ways the smaller sample precludes.

27. One might argue with these findings, claiming that the nature of the sample, one that includes only families with at least one female millhand, necessarily biases any comparison of male and female children. With this in mind I also compared the work and school experiences of siblings of millhands, thus excluding sample members themselves. While the differences evident in tables 10.6 and 10.7 diminished somewhat, daughters still worked more and attended school less than sons. In the critical 10-13 age group fully 29 percent of female siblings worked, compared to only 13 percent for males. School attendance differences declined, but the proportion of boys 10-13 attending school and not working remained fully 10 percent larger than that for girls. See also Mitchell, "Irish Family Patterns," p. 328; Anderson, *Family Structure*, p. 75; Katz, *People of Hamilton*, pp. 285-88; Katz and Davey, "Youth and Early Industrialization," pp. 16, 34.

28. The small numbers of sons and daughters in native mill families led me not to produce separate tables for native and immigrant families. In all, there were 19 male children and 81 females over 13 in native mill families, compared to 245 males and 368 females of similar ages in immigrant families.

29. This pattern of earlier male departure holds even if we exclude sample members and examine the proportions of males and females among their siblings. The proportion of males among siblings declined from more than 52 percent for 10-13 year olds, to 43 percent for 14-17 year olds, to less than 34 percent for those 18 and over. Although table 10.8 presents combined data, the pattern of early male departure held equally for native and immigrant families.

30. Mitchell, "Irish Family Patterns," p. 290; Glasco, "Life Cycles and Household Structure," pp. 347, 357; Pernicone, "The 'Bloody Ould Sixth,'" p. 75.

31. Dubnoff also finds evidence of a declining proportion of males among children with increasing age in families of Hamilton operatives in 1860. Coupling age distribution data with an analysis of regularity of attendance in the mills, Dubnoff argues that sons remained living at home longer and worked more regularly in female-headed households, while daughters stayed longer and worked more faithfully in male-headed ones. Dubnoff attributes this pattern to the persistence of Old World affective bonds that made for particularly strong

father-daughter and mother-son bonds in Irish culture. "Family and Absence from Work," pp. 75-79, 103-26. See also Mitchell, "Irish Family Patterns," p. 339; Anderson, *Family Structure*, p. 126. Interesting contrasting patterns are evident in Buffalo, New York, where the primary occupation of Irish women, domestic service, required that they leave home and take up residence with their employers. See Glasco, "Life Cycles and Household Structure," pp. 355-57.

11. CAREERS OF OPERATIVES, 1836-1860

1. Based on Hamilton Company payrolls for July 1836, August 1850, and June 1860, BL, and linkage to the 1850 federal manuscript census for Lowell, M432, roll 326.

2. Mass. House Document No. 50 (1845), in Commons et al., *Documentary History*, 8:146; Miles, *Lowell As It Was*, pp. 165-86; Elisha Bartlett, *A Vindication of the Character and Condition of Females*, p. 14, as quoted in Ray Ginger, "Labor in a Massachusetts Cotton Mill, 1853-1860," p. 89.

3. Appleton, *Introduction of the Power Loom*, p. 13; Miles, *Lowell As It Was*, pp. 75-76.

4. For a fuller discussion of the choice of Mill A for this analysis see appendix 1.

5. The figures for previous work experience at Hamilton are somewhat less than those presented by contemporaries. See Commons et al., *Documentary History*, 8:146; Miles, *Lowell As It Was*, pp. 165-86. These other data were derived by asking operatives how long they had been employed, and probably included periods of work at more than one firm. Data from Hamilton alone undoubtedly understate work experience, but can provide a basis for discussion of trends over time. The trend is what concerns us here, not the precise findings for a single point in time.

6. Mary Hall Diary, *passim*, NHHS.

7. Prude, "Coming of Industrial Order," p. 120, shows that in Samuel Slater's Green Mill in 1830 continuous employment averaged 1.8 years, although he gives no breakdown by sex.

8. Ideally, one would like to compare these data to findings for other Waltham-Lowell type firms, but there are no comparable studies of women's wages over the course of their careers. The most relevant study examines skilled Scottish weavers in a Holyoke, Massachusetts, textile firm in the 1850s: Ginger, "Labor in a Massachusetts Cotton Mill." For related data on the Irish at the Boston Manufacturing Company, see Gitelman, "The Waltham System," and "'No Irish Need Apply.'"

9. Layer, "Wages, Earnings, and Output," pp. 348-83, provides fuller data on daily earnings of women in the major departments of Hamilton that corroborate the findings here. See also Gitelman, "The Waltham System," table 3, p. 243.

10. Robinson, *Loom and Spindle*, pp. 30, 39, 73; Larcom, *New England Girlhood*, pp. 153-54, 175-76, 226, 229.

11. Persistent workers were determined by alphabetically sorting and then merging the names of operatives employed at Hamilton in these two months. All pairs of identical or similar names were checked for signatures in the appropriate payroll volumes. Where signatures matched, the individuals were considered a linked pair; where either signature was missing, register volumes were consulted to test the linkage. In this manner 46 linked pairs were found, about 4 percent of the Hamilton work force in 1836. These workers did not necessarily work continuously over the interval but had undoubtedly worked several distinct stints. Gitelman, "The Waltham System," p. 251, provides relevant data on persistence at the Boston Manufacturing Company for the period 1850-1865.

12. In actuality male workers at Hamilton moved up the job hierarchy one step at a time. Over the fourteen-year interval, 5 operatives became second hands and 3 second hands became overseers. Thus, while the number of second hands did not change greatly, there was a complete turnover in the members of this group.

13. Mary Paul noted in a letter to her father that the companies had increased the rate of board in company boardinghouses to $1.375. Mary Paul to Bela Paul, Nov. 5, 1848, Mary Paul Letters, VHS. For corroboration on the relation of mill income to expenses see Ginger, "Labor in a Massachusetts Mill," p. 78. He found that for Scottish women weavers room and board accounted for less than a third of income. The rapidity with which they paid off their debts suggested a savings ratio of 25 to 50 percent of their earnings, a finding comparable to the savings figures for Yankee operatives in Lowell in the mid-1830s.

14. Based on linkage of company payrolls for July 1836 with savings account records of the Lowell Institution for Savings. Names were traced in bank records of accounts established between 1829 and 1838. This procedure undoubtedly understates the proportion of women with savings accounts because those who opened accounts between 1839 and 1850 are excluded. This linkage was carried out in the course of related research and the exponential increase in the number of accounts opened after 1838 precluded further tracing of persistent workers in succeeding years.

15. Josiah Curtis, "Brief Remarks on Hygiene of Massachusetts," p. 28, provides turnover data for one Lowell firm between 1840 and 1848, noting that on average women worked 8.95 months at a time. Ginger, "Labor in a Massachusetts Mill," p. 85, has more comparable data (though not broken down by sex) for the Lyman Mills in Holyoke in 1860. Analyzing the work stints of 440 operatives employed in September 1860, he came up with the following frequency distribution:

0-1 years	57%
1-2	14
2-3	5
3 +	23

If one assumes a midpoint for the 3+ group at 5 years, one can compute a mean work length of 1.64 years, a figure consistent with the overall finding of 2.5

for Hamilton at this date. Ginger did not trace workers after the payroll date and thus his results understate the overall length of work stints.

16. The linkage of the 1850 and 1860 payrolls used the same criteria as the 1836-1850 linkage described above. For pairs of entries with similar or identical names, signatures were checked. For illiterate operatives, register book entries were examined to verify that the two individuals had the same nativity, and for one date, at least, the same local address. This process resulted in 72 linked pairs of payroll entries.

12. THE OPERATIVES' RESPONSE, 1850-1860

1. It is likely that a significantly greater proportion of the Hamilton 1860 work force than of the millhand sample lived at home, so the figure of 35 percent probably understates the full extent of the change over this period. See appendix 5 for a fuller comparison of the millhand sample with the Hamilton work force.

2. Lowell *American*, Nov. 15, 22, 29, 1851; Benjamin F. Butler, *Butler's Book*, pp. 98-107. As evidence of company efforts to influence the votes of workers, Butler (p. 99) quoted a broadside posted in one of the mills: "Whoever, employed by this corporation, votes the Ben Butler ten-hour ticket on Monday next, will be discharged."

3. Petitions 1587/8 and 1587/9 (1845), 11983 (1846), 13145/1 and 13145/2 (1851), Mass. State Archives. Among 1851 petition signers, 82 of 137 whose sex could be determined were males. An additional 51 signed with first initials and surnames. My previous experience with payroll signatures suggests that these others were virtually all male. If such were the case, the proportion of males among petition signers would reach 70 percent.

4. Lowell *American*, Oct. 6, 14, 1853.

5. *Ibid.*, Oct. 6, 1853.

6. *Ibid.*, March 11, 25, 1853; Lowell *Advertiser*, March 9, 1853; Lowell *Weekly Journal and Courier*, March 25, 1853. The *Courier*, March 4, 1853, also reported a ten-hour strike in Mechanics' Mill in Lowell just before the turn-out at the Machine Shop. Both strikes involved skilled male machinists.

7. Lawrence Co., vol. MA-1, Sept. 5 and 11, 1853; Hamilton Co., vol. 670, Sept. 2, 1853, Directors' Records, Sept. 14, 1853; Tremont-Suffolk Mills, vol. FB-5, Sept. 16, 1853 (hereafter cited as T-S Mills). All BL. Lowell *Weekly Journal and Courier*, Sept. 23, Oct. 7, 1853. Workingmen active in the Ten Hour Movement were not satisfied with this concession, however, and continued their rallies in Lowell and their lobbying in the legislature.

8. Persons, "Early History," pp. 88-89, 123-25.

9. Hamilton Co., vol. 670, Sept. 20, 1850, BL; T-S Mills, vol. FB-5, Sept. 17, 1850, Jan. 12, 1855, BL; Appleton Co., Agent's letter book, Sept. 24, 30, 1850, MVTM; Lawrence Co., vol. MA-2, Aug. 30, 1850, Oct. 17, 1857, BL.

10. Calculations based on data in *Statistics of Lowell Manufactures*, 1850 and 1860, BL.

11. Lowell *Weekly Journal and Courier*, Feb. 11, 1859; Boston *Post*, Feb. 8, 9, 1859;

quote, Lowell *American Citizen*, Feb. 11, 1859. For evidence of further strike activity stimulated by the Lowell outbreak, see Lowell *American Citizen*, Feb. 18, March 11, 1859; Shlakman, *Economic History*, p. 146.

12. For the 1834 and 1836 proportions see chapter 6, notes 33, 41; for 1859, *Statistics of Lowell Manufactures* (1859), BL, sets the number of female operatives in the Lowell mills at 8,900.

13. Lowell *American Citizen*, Feb. 11, 1859.

14. Mass. Bureau of Statistics of Labor, *Eleventh Annual Report* (1880), pp. 9-14; Thomas Franklin Currier, "Whittier and the Amesbury-Salisbury Strike," *New England Quarterly* (1935), 8:105-12. For evidence on the limited impact of the Lowell turn-out on one of the affected companies, see T-S Mills, vol. FA-1, Aug. 6, 1859, vol. FA-4, Aug. 9, 1859, BL.

15. N. Ware, *Industrial Worker*, chs. 14, 15.

16. Persons, "Early History," pp. 90-125; Montgomery, *Beyond Equality*, pp. 114-26, 265-95.

17. See note 16 above.

18. See note 14 above.

19. Handlin, *Boston's Immigrants*, ch. 7; David Montgomery, "The Shuttle and the Cross: Weavers and Artisans in the Kensington Riots of 1844," *Journal of Social History* (1972), 5:411-46; Michael Holt, "The Politics of Impatience: The Origins of Know-Nothingism," *Journal of American History* (1973), 60:309-31.

APPENDIX 1

1. Lawrence Co., volumes in G Series; Hamilton Co., vols. 251-479, BL.

2. Hamilton Co., vols. 481-505. Only fragmentary collections of register volumes are extant for other Waltham-Lowell firms. Lawrence Co., vol. GN-1 (1870-72); Hadley Falls Co. (1849-1854), and Lyman Mills (1858-1860, 1866-1869) in Lyman Mills Collection, vols. LB1-8; Dwight Co., vols. HY1-2 (1880-86); Nashua Co., Contract Books, vols. BO1-3 (1837-39). All BL. For the Amoskeag Company see "Register of the Residents of Manchester, N.H., 1846," MHA. The Hadley Falls records are analyzed in Green, *Holyoke*, p. 30n.

3. Although the consolidation of payroll entries preceded register linkage, a certain number of double entries were only discovered during the linkage process, as in cases in which a name was spelled differently in two places in the payrolls. For purposes of clarity, the discussion focuses on the basic outline of the procedures followed.

4. There has been considerable work done with computerizing nominal record linkage in the past few years. While it did not seem practicable, given the scale and financial support of the study, to employ a computer linkage program, efforts have been made to incorporate the principles of these programs into the work. In using the register books, for instance, it was not possible to keypunch the entire source, but it was possible to apply the principles of soundex coding to the hand linkage. Although I did not use objective weighting scales for the linkage variables, by requiring agreement on two of the three variables, I did

attempt to deal with discrepant data in a consistent manner. See Theodore Hershberg, Allan Burstein, and Robert Dockhorn, "Record Linkage," *Historical Methods Newsletter* (1976), 9:137-63; Terry Stickel, "A Computerized Nominal Record Linkage System," M.A. thesis, Moore School of Electrical Engineering, University of Pennsylvania, 1971; Michael Katz and John Tiller, "Record Linkage For Everyman: A Semi-Automated Process," *Historical Methods Newsletter* (1972) 5:144-50; Ian Winchester, "The Linkage of Historical Records by Man and Computer: Techniques and Problems," *Journal of Interdisciplinary History* (1970), 1:107-24; M. H. Skolnick, "A Computer Program for Linking Records," *Historical Methods Newsletter* (1971), 4:114-25; Dennis Kelley, "Linking Nineteenth-Century Manuscript Census Records: A Computer Strategy," *Historical Methods Newsletter* (1974), 7:72-82.

5. *Lowell Directory* (1836); *Female Supplement to the Lowell Directory* (1836).

6. Hamilton Co., vol. 258, BL. Payroll data for each of the company's three mills were graphed and compared to the graph for the company payroll as a whole for the period, January-December 1836.

7. This exclusion had the additional advantage that the resulting sample was comparable to that analyzed by Robert Layer in "Wages, Earnings, and Output." The Mill A Sample appears to have been quite representative of the larger Hamilton work force at this date. Table N.4 indicates that differences between the two populations are minor.

TABLE N.4. COMPARISON OF THE 1836 MILL A SAMPLE TO THE WORK FORCE AS A WHOLE

Variable	Mill A Sample	Overall Work Force
percent male	12.6	14.4
percent native-born	97.6	96.3
percent in company housing	72.2	73.7
Total cases[a]	271	1030

[a] Missing cases vary on each variable for each population.

8. Although the payrolls for six months were keypunched and sorted, only those individuals employed during July were studied in detail. About as many operatives had been employed at some time in the six-month period, but not in July. They were excluded because they still required linkage in company register volumes to make them comparable to sample members.

9. Hamilton Co., vols. 481-483, BL.

10. The most likely bias in this procedure, based on the requirement that name and nativity agree, is that the first entrance data understate the length of time individuals worked at the company prior to July 1836. The frequency of common names, both among Yankee women in 1836 and the Irish later, made

such a requirement necessary to minimize linkage errors. Data on experience should be comparable among groups at the same date and across time since I used the same linkage requirements throughout.

11. Hamilton Co., vols. 506-508, BL.

APPENDIX 2

1. The leading towns in the numbers of operatives entering the Hamilton Company between January and June 1836 were:

Lyndboro, N.H.	13	Greenfield, N.H.	7
Canterbury, N.H.	12	Warner, N.H.	7
Boston, Mass.	12	Alexandria, N.H.	7
Dover, N.H.	11	Bradford, N.H.	7
Sutton, N.H.	9	Hudson, N.H.	7
Freedom, N.H.	9	Loudon, N.H.	7
Canaan, N.H.	8	Westford, Mass.	7

Lowell residences, totaling 48, led all towns, but gave no indication where mill-hands had come from earlier. Given the rapid growth of Lowell, I doubt that such workers had lived long in the city. Boscawen sent only 6 workers to Hamilton in this period but was included among the sampled towns because of its fine genealogical and vital records. It proved a helpful decision, as Boscawen provided 75 of the 175 women included in the sample.

2. Hurd, *History of Merrimack County*, p. 1.

3. Hamilton Co., vols. 481-491, BL.

4. On occasion these notations indicated when the individual had worked at the other company. For these cases, the entry date was recoded to reflect the earlier work. When a specific date was not given, it was assumed that the individual had begun work at the other firm one year earlier and the entry date was modified accordingly. In this way, career data reflect not simply individuals' work at Hamilton, but the entire career of operatives as far as can be determined from Hamilton records alone.

5. Nashua Co., Contract Books, vols. BO-1-3, BL; "Register of the Residents of Manchester, N.H., 1846," MHA.

6. For published genealogical sources see chapter 3, note 14.

7. Lyford, *History of Canterbury*, pp. xiv, provides confirming evidence: "Some of the early families are either extinct or the residences of their descendants are unknown. The offspring of others have widely scattered, and, when they have been located, too often they have been indifferent to this work." See also David C. Dearborn, "New Hampshire Genealogy: A Perspective," *New England Historical and Genealogical Register* (1976), 130:244-58.

8. The largest collections of these additional sources were found at the New Hampshire Historical Society and the New England Historical and Genealogical Library in Boston. For access to the Boscawen vital record card file I would like to express my appreciation to Dorothy Sanborn, assistant town clerk.

9. *Vital Records of Lowell, Massachusetts, To the End of the Year 1849.* These records are undoubtedly incomplete and additional linkages were found in manuscript vital records on deposit at the City Clerk's Office in Lowell. The records of the state registration system appear to be simply duplicates of Lowell records after 1841.

10. Federal Manuscript Censuses for Merrimack County, New Hampshire, Microcopy 432, Roll 436 (1850); M653, Roll 676 (1860).

11. *Laws of the State of New Hampshire . . . Published by Authority* (Hopkinton: Isaac Long Jr., 1830), pp. 551-59; *General Statutes of the State of New Hampshire* (Concord: B. W. Sanborn, 1867), pp. 115-23. My thanks to Art McEvoy for finding these sources.

12. My thanks to Gary Nash for discussing some of the issues involved in working with assessment records at an early point in the analysis. For considerations of methodology in dealing with tax inventories see James Lemon and Gary B. Nash, "The Distribution of Wealth in Eighteenth-Century America: A Century of Change in Chester County, Pennsylvania, 1693-1802," *Journal of Social History* (1968), 2:1-24; Alice Hansen Jones, "Wealth Estimates for the New England Colonies About 1770," *Journal of Economic History* (1972), 32:98-127; John Waters, "Patrimony, Succession and Social Stability: Guilford, Connecticut in the Eighteenth Century," *Perspectives in American History* (1976), 10:131-60.

13. For a number of studies the specific unit of analysis is crucial. The mean number of children in millhands' families is considerably larger if every millhand is counted separately than if each family is counted only once. For a discussion of this general principle see Samuel Preston, "Family Sizes of Children and Family Sizes of Women," *Demography* (1976), 13:105-14. My thanks to Daniel Scott Smith for pointing out this problem to me.

APPENDIX 3

1. Federal Manuscript Census (1850), M653, Roll 507.

2. Hamilton Co., vols. 317-321, BL. The decision to exclude Print Works employees made a considerable difference in the composition of the work force. The Print Works employed 129 workers in 1850 and had a much higher proportion of immigrants than the mill work force. Since so many operatives in the Print Works remained unlinked in register volumes and since the 1836 Hamilton payrolls had not provided data on these workers, I excluded them from the analysis.

3. Relevant registers include Hamilton Co., vols. 489-493, BL.

4. The effort to trace Hamilton 1850 workers to their dates of first employment at the company actually preceded the similar work for the 1836 Mill A Sample. This nominal record linkage proved incredibly time consuming and led to the subsequent decision to trace only samples of operatives for 1836 and 1860.

5. See appendix 5 for discussion of this difficulty and an effort to correct the age distribution of the 1850 Hamilton work force by taking into account the unrepresentativeness of the linked group.

6. Hamilton Co., vols. 349-351, 493-498, BL.

7. Federal Manuscript Census of Lowell (1860), M653, Roll 507. In 1860 only a third of the Hamilton work force resided in company housing compared to three fourths in 1836, a change that called for a different strategy in analyzing the age distribution of operatives than had been employed earlier. The fact that the 1860 census was the first to list women's occupations permitted analysis of a sample drawn entirely from that source. See chapter 10 and appendix 4 for more on that sample.

8. My thanks to Steven Dubnoff who prepared the yearly payroll of the Mill AB Sample in the course of his own research for sharing that resource with me.

APPENDIX 4

1. Federal Manuscript Census of Lowell (1860), M653, Roll 507.

2. Counting was not always straight forward, and in two cases I found errors where enumerators listed children in their own household as if they lived alone. I corrected these errors in the coding process. Of considerable assistance in coding variables requiring inferences from the historical record was Wright, *History and Growth of the United States Census*.

3. For a good discussion of the issues involved here, see Laurence Glasco, "Computerizing the Manuscript Census," *Historical Methods Newsletter* (December 1969), 3:1-4, (March 1970), 3:1-2. I have not used set parameters for determining the relationship of individuals to the household head, as I had no basis for choosing particular numbers. Had I coded the entire city I might have analyzed a smaller sample first and then have used the findings to code the remainder. In making individual inferences I did find Glasco's discussion helpful, although I did not follow his suggestions to the letter.

4. The lack of a city directory for Lowell in 1860 made this strategy necessary. Peter Knights, *The Plain People of Boston, 1830-1860: A Study in City Growth* (New York: Oxford University Press, 1971), pp. 127-39, has a useful discussion of census mapping.

5. Numbers exclude 12 sample members living in single-person households and boarders in households with six or more boarders.

APPENDIX 5

1. Davis and Stettler, "New England Textile Industry," p. 217.

2. The most recent cuts had been in March 1834, October 1848, and October 1857, respectively.

3. Montgomery, *Practical Detail*, p. 174; *Timetable of the Lowell Mills*, BL.

4. See table 10.3 for data on nativity of sample members living at home and of their parent-household heads.

5. See table 8.2 for the breakdown of ethnicity in the Hamilton Company work force as derived from company registers.

6. Dubnoff, "Family and Absence from Work," table 4, p. 76.

Selected Bibliography

PRIMARY SOURCES

Manuscript Materials in Depositories or Privately Owned
  Includes corporation records, genealogical records, church records, letters, and diaries.

BL   Baker Library, Harvard Graduate School of Business
        Administration, Boston, Massachusetts
      Hamilton Manufacturing Company Records.
            Payrolls, 1826-1863, vols. 240-353.
            Register books, 1830-1862, vols. 481-498.
            Rental volumes, 1830-1868, vols. 506-508.
            Treasurers' letters, 1839-1864, vols. 670-672.
            Directors' records, 1824-1864, vols. A and B.
      Lawrence Manufacturing Company Records.
            Payrolls: vols. in G series.
            Correspondence: vols. MA-1, MAB-1, MD-1. 1832-1857.
            "Regulations to be Observed by all persons employed by the
                Lawrence Manufacturing Company," May 1833.
            "General Regulations to be observed by persons employed
                by the Lawrence Manufacturing Company in Lowell," n.d.
            "Regulations of Boarding Houses," n.d.
      Massachusetts Cotton Mills.
            Directors and Proprietors' records, 1839-1916, 1 vol., in
                Pepperell Manufacturing Company Records.
      Merrimack Manufacturing Company Records.
            Directors' records, 1822-1843, vol. 1.
            "Buildings and Machinery," vol. 58A.
      Nashua (N.H.) Manufacturing Company.
            Correspondence of agent, vols. GA-1, GB-1, GC-1.
            Contract books, vols. BO-1-3.
      Proprietors of Locks and Canals.
            Correspondence, vol. 1.
            Directors' records, 1821-1842, microfilm.

Payrolls, volumes in R series, outdoor hands and machine
    shop.
Rental volumes, OB series.
Statistics of Lowell Manufactures. Microfilm of broadsides printed in
    Lowell, 1835-1860.
Timetable of the Lowell Mills, broadsides, various years.
Tremont-Suffolk Mills.
    Correspondence: vols. FA-1-4; FB-1, 2; FN-1.

HPL   Haverhill, Massachusetts, Public Library
Bennett Family Letters, 1835-1852.

JHL   John Hay Library, Brown University, Providence, Rhode Island
Thomas Dorr Letters.

LHSC   Lowell Historical Society Collection, University of Lowell,
    Lowell, Massachusetts
Clark, John. Letter from Merrimack Company agent to Jesse
    Huse, July 27, 1847.
"The Lowell Factory Girl," broadside.
"Regulations of Boarding Houses," n.d., Lawrence Company.
"Regulations for the Boarding Houses of the Middlesex
    Company," n.d.
"Regulations to be observed by all persons employed in the
    factories of the Middlesex Company," 1846.
"Regulations to be Observed by all Persons Employed by the
    Suffolk Manufacturing Company," n.d.

LIS   Lowell Institution for Savings, Lowell, Massachusetts
Savings account ledgers, vols. a and b.

MHA   Manchester (N.H.) Historic Association
Ann Swett Appleton Letters.
"Register of the Residents of Manchester, N.H., 1846."

MHS   Massachusetts Historical Society
Nathan Appleton Papers.
A. A. Lawrence Papers.

MVTM   Merrimack Valley Textile Museum, North Andover,
    Massachusetts
Appleton Manufacturing Company Records.
    Stockholders' meetings, 1827-1925, MS 314.
    Agent's letter book, June 1844-May 1859, MS 206. 5.
    Unbound papers, 1 vol.

Essex Company Records.
   Samuel Lawrence to Charles Storrow, March 6, 1847, MS
   306.

NEHGS   New England Historical Genealogical Society, Boston,
   Massachusetts
Canterbury Records Index, vols. 3, 7.
"Cemetery Inscriptions of Twelve Private Cemeteries."
"Shell Meeting House Cemetery, Canterbury, N.H."
"Some Gravestone Inscriptions from Canterbury, N.H."
"Vital Records from an Old Notebook kept by Jeremiah Clough
   of Canterbury and Loudon, N.H." Typescript.

NHHS   New Hampshire Historical Society, Concord
Book of Records, First Congregational Society in Canterbury, New
   Hampshire, 1832-1924.
Canterbury Inventory of Taxes and Property, 1820-1853, 2 vols.
"Cemetery Inscriptions of Sutton, N.H."
"Deaths in Boscawen." Manuscript.
Freewill Baptist Society Records, 1848-1919 (Canterbury).
Dover Manufacturing Company.
   Letter books, 1825-1828, 3 vols.
Mary Hall Diary, 1821-1836, 1 vol.
Hodgdon Letters, 1830-1840.
Records of the Baptist Church (Sutton), vol. 3.

OSV   Old Sturbridge Village, Sturbridge, Massachusetts
Lummus, Aaron. "Records of Some of the Principal Events in the
   Life of Aaron Lummus." Manuscript, written 1850-57.

Private   Private Collections.
Eliza Adams, Lowell, to John Karr, Londonderry, New
   Hampshire, February 27, 1842. Courtesy of Joanne Preston,
   Cambridge, Massachusetts.
Dutton Family Letters, 1827-1855.
   Letters of Lucretia Wilson Dutton and family, Colchester,
      Vermont. Include a number written by daughter, Julia A.
      Dutton, while working in Clintonville, Massachusetts.
      Courtesy of Mrs. Aileen Eurich, Waitsfield, Vermont.
Jennison Letters, 1849-1861.
   Three letters from Eben Jennison, Charleston, Maine, to his
      daughters Elizabeth and Amelia while they were working
      in the Lowell mills. Courtesy of Harry and Mary Dinmore,
      Lowell, Massachusetts.

Delia Page Letters, 1859-1861.
    Manuscript letters from Luther Trussell and family to his
    foster daughter, Delia Page, while she was working in the
    Manchester mills. Courtesy of Mildred Tunis, New
    London, New Hampshire.

SL   Arthur and Elizabeth Schlesinger Library on the History of
    Women in America, Radcliffe College, Cambridge,
    Massachusetts
Harriet Hanson Robinson Collection.

UL   University of Lowell, Special Collections
Locks and Canals Collection.
    Architectural drawings of mills and boardinghouses.
    Photographic views of Lowell.

VHS   Vermont Historical Society, Montpelier, Vermont
Mary Paul Letters, 1845-1862.
Plimpton, Gardiner. Letter from Whitinsville, Massachusetts,
    January 10, 1847, to Werden Babcock.

                    Government Records and Publications
Local Records
Boscawen (N.H.). Vital Records. Card File Index, Town Clerk's Office.
—— Inventory of Taxes and Property, 1830-1860.
Canterbury (N.H.). Vital Records, Town Clerk's Office.
    "Births, Marriages, and Deaths," vol. 1.
    "Early Records to 1900."
    Marriage Intentions.
Lowell (Mass.). School Committee Reports, 1827-1860. Lowell School
    Committee. Manuscript reports, 1827-1835. Printed, 1836-1860.
—— Town Record, 1826-1836. Manuscript record of town meetings,
    elections, reports of committees. City Clerk's Office.
—— Valuations of Lowell, 1826-1860. Assessors' Office.
—— Vital Records, 1826-1860. City Clerk's Office.
Vital Records of Lowell, Massachusetts, To the End of the Year 1849. 4 vols.
    Salem, Mass.: The Essex Institute, 1930.
Sutton (N.H.). Inventory of Taxes and Property, 1830-1860.

State Records
Massachusetts. Bureau of Statistics of Labor. *Annual Reports.* Boston:
    1869-1900.

—— Department of Vital Statistics. Indexes of Births, Marriages and Deaths.

—— General Court. *House Documents*. Nos. 50 (1845); 153 (1850); 185, 230 (1852); 122 (1853); 80 (1855); 107, 112 (1856).

—— General Court. *Senate Documents*. Nos. 81 (1846); 107, 122 (1856).

—— State Board of Education. *Fifth Annual Report*. Boston: 1841.

—— Ten Hour Petitions: 1587/8, 1587/9 (1845); 11983 (1846); 13145/1, 13145/2, 13145/3 (1851). State Archives.

Statistical Tables Exhibiting the Condition and the Products of Certain Branches of Industry in Massachusetts for the Year Ending April 1, 1837. Boston: Dutton and Wentworth, 1838.

Statistics of the Condition and Products of Certain Branches of Industry in Massachusetts for the Year Ending April 1, 1845. Boston: Dutton and Wentworth, 1846.

New Hampshire. Bureau of Health. Department of Vital Statistics. State Vital Records Registration System.

Federal Records

Abstract of the Statistics of Manufactures According to the Seventh Census. Washington: 1859.

Compendium of the Enumeration of the Inhabitants and Statistics of the United States, as Obtained at the Department of State, From the Returns of the Sixth Census. Washington: Thomas Allen, 1842.

DeBow, J. D. B. *Statistical View of the United States . . . Being a Compendium of the Seventh Census*. Washington: 1854.

Digest of Accounts of Manufacturing Establishments in the United States and of Their Manufactures. Washington: Gales and Seaton, 1823.

Fifth Census: Or, Enumeration of the Inhabitants of the United States, as Corrected at the Department of State, 1830. Washington: Duff Green, 1832.

Manuscript Censuses of Lowell.
    1830: Microcopy 19, Roll 167. 1840: Microcopy 704, Roll 187. 1850: Microcopy 432, Rolls 326, 327. 1860: Microcopy 653, Roll 507.

Manuscript Censuses of Merrimack County.
    1830: Microcopy 19, Roll 76. 1840: Microcopy 704, Rolls 240, 241. 1850: Microcopy 432, Roll 436. 1860: Microcopy 653, Roll 676.

United States. Bureau of the Census. *Manufactures of the United States in 1860: Compiled from the Original Returns of the Eighth Census*. Washington, 1865.

—— Bureau of the Census. *Historical Statistics of the United States: Colonial Times to 1957*. Washington: Government Printing Office, 1960.

—— Department of Treasury. *Documents Relative to the Manufacture of the United States*. Washington: D. Green, 1833.

Contemporary Published Works, Reminiscences, and Genealogical Sources

Appleton, Nathan. *Introduction of the Power Loom and Origin of Lowell*. Lowell: B. H. Penhallow, 1858.

Ayer, J[ames] C[ook]. *Some of the Usages and Abuses in the Management of Our Manufacturing Corporations*. Lowell: C. M. Langley, 1863.

Baird, Robert H. *The American Cotton Spinner, and Managers' and Carders' Guide: A Practical Treatise on Cotton Spinning*. Philadelphia: A. Hart, 1851.

Batchelder, Samuel. *Introduction and Early Progress of the Cotton Manufacture in the United States*. Boston: Little, Brown, 1863.

Blake, Francis, comp. *History of the Town of Princeton . . . Massachusetts*. Princeton: by the Town, 1915.

Boston *Daily Times*. October-November 1836, February-March 1859.

Boston *Evening Transcript*. February-March 1834, October-November 1836, October 1850, January 1855, October-December 1857, and February-March 1859.

Boston *Pilot*, 1829-1860. After 1858 published as *The Pilot*.

Boston *Post*. February-March 1859.

Boston Quarterly Review, vol. 3 (July 1840).

Burke, William. "Statistics Relating to the Cost of Manufacturing Drillings and Standard Sheetings in 1838 and 1875." *Proceedings of the New England Cotton Manufacturers' Association* (October 1876), no. 21, pp. 6-7.

Burton, Willis. *History: Boscawen-Webster, Fifty Years, 1883-1933*. Penacook, N.H.: W. B. Ranney, n.d.

Butler, Benjamin F. *Butler's Book: Autobiography and Personal Reminiscences of Major-General Benjamin F. Butler*. Boston: A. M. Thayer, 1892.

Chelmsford *Courier*. 1824-1825.

Chelmsford *Phoenix*. 1825-1826.

Coffin, Charles. *The History of Boscawen and Webster, From 1733 to 1878*. Concord: Republican Press Association, 1878.

Cowley, Charles. *A Handbook of Business in Lowell With a History of the City*. Lowell: E. D. Green, 1856.

Curtis, Josiah. "Brief Remarks on Hygiene of Massachusetts, But More Particularly of the Cities of Boston and Lowell, Being a Report to the American Medical Association." *Transactions of the American Medical Association*, vol. 2 (1849).

Draper, George. *Facts and Figures for Textile Manufacturers*. Hopedale, Mass.: George Draper, 1896.

Exercises of the Fiftieth Anniversary Commemorative of the Incorporation of the City of Lowell. Lowell: Vox Populi Press: S. W. Huse, 1886.

The Experiment. Published in Lowell, February-March 1832.

A Factory Girl. *Lights and Shadows of Factory Life in New England*. New York: J. Winchester, 1843.

Farley, Harriet. *Operatives' Reply to Hon. Jere. Clemens, Being a Sketch of Factory Life and Factory Enterprise and a Brief History of Manufacturing by Machinery*. Lowell: S. J. Varney, 1850.

Handbook for the Visiter [sic] *to Lowell*. Lowell: D. Bixby, 1848.

Hayes, John L. *American Textile Machinery: Its Early History, Characteristics, Contributions to the Industry of the World, Relations to Other Industries, and Claims for National Recognition*. Cambridge: University Press, John Wilson, 1879.

Hopkins, G. M. *City Atlas of Lowell*. Philadelphia: published by the author, 1879.

Hurd, D. Hamilton. *History of Merrimack and Belknap Counties, New Hampshire*. Philadelphia: D. L. Lewis, 1885.

Larcom, Lucy. *An Idyl of Work*. Boston: James R. Osgood, 1875.

—— *A New England Girlhood*. Boston: Houghton Mifflin, 1889.

Lowell *Advertiser*. 1838-1860.

Lowell *American*. 1849-1853.

Lowell *American Citizen*. February-March 1859.

Lowell *Courier*. 1837.

The Lowell Directory, various titles and compilers, 1832-1860. Originals at Lowell City Library.

Lowell Historical Society. *Contributions*, 2 vols. Lowell: Butterfield, 1913 and 1926.

Lowell *Journal*. 1830-1834.

Lowell *Mercury*. 1831-1834.

The Lowell Offering. 1840-1845. Three single issues and five bound volumes.

Lowell *Weekly Compend*. 1832-1833.

Lowell *Weekly Journal and Courier*. 1854-1859.

Luther, Seth. *An Address to the Working-Men of New-England*. Boston: published by the author, 1832.

Lyford, James Otis. *History of the Town of Canterbury, New Hampshire, 1727-1912*, 2 vols. Concord: Rumford Press, 1912.

Merrimack *Journal*. 1826-1827. Published in Lowell.

Miles, Henry A. *Lowell As It Was and As It Is*. Lowell: Powers and Bagley, 1845.

Montgomery, James. *A Practical Detail of the Cotton Manufacture of the United States of America*. Glasgow: John Niven, 1840.

New England Cotton Manufacturers' Association. *Proceedings*. Nos. 1-56, 1866-1897.

Old Residents' Historical Association (ORHA). *Contributions*, vols. 1-6. Lowell, 1874-1904.

One Hundred and Fiftieth Anniversary of the Settlement of Boscawen and Webster, Merrimack Co., N.H. Concord: Republican Press Association, 1884.

An Operative. *Factory Life As It Is*. Lowell, Mass.: Lowell Female Labor Reform Association, 1845.

The Operative. 1844-1845. Published in Lowell.

Proceedings in the City of Lowell at the Semi-Centennial Celebration of the Incorporation of the Town of Lowell. Lowell: Penhallow, 1876.

Robinson, Harriet Hanson. *Loom and Spindle; or Life Among the Early Mill Girls*. New York: Crowell, 1898.

Scoresby, William. *American Factories and Their Female Operatives*. London: Longman, Brown, Green and Longmans, 1845.

Thompson, Zadock. *The History of Vermont, Natural, Civil, and Statistical, in Three Parts*. Burlington: Chauncey Goodrich, 1842.

Voice of Industry. 1845-1848. Published in Fitchburg, Lowell, and Boston by the New England Working Men's Association.

Vox Populi. 1844-1846.

Webber, Samuel C. *Manual of Power For Machines, Shafts, and Belts, with The History of Cotton Manufacture in the United States*. New York: D. Appleton, 1879.

White, George S. *Memoir of Samuel Slater: The Father of American Manufactures, Connected with a History of the Rise and Progress of the Cotton Manufactures in England and America*. Philadelphia: published by the author, 1836.

Worthen, Augusta Harvey. *The History of Sutton, New Hampshire: Consisting of the Historical Collections of Erastus Wadleigh, Esq., and A. H. Worthen*, 2 parts. Concord: Republican Press Association, 1890.

Zion's Herald. October 1836. Published by the New England Conference of the Methodist Episcopal Church.

SECONDARY SOURCES

Abbott, Edith. *Women In Industry: A Study in American Economic History*. New York: D. Appleton, 1913.

Anderson, Michael. *Family Structure in Nineteenth-Century Lancashire*. Cambridge: Cambridge University Press, 1971.

Andrews, John B. and W. D. P. Bliss. *History of Women in Trade Unions*. Washington: Government Printing Office, 1911.

Armstrong, John. *Factory Under the Elms: A History of Harrisville, New Hampshire, 1774-1969*. Cambridge: M. I. T. Press, 1969.

Bagnall, William R. *Samuel Slater and the Cotton Manufacture*. Middletown, Connecticut: J. B. Stewart, 1890.

Bender, Thomas. *Toward an Urban Vision: Ideas and Institutions in Nineteenth-Century America*. Lexington: University Press of Kentucky, 1975.

Bidwell, Percy. "The Agricultural Revolution in New England." In L. B. Schmidt and E. D. Ross, eds., *Readings in the Economic History of American Agriculture*. New York: Macmillan, 1925.

Brigham, Loriman S. "An Independent Voice: A Mill Girl from Vermont Speaks her Mind." *Vermont History* (1973), 41:142-46.

Bruck, David J. "The Schools of Lowell, 1824-1861: A Case Study in the Origins of Modern Public Education in America." Undergraduate honors thesis, Harvard College, 1971.

Bryant, Blanche Brown and Gertrude Elaine Baker, eds. *The Diaries of Sally and Pamela Brown*. Springfield, Vt.: William L. Bryant Foundation, 1970.

Cameron, E. H. *Samuel Slater: Father of American Manufactures*. N.P.: Bond Wheelwright, 1960.

Cantor, Milton and Bruce Laurie, eds. *Class, Sex, and the Woman Worker*. Westport, Conn.: Greenwood Press, 1977.

Clark, Victor S. *History of Manufactures in the United States*, vol. 1. New York: Peter Smith, 1949. Originally published in 1916.

Coburn, Frederick W. *History of Lowell and Its People*, vol. 1. New York: Lewis Historical Publishing, 1920.

Cole, Arthur H. *The American Wool Manufacture*, vol. 1. Cambridge: Harvard University Press, 1926.

Coleman, Peter J. *The Transformation of Rhode Island, 1790-1860*. Providence: Brown University Press, 1963.

Commons, John R. et al. *History of Labour in the United States*, vol. 1. New York: Macmillan, 1946. Originally published in 1918.

—— *A Documentary History of American Industrial Society*, vols. 5-8. Cleveland: Arthur H. Clark, 1910.

Coolidge, John. *Mill and Mansion: A Study of Architecture and Society in Lowell, Massachusetts, 1820-1865*. New York: Columbia University Press, 1942.

Cott, Nancy F. *The Bonds of Womanhood: "Woman's Sphere" in New England, 1780-1835*. New Haven: Yale University Press, 1977.

Dalzell, Robert F. "The Rise of the Waltham-Lowell System and Some Thoughts on the Political Economy of Modernization in Antebellum Massachusetts." *Perspectives in American History* (1975), 9:229-68.

Davis, Lance E. "Capital Mobility and American Growth." In Stanley Engerman and Robert Fogel, eds., *The Reinterpretation of American Economic History*, pp. 285-300. New York: Harper and Row, 1971.

—— "The New England Textile Mills and the Capital Market: A Study in Industrial Borrowing, 1840-1860." *Journal of Economic History* (1960), 20:1-30.

—— "Sources of Industrial Finance: The American Textile Industry, A Case Study." *Explorations in Entrepreneurial History* (1957), 1st ser., 9:189-203.

—— "Stock Ownership in the Early New England Textile Industry." *Business History Review* (1958), 32:204-22.

Davis, Lance E. and H. Louis Stettler. "The New England Textile Industry, 1825-1860: Trends and Fluctuations." Conference on Research in Income and Wealth. *Output, Employment, and Productivity in the United States After 1800*. New York: National Bureau of Economic Research, 1966.

Dawley, Alan. *Class and Community: The Industrial Revolution in Lynn*. Cambridge: Harvard University Press, 1976.

Dubnoff, Steven Jan. "The Family and Absence from Work: Irish Workers in a Lowell, Massachusetts, Cotton Mill, 1860." Ph.D. dissertation, Brandeis University, 1976.

Engerman, Stanley and Robert Fogel, eds. *The Reinterpretation of American Economic History*. New York: Harper and Row, 1971.

English, Walter. *The Textile Industry: An Account of the Early Invention of Spinning, Weaving, and Knitting Machines*. London: Longmans, Green, 1969.

Eno, Arthur L. Jr., ed. *Cotton Was King: A History of Lowell, Massachusetts.* N.P.: New Hampshire Publishing Company, 1976.

Evans, Bryn E. "Sutton, New Hampshire, and the Kearsarge Valley: Life and Wealth in Rural New England, 1810-1870." M.A. thesis, Salem (Mass.) State College, 1975.

Faler, Paul and Alan Dawley. "Working-Class Culture and Politics in the Industrial Revolution: Sources of Loyalism and Rebellion." *Journal of Social History* (1975), 9:466-80.

Fogg, Alonzo J. *The Statistics and Gazetteer of New Hampshire.* Concord: D. L. Guernsey, 1874.

Foner, Philip S. *History of the Labor Movement in the United States,* vol. 1. New York: International, 1947.

—— *The Factory Girls.* Urbana: University of Illinois Press, 1977.

Gersuny, Carl. "'A Devil in Petticoats,' and Just Cause: Patterns of Punishment in Two New England Textile Factories." *Business History Review* (1976), 50:131-52.

Gibb, George Sweet. *The Saco-Lowell Shops: Textile Machinery Building in New England, 1813-1949.* Cambridge: Harvard University Press, 1950.

Ginger, Ray. "Labor in a Massachusetts Cotton Mill, 1853-1860." *Business History Review* (1954), 28:67-91.

Gitelman, Howard M. "'No Irish Need Apply': Patterns and Responses to Ethnic Discrimination in the Labor Market." *Labor History* (1973), 14:56-68.

—— "The Waltham System and the Coming of the Irish." *Labor History* (1967), 8:227-53.

—— *Workingmen of Waltham: Mobility in American Urban Industrial Development, 1850-1890.* Baltimore: Johns Hopkins University Press, 1974.

Glasco, Laurence. "The Life Cycles and Household Structure of American Ethnic Groups: Irish, Germans, and Native-born Whites in Buffalo, New York, 1855." *Journal of Urban History* (1975), 1:339-64.

Green, Constance McLaughlin. *Holyoke, Massachusetts: A Case History of the Industrial Revolution in America.* New Haven: Yale University Press, 1939.

Gregory, Frances. *Nathan Appleton: Merchant and Entrepreneur, 1779-1861.* Charlottesville: University Press of Virginia, 1975.

Gutman, Herbert G. "Work, Culture, and Society in Industrializing America, 1815-1919." *American Historical Review* (1973), 78:531-68.

Handlin, Oscar. *Boston's Immigrants: A Study in Acculturation.* New York: Atheneum, 1968. Originally published in 1941.

Hareven, Tamara. "The Dynamics of Kin in an Industrial Community: A Historical Perspective." Davis Center Seminar, April 1977. Manuscript.

Harris, Marc. "A Demographic Study of Concord, Massachusetts, 1750-1850." Undergraduate honors thesis, Brandeis University, 1973.

Hedges, James B. *The Browns of Providence Plantations: The Nineteenth Century,* vol. 2. Providence: Brown University Press, 1968.

Hogan, William. "Demographic Aspects of a Maturing Economy: New England, 1850-1900." Ph.D. dissertation, Cornell University, 1976.

Holbrook, Stewart. *The Yankee Exodus, an Account of Migration from New England.* New York: Macmillan, 1950.

Jeremy, David. "Innovation in American Textile Technology During the Early 19th Century." *Technology and Culture* (1973), 14:40-76.

Josephson, Hannah. *The Golden Threads: New England's Mill Girls and Magnates.* New York: Duell, Sloan, and Pearce, 1949.

Katz, Michael B. *The People of Hamilton, Canada West: Family and Class in a Mid-Nineteenth-Century City.* Cambridge: Harvard University Press, 1975.

Katz, Michael B. and Ian Davey. "Youth and Early Industrialization in a Canadian City." Davis Center Seminar, 1977. Manuscript.

Keith, E. Gordon. "The Financial History of Two Textile Cities." Ph.D. dissertation, Harvard University, 1936.

Kenngott, George F. *The Record of a City: A Social Survey of Lowell, Massachusetts.* New York: Macmillan, 1912.

Kulik, Gary. "Pawtucket Village and the Strike of 1824: The Origins of Class Conflict in Rhode Island." *Radical History Review* (1978), no. 17, pp. 5-37.

Kull, Nell, ed. "'I Can Never Be So Happy There Among All Those Mountains': The Letters of Sally Rice." *Vermont History* (1970), 38:49-57.

Lahne, Herbert J. *The Cotton Mill Worker.* New York: Farrar and Rinehart, 1944.

Layer, Robert G. *Earnings of Cotton Mill Operatives, 1825-1914.* Cambridge: Harvard University Press, 1955.

—— "Wages, Earnings, and Output of Four Cotton Textile Companies in New England, 1825-1860." Ph.D. dissertation, Harvard University, 1952.

Leavitt, Thomas W., ed. *The Hollingworth Letters: Technical Change in the Textile Industry, 1826-1837.* Cambridge: M. I. T. Press, 1969.

Lebergott, Stanley. *Manpower in Economic Growth: The American Record Since 1800.* New York: McGraw-Hill, 1964.

Lerner, Gerda. "The Lady and the Mill Girl: Changes in the Status of Women in the Age of Jackson." *Mid-Continent American Studies Journal* (1969), 10:5-15.

Levine, David. *Family Formation in an Age of Nascent Capitalism.* New York: Academic Press, 1977.

Luft, Harold. "New England Textile Labor in the 1840's: From Yankee Farm Girl to Irish Immigrant." Graduate seminar paper, Harvard University, 1971. Manuscript.

Mathews, Lois Kimball. *The Expansion of New England: The Spread of New England Settlement and Institutions to the Mississippi River, 1620-1865.* New York: Russell and Russell, 1962. Originally published in 1909.

McCauley, Elfrieda B. "The New England Mill Girls: Feminine Influence in the Development of Public Libraries in New England." D.L.S. dissertation, Columbia University, 1971.

McGouldrick, Paul F. *New England Textiles in the Nineteenth Century: Profits and Investments.* Vol. 131 in Harvard Economic Studies. Cambridge: Harvard University Press, 1968.

Mitchell, A. Gibbs Jr. "Irish Family Patterns in Nineteenth-Century Ireland and Lowell, Massachusetts." Ph.D. dissertation, Boston University, 1976.

Monahan, Thomas P. *The Pattern of Age at Marriage in the United States*, 2 vols. Philadelphia: published by author, 1951.

Montgomery, David. *Beyond Equality: Labor and the Radical Republicans, 1862-1872.* New York: Knopf, 1967.

Nickless, Pamela Jean. "Changing Labor Productivity and the Utilizing of Native Women Workers in the American Cotton Textile Industry, 1825-1860." Ph.D. dissertation, Purdue University, 1976.

North, Douglass C. *The Economic Growth of the United States, 1790-1860.* Englewood Cliffs: Prentice-Hall, 1961.

O'Dwyer, George F. *The Irish Catholic Genesis of Lowell*, Rev. ed. Lowell: Sullivan, 1920.

Osterud, Nancy and J. Fulton. "Family Limitation and Age at Marriage: Fertility Decline in Sturbridge, Massachusetts, 1730-1850." *Population Studies* (1976), 30:481-94.

Pernicone, Carol Groneman. "The 'Bloody Ould Sixth': A Social Analysis of a New York City Working-Class Community in the Mid-Nineteenth Century." Ph.D. dissertation, University of Rochester, 1973.

Persons, Charles. "The Early History of Factory Legislation in Massachusetts: From 1825 to the Passage of the Ten Hour Law in 1874." In Susan M. Kingsbury, ed., *Labor Laws and Their Enforcement, With Special Reference to Massachusetts*. New York: Longmans, Green, 1911.

Prude, Jonathan. "The Coming of Industrial Order: A Study of Town and Factory Life in Rural Massachusetts, 1813-1860." Ph.D. dissertation, Harvard University, 1976.

Rivard, Paul E. "Textile Experiments in Rhode Island, 1788-1789." *Rhode Island History* (1974), 33:35-45.

Sande, Theodore. "The Architecture of the Cotton Textile Mills of Lowell, Mass., 1822-1860." Special Collections, University of Lowell. Manuscript.

Scott, Joan W. and Louise A. Tilly. "Women's Work and the Family in Nineteenth-Century Europe." *Comparative Studies in Society and History* (1975), 17:36-64.

Shlakman, Vera. *Economic History of a Factory Town: A Study of Chicopee, Massachusetts*. New York: Octagon Books, 1969. Originally published in *Smith College Studies in History* (1934-35), vol. 10, nos. 1-4.

Shorter, Edward, "Female Emancipation, Birth Control, and Fertility in European History." *American Historical Review* (1973), 78:605-40.

Sloat, Caroline. "The Dover Manufacturing Company and the Integration of English and American Calico Printing Techniques, 1815-1829." *Winterthur Portfolio* (1975), 10:51-68.

Smith-Rosenberg, Carroll. "Beauty, the Beast, and the Militant Woman: A Case Study in Sex Roles and Social Stress in Jacksonian America." *American Quarterly* (1971), 23:562-84.

—— "The Female World of Love and Ritual: Relations Between Women in Nineteenth-Century America." *Signs* (1976), 1:1-29.

Spalding, Robert Varnum. "The Boston Mercantile Community and the Promotion of the Textile Industry in New England, 1813-1860." Ph.D. disseration, Yale University, 1963.

Stilwell, Lewis. *Migration From Vermont*. Montpelier: Vermont Historical Society, 1948.

Sumner, Helen. *History of Women in Industry in the United States.* Washington: Government Printing Office, 1910.

Taylor, George Rogers. *The Transportation Revolution: 1815-1860,* Volume IV in The Economic History of the United States. New York: Harper and Row, 1951.

Thernstrom, Stephan. *Poverty and Progress: Social Mobility in a Nineteenth-Century City.* Cambridge: Harvard University Press, 1964.

Thompson, E. P. *The Making of the English Working Class.* New York: Vintage Books, 1966.

—— "Time, Work-Discipline, and Industrial Capitalism." *Past and Present* (1967), no. 38, pp. 56-97.

Tilly, Louise, Joan Scott, and Miriam Cohen. "Women's Work and European Fertility Patterns." *Journal of Interdisciplinary History* (1976), 6:447-76.

Tryon, Rolla. *Household Manufactures in the United States, 1640-1860: A Study in Industrial History.* Chicago: University of Chicago Press, 1917.

Tunis, Elizabeth. "Beverly and Metheun Daughters at Lowell, 1830-1840." Graduate seminar paper, University of Massachusetts, 1974.

Tunis, Mildred. "Two Young Factory Girls from New London." Paper read to Business and Professional Women's Group of New London (N.H.) Baptist Church, 1970.

Uhlenberg, Peter. "A Study of Cohort Life Cycles: Cohorts of Native-Born Massachusetts Women, 1830-1920." *Population Studies* (1969), 23:407-20.

Vogel, Lise. "Humorous Incidents and Sound Common Sense: More on the New England Mill Women." *Labor History* (1978), 19:280-86.

Walkowitz, Daniel J. "Working-Class Women in the Gilded Age: Factory, Community, and Family Life Among Cohoes, New York, Cotton Workers." *Journal of Social History* (1972), 5:464-90.

Ward, Nicholas Hayes. "Pianos, Parasols, and Poppa: The Migration of Vermont Farm Girls to the Massachusetts Mill Towns." M.A. thesis, Brown University, 1974.

Ware, Caroline F. *The Early New England Cotton Manufacture: A Study in Industrial Beginnings.* New York: Russell and Russell, 1966. Originally published in 1931.

Ware, Norman. *The Industrial Worker, 1840-1860: The Reaction of American Industrial Society to the Advance of the Industrial Revolution.* Gloucester: Peter Smith, 1959. Originally published in 1924.

Welter, Barbara. "The Cult of True Womanhood." *American Quarterly* (1966), 18:151-74.

Wilson, Harold Fisher. *The Hill Country of Northern New England.* New York: Columbia University Press, 1936.

Wolfe, Allis Rosenberg, ed. "Letters of a Lowell Mill Girl and Friends, 1845-1846." *Labor History* (1976), 17:96-102.

Wright, Carroll D. *The History and Growth of the United States Census.* Washington, D.C.: Government Printing Office, 1900.

Yasuba, Yasukichi. *Birth Rates of the White Population in the United States, 1800-1860: An Economic Study.* Baltimore: Johns Hopkins University Press, 1962.

Zevin, Robert Brooke. "The Growth of Cotton Textile Production After 1815". In Stanley Engerman and Robert Fogel, eds., *The Reinterpretation of American Economic History*, pp. 122-47. New York: Harper and Row, 1971.

Zwarg, Christina Lynne. "Woman as Wife or Worker: The Success and Failure of Feminism in the Lowell Female Labor Reform Association, 1845-1848." M.A. thesis, Brown University, 1975.

Index

Wage differentials: sexual, 66, 148, 185,
190, 195; ethnic, 147-53, 157-58, 195-97,
279; educational, 149-51; departmental,
159; experiential, 185-88, 190-92
Wage slavery, 98-99, 106
Waltham, Mass., 5, 17-18
Waltham-Lowell system, 9-12, 17, 58-59,
73, 75-79, 105, 137, 239-40
Ward, Henry, 10
Warping, 64
Waterpower, 15, 19-20, 61, 134-35, 145
Weaving, 64, 67, 142
Women: marriage, 31-32, 50-54, 126-30,
168, 282; families, 31-35, 41-49, 167-82;
motivations, 35-40, 197; savings, 38, 53,

55, 188; careers, 49, 151-53, 160-61,
183-97, 263; socialization of, 71-72,
81-83
Women's rights, 91-92, 127, 130
Working conditions, 62-64, 67-69, 109-12,
114, 137, 202
Worksharing, 72

Yankees, proportions in mills, 26, 138-39;
housing of, 27, 143, 155, 166-67; cultural
traditions of, 81, 93-95; wages of, 148,
158, 197; job placement of, 152-54,
195-97; and family economy, 175-76,
180; careers of, 189